A Journey *of* Trials Strengthened Through Faith

A Journey *of* Trials Strengthened Through Faith

BIOGRAPHY *of a* NEW ENGLAND GIRL

JOYCE A. LEONARD

A Journey of Trials Strengthened Through Faith
Copyright © 2021 by Joyce A. Leonard. All rights reserved.
www.JoyceALeonard.com

No part of this publication may be reproduced, stored in a retrieval system or transmitted in any way by any means, electronic, mechanical, photocopy, recording or otherwise without the prior permission of the author except as provided by USA copyright law.

The opinions expressed by the author are not necessarily those of URLink Print and Media.

1603 Capitol Ave., Suite 310 Cheyenne, Wyoming USA 82001
1-888-980-6523 | admin@urlinkpublishing.com

URLink Print and Media is committed to excellence in the publishing industry.

Book design copyright © 2021 by URLink Print and Media. All rights reserved.

Published in the United States of America

Library of Congress Control Number: 2021910366
ISBN 978-1-64753-819-4 (Paperback)
ISBN 978-1-64753-820-0 (Digital)

07.05.21

Contents

Acknowledgement 7
Introduction 9

Chapter 1: My Earliest Childhood Memories 13
Chapter 2: Blueberry Hill 1950 21
Chapter 3: Moving On 24
Chapter 4: Physical & Spiritual Eye Sight 30
Chapter 5: Growing Up in Center Conway 33
Chapter 6: "The In-Between Years" 1960-1964 56
Chapter 7: "The Dark Silence" 64
Chapter 8: A Rebel's Mischief 70
Chapter 9: Hormones Gone Crazy 75
Chapter 10: Contentions-Prickly Communication 78
Chapter 11: Sweet Sixteen 85
Chapter 12: Defiance - Manipulation - Deception 93
Chapter 13: "Demons of the Mind" 97
Chapter 14: Cherry Creek 111
Chapter 15: A Broken Heart – And No Where to Go. 117
Chapter 16: Tammy Marie -My Baby Girl 138
Chapter 17: From Pleasant St. to Main St. to Roak St. 144
Chapter 18: Roak Street 154
Chapter 19: My Third Child 174
Chapter 20: 1971-1972 187
Chapter 21: Mama, My Precious Mama 196
Chapter 22: Am I Going to Die? 210
Chapter 23: 12 High St – Bog Hoot 213
Chapter 24: 201 Main St 1977-1978 222

Chapter 25: 1979 - Tragedy Strikes 237
Chapter 26: Don't Cry Out-Loud 243
Chapter 27: Hope Drained - Emotions Torn...........................247
Chapter 28: The Whispered Promise 253
Chapter 29: Memories of Laughter and Tears 259
Chapter 30: Gift Wrapped Words 264

Acknowledgement

The art work for the cover of this book was created and inspired by Eric D. Calvin, an inmate of Louisiana State Penitentiary. I have corresponded with Eric for over fifteen years. He is a good Christian man, and a wonderful friend. I appreciate his friendship and great artistic talent.

My friend Pauline Nota, (Founder) and Jesus Christ (CEO) of our prison ministry called "Freedom Within" Worldwide Prison Outreach Ministry, which included a newsletter, of which I was editor. We corresponded with numerous inmates, which was how Eric and I became pen-friends.

The title of this book, "A Journey of Trials Strengthened Through Faith," was given to me under inspiration, from my dear friend, Pauline Nota. Her insights give credit to my thoughts and I owe her a debt of gratitude for the many hours counseling me and helping me with the outcome of this book thus making it possible for publication. This journey has been to the honor and glory of our Lord and Savior Jesus Christ. In the words of Oswald Chambers, "And every virtue we possess is His alone. (*My Utmost for His Highest,*" Devotional December 30)

Introduction

"Go ye therefore into the highways, and as many as you shall find, bid to the marriage.

So those servants went out into the highways, and gathered all as many as they found, both bad and good; and the wedding was furnished with guests.

And the King came to see His guests, he saw there a man which had not the wedding garment.

And He said unto him, Friend, how camest thou hither not having a wedding garment?

And he was speechless."

(Matthew 22:9-12 NKJV)

Everyone has a story to tell, some write to have a voice because they have been silenced for so long. Some write for therapeutic reasons or to heal from their demons. Some write for the sake of sharing their opinion or out of desire to help others to become all they can be, but everyone has a story. I write for all of the reasons above, but mainly because I want others to know that no matter how bad circumstances may be in your life, there is healing in Christ. I want people to know I have become the person I am today, because of the prayers of family and friends, who loved me unconditionally, and who never gave up on me.

There is a wedding feast coming, and you are invited, no matter how good or bad you are. All you have to do is put on the wedding garment, Jesus' Robe of Righteousness. (see Matthew 22:9-12) He covers all the horrors, and the battered and brokenness that is deep inside. He covers the scars, and the filth, and heals the pain, and teaches us forgiveness. I read from another author a profound statement – "we can never forgive any more than Jesus has already forgiven us."

Some authors have connections for publications. Some take the road of self-publishing. I have no connections and no confidence that this book will be snatched up because of its profound writing or its expertise. But I have the Divine Publisher that expressly told me in 1989 to write this book as clearly and audibly as if I were talking to another human being sitting next to me.

I drove for a company called Western Maine Transportation for six years, and the last two and a half years I drove a bus route that took me to the outskirts of surrounding towns, when I picked up mentally challenged clients, and took them to day jobs, and schools where they spent their day interacting with others, and trying to enjoy some normalcy in their lives.

I had to leave very early in the morning as my pick up was at 6 a.m. It was my custom to get up around 3:30 in the morning to have my devotions first, as I spent at least an hour with my Jesus before heading out in the morning, then dressing, checking the oil in my bus and starting it, and so forth, as part of my daily routine before I left at 5:30 a.m. I was alone in the bus, as I had not arrived at my first destination yet. I spent many hours in the bus, and often I felt like it was home away from home. It was before sunrise, as the sun was beginning to make its way to peek over the foothills, and the sky was beautifully glazed like frosting, with streaks of pink breaking through the deep hues of blue. I heard a voice, "Joyce! Joyce! I want you to write a book." It was so audible that I thought someone had been hiding in the bus that I wasn't aware of. I pulled to the side of the road as quickly as possible, unfastening my seat belt, and walked through the bus looking for the owner of the voice. There was none there! I sat down chilled by the encounter, when I heard it again. "I want you to write a book, may you never forget." I sat in awe, and then I spoke aloud to the darkness, "Is that You Lord?" There was no answer. I took that as a command, not to forget to write the book. Tears came to my eyes, and I rehearsed the encounter over and over again in my mind, and pondered it all in my heart. I know that it was definitely God speaking to me!

Since the encounter, and as the years have passed, I began having doubts, and then I thought of Abraham and how God told him he would be the father of many nations, but then Abraham took matters into his own hands, not quite understanding or trusting God's timeline. Along the way, many people have said to me, "Joyce you need to write a book." Well, I believe the time has arrived!

One Christmas, Kathy, my youngest daughter, gave me a picture of an old typewriter that looks much like the one I used to own. The caption under the picture says, "Write your own story." After watching me henpeck the sticking keys on the antiquated one, my husband Dave, bought me the elite Brother Word Processor that Christmas.

I dedicate this book to my children. They are the most precious treasures God has given me. I don't think I always recognized that as emphatically as I do now. That is what age does. They are the reason I kept going in life. They are the love I cherished, and are my heritage. They are gifts.... each one! It is my children, and now my grandchildren, that have given me meaning to life, and kept me faithful. I have felt that without them, I would be nobody, but with them I am somebody. Just being a child of God makes each of us "somebody," and this was an area I had to come to terms with to feel some self-worth. For with Jesus I am a princess, and they are the heirs that God has given me for His honor and glory to come to the marriage feast. Good or bad, He has called them and us! Every day I pray for them to put on the Robe of Righteousness, and be ready to enter in, and sit at the table with Jesus. He is calling you too.... please come!

> *"But seek first the Kingdom of heaven and His Righteousness, And all these things will be added to you."*
> *(Matthew 6:33 NKJV)*

In the pages ahead it will be revealed that my life took on many dimensions that conditioned me for conflict, endurance, perseverance, and ultimately taught me commitment, and what that meant. Somewhere while in my mother's womb the seed of faith was planted, and my faith has grown to immeasurable depths that was watered, and still being harvested by God's powerful interacting with me. I feel so unworthy for only He is worthy, and it is by His instruction that these pages can be written.

Chapter One

My Earliest Childhood Memories

*Train up a child in the way he should go:
and when he is old, he will not depart from it."*
(Proverbs 22:6 NKJV)

North Pembroke, New Hampshire 1948-1951

I grew up in the formative years of my life in North Pembroke, New Hampshire. We were all related on that old country road. There was my cousin Betty and her husband, Clarence, & their children, Daniel & Jeannie, and it was where we went to watch television. Jeannie was my playmate, and we were the same age. Across from their home was Pop & Ma Saturley, who were the parents of other cousins on the road. Pop's wife, Ella, was my grandfather's sister. Pop was a very crude man always clenching a fat cigar between his teeth. They had a farm on the hill with lots of horses and cows and I remember going there often. Pop was loud with a harsh voice that always sent a chill through me. Just beyond the cemetery, was my great Aunt Cora, who was my grandfather's sister as well. I can recall how she would let Jeannie and I have a bottle of milk on her bed at nap time, which was against Mama's wishes, but we were careful to keep her secret and giggled as we knew this was not allowed. Aunt Cora was always old, or so it seemed. Her son, Doug, lived across the road from her small cape, in a huge brick house. He had goats and Aunt Cora milked the nanny goat that filled our bottles.

"HENRY"

Great Aunt Cora brought Henry up as her own, and he became part of the family through foster care. His mother was a white girl who was impregnated by a black man. It was a disgrace then to be involved with a person of color, and this woman would have been shunned by society. I never learned the full details, only knew Henry was my cousin, and I accepted him as he was. He often wheeled me in the old, black, baby buggy up and down the road, which was great fun and I just loved Henry. Children only see what is sincere in the heart. Great Aunt Cora was my cousin Betty's mother, so by caring for Henry as her own, he became Betty's brother, and they loved each other always. Aunt Cora also had a foster daughter, Florence. We called her Flo, and she and Betty were like sisters, and we always thought of Flo as our cousin as well.

"Margaret & Cliff"

As you kept going down the road you came to cousin Margaret and her husband Cliff's home. Margaret and Cliff always had a houseful of kids. I never questioned why there were so many, but realized much later on in life that they were foster parents. She was a school bus driver for many years. I remember walking up the pasture and Cliff let me ride the old cow when it was time for the cows to come to the barn. I was called Jojo, as a fond nickname. Mama didn't like nick names, but Cliff ignored that fact.

"Uncle Walter & Aunt Florence"

It was just a stone's throw further, where Uncle Walter and Aunt Florence lived. Walter was Daddy's brother. Aunt Florence was doubly related since Pop & Aunt Ella were also Aunt Florence's parents, making Aunt Florence my second cousin on Mama's side, and my aunt on Daddy's side, by marrying his brother. Cliff and Uncle Walter were great friends. They often talked about the "end times," and how they would meet on the Allegany Trail during the "great time of trouble," and lead God's people through the wilderness till He came. I took their conversations as gospel, and wondered how they would know when to do this, and if they had to hike there, and how far it was. We all often hiked the mountains in New Hampshire.

"Bessie & Jennie"

Bessie and Jennie's home, which was a little cape, about a quarter of a mile from Uncle Walter's home, were two old ladies, who were sisters that lived together. They kept chickens, and an old cow in the barn. I remember hearing Mama & Daddy talking about the hooves of that old cow being so long that it was unhealthy, but they would do nothing to disturb its presence in their barn. It was never let out, but faithfully fed. Bessie cared for me and my sister while Mama was working. Then a little further down the road was this lady, who was called the "dog lady," because she had so many dogs. She was good friends with Bessie & Jennie. Jennie was our cousin Margaret's husband's mother (Cliff) and Bessie was a widow. We called them "aunt" even though they were not blood related. We never knew the difference.

"Grampa & Gramma Hutchinson"

My Grampa and Gramma Hutchinson lived in a beautiful ranch home beyond where the "dog lady" lived, and my only memory of my grandmother, Emma, was her standing in the doorway when we went to visit her. She wore a long pink night gown with a little quilted jacket around her shoulders. It was not long after that I heard she died. She was a severe diabetic. Between Bessie's and the "dog lady" is a cemetery and that is where my Grandmother Hutchinson is waiting for Jesus to wake her from her grave of rest. (see I Thessalonians 4:13-16 NKJV)

(The following story is written, as my imagination has seen the events, that were told by my mother, and my Aunt Thelma Lou and the horror of that event.)

"The Fire"

The year was 1941. . . .. The old wood stove had burned out or so she thought. Priscilla, my Mama, carefully laid some kindling & firewood to restart the stove on the chilly May morning, she decided to put a bit of kerosene on it to get it started. The flames hadn't completely died from the previous fire, and it blew like a blow torch, before her very eyes, and spewed the flames that caught the curtains and then the pillows that decorated the couch. Frantically beating the flames with anything she could get in her hands, to no avail, she scooped up her a baby girl, my sister, and placed her in the wicker baby buggy, along with her wedding dress, Daddy's Sabbath suit, their Bible, and the mother cat & kittens. She pressed her way to safety as tears burned as hot as the flames that licked up her little home. Their neighbor, down the road, the only one on the road with a phone, called the State Police, and gave her a place of refuge, while the flames consumed the tall grass in the field, as well as the mama cat, and the baby kittens that had been placed there for safety, leaving her and her little family homeless. There was no hope but to let it burn. Her beloved books were to be left in a charred rubble. This was during the Depression, and she had just received their rations from the City of Concord for sugar, flour, coffee, peanut butter and butter.

Daddy was on his way to work to the Portsmouth, New Hampshire Navy Ship Yard. The State Troopers stopped him on the road, and told him his home was on fire. He looked, into the distance and saw black smoke billowing, as his heart sank he realized this was his home. When he arrived home, he found his home burned to the ground, and no one around. His heart hit the pit of his stomach as he only imagined the worst. What torment he endured until he found Mama and his baby girl safe at the neighbor's home. When Mama went back to the City of Concord for rations, since theirs had been lost, they refused to believe her.

During this time, my Daddy's sisters, Alta, Thelma Lou and Alice, along with their brother, Walter, were preparing to visit their brother, Stan. Even though his name was William, he was called Stan, from his middle name, as there was a line of Williams in the family. Walter had mounted and strapped with rope, seven tires on top of his old two-seater, Ford car, and drove from Buck Tooth Run in New York State to N. Pembroke, New Hampshire.

By this time Daddy and his little family were living in a chicken coop until a house was built. When everyone arrived, they stayed in the chicken coop for a few days, and slept on wooden pallets with old quilts as their padding, while the new place was being built. Daddy rebuilt another home again eight years later on Blueberry Hill.

As I write this story of their great courage, and heartbreak, during this time in their life, I am so thankful that God spared my mother and my sister. The ending of this story could have been much more tragic. I am thankful to God, that He had a neighbor nearby prepared to care for Mama and my sister. I am thankful for my parent's inner strength that held them together during such a horrific time.

"Navy Ship Yard"

Daddy was drafted into the Navy, and was assigned to work at the Navy Ship Yard during World War II. Being a Seventh-day Adventist Christian man, he was brought up to believe that you never took a life, but he would serve as a medic. They began to threaten to send him out to the front lines, if he would not bear arms. There was one other man that worked with him that also believed the same. The threat came again that if he refused to bear arms then he would be sent out on the front lines. Daddy's response was, "if you are laying out there wounded, on those front lines, you would be mighty glad to see me crawling to get you."

With that response they never pursued his being on active duty again. They allowed him to continue to work in the ship yard as a welder on battle ships. But his comrade of faith, gave in to their demand and went out to fight, later losing his life.

"Buster"

My memories continue with "Buster," our Chow dog. Our house was located by the side of the road, and even though there was little traffic, there was always other menaces around out in the country. Mama always felt safe leaving me outside with Buster because he was a wonderful watch dog. If I wandered too close to the road, he would take hold of my dress and calmly pull me back within safety limits. Mama taught him to take bread from her mouth. He would gently take his prize as she offered it to him. He was such a beauty with his thick, lush, brown coat. She often showed others how gentle he was, but as good a dog, as he was, he was very possessive of his family, and when anyone came we had to be careful that they didn't tease him because he was apt to bite. A cousin came to visit and one of the kids, my age, (around two years old), teased him, and sure enough was bitten and drew blood. Mama & Daddy said he had to be put to sleep. My sister and I sat in the upstairs window when the veterinarian came to put Buster to sleep. My sister covered my eyes expecting it to be a gruesome event. I cried because Buster had been my protector and playmate, and I really missed him.

"Snakes"

My cousin Jeannie & I, were playing hide and seek. I was giggling to myself that I had found the perfect hiding spot, while Jeannie was walking around hunting for me. I felt a tickle on my leg, and thinking it was the tall grass I was in, I reached down to scratch my leg when I, shockingly, realized that it was a snake crawling up my leg. I let out a shriek and Mama came running. I watched her take a shovel, and beat that snake to death, while from its tail came oodles of baby snakes. It was a harmless milk adder, but Mama had a, deathly, fear of snakes, and hated them intensely.

We had chickens, and snakes were a menace to them so the baby snakes were killed too.

"Fleas"

Sometimes I would stay at Jeannie's house, and sleep in a twin bed in a pretty room. It was special since I shared an iron bunk bed with my sister. They had a dog called Susie. She had short, white fur with black patches on her, and she was a mutt! Susie was part of the family, just like Buster had been, but she was a small dog, and slept on the beds with the kids. This particular night at Jeannie's, I woke up to see bugs jumping all over the bed. I was in horror because it was the first time I ever saw such a sight! I squealed at Jeannie to look at the bugs jumping, as I cowered under the covers. Laughingly, Jeannie regaled, "Oh those are Susie's fleas. Don't worry! They won't hurt you." She thought I was just being silly to be scared of them, and even though she reassured me that they were harmless, I didn't like staying there overnight anymore.

"The Black Snake"

There was another incident with a snake. Daddy was on the roof of the cabin he was building for us on Blueberry Hill, when Mama came screaming on a dead run, while a huge black snake chased her. It was long, and bowed its back in a hump, and stretched out again, bounding after her. Daddy jumped off the roof, as I was standing beside the high bush blueberry bushes, stunned by the scene. He grabbed a shovel, chased the snake, and killed it.

> *The wolf and the lamb shall feed together; The lion shall eat straw like the ox.*
>
> *And dust shall be the serpent's food.*
>
> *They shall not hurt or destroy in all My holy mountain,*
>
> *Says the Lord."*
>
> (Isaiah 65:25 NKJV)

"Listening to Grampa Hutchinson Preach"

We attended the Concord, New Hampshire Seventh-day Adventist Church. Grampa Hutchinson, Mama's Daddy, used to preach there. He was a lay pastor and spoke quite regularly. I remember sitting on Daddy's lap and drawing pictures of Daddy on tithe envelopes, while he was listening to Grampa's sermon. I remember cousin Margaret used to chew gum constantly while listening to the sermon as she snapped her gum, and there were a few whispers about how rude she was being during the worship service. I was about two-three years old during this time and this is where I learned how to be reverent in church. On Daddy's lap there was no wiggling around, fussing or whining, but I can say, I felt very secure sitting with him, and I knew better than to cause a fuss. I am thankful I learned this at a very young age.

> *"Since we are receiving a Kingdom that cannot be destroyed, let us be thankful and please God by worshipping Him with holy fear and awe."*
> (Hebrews 12:28 NLT)

Chapter Two

Blueberry Hill
1950

The Lord guards. . .. The lives of His faithful ones."
(Psalms 97:10 NIV)

We lived on what was known, and still is today, as "Blueberry Hill" in North Pembroke, New Hampshire, just eight miles outside of Concord, the state capital. My grandfather owned the "Hill" and sold it to our family, as my mother was fond of the location that spanned a mountainous view and overlooked the family cemetery. Of course, the high-bush blueberries added to the attraction. Our cabin on "Blueberry Hill" didn't have electricity, or an indoor bathroom, and of course, no running water! The lofty Pines protected our little home as well as the high-bush blueberries. It was an ideal place for a bird sanctuary, and the serenading of their song made it our own paradise haven.

We had to carry our water from a spring, climbing the hill on a well-worn dirt path using uncovered tree roots and fallen broken limbs as our stairway. Daddy had a wooden yoke that he carried across his shoulders supporting a couple pails of water. I carried a tea kettle and my sister carried two water jugs, since she was older, her load was heavier. Daddy rewarded my efforts with a penny.

This night, we went to our cousin's home to watch television. I even remember the program, "The Lone Ranger." Daddy loved westerns and that was a treat. I believed that the characters on the T.V. screen could see you as well as you could see them! So I was careful how I sat so I would be respectful. It was the spring of the year when rain was plentiful, and this night, it was pouring very hard. We had driven to our cousin's home in our old truck. I don't remember the make or model, just that it was old and, sort of, beat up, but it got us to church, Daddy to work and so forth. I sat on Mama's lap, my sister in the middle, while Daddy drove. The entrance to our "hill" was a dirt road, quite bumpy with rocks.

As you would approach the crest of the hill, you had to turn right on a continued dirt roadway that leaned toward the downside of the hill, which bordered a ravine below, with brush, blueberries, bramble bushes, rocks and shrubs that blanketed the wall, that fell down into the ravine. The roadway was treacherous, when not absolutely dry. Tonight it was slippery mud, and as we continued across to reach our cabin, the truck began to slide. Frantically, Daddy jumped out of the truck and pulled my sister out on his side. He called to Mama, "Hand Joyce over to me, and slide this way carefully." There was terror in his voice! Before Mama passed me over to him, I glanced out the rain-streaked side window of the truck and saw only the black hollow below threatening to swallow us up. I could feel the truck inching sideways in a menacing slide. Daddy cautioned Mama to move cautiously for any extra movement was a danger of sending the old truck plummeting into the darkness below.

I began to whimper. Daddy commanded my sister, "Take Joyce and go to the cabin. Don't look back." My sister firmly took my hand, and in control, marched me the endless quarter mile to our home. I didn't look back and neither did she. I could hear the truck engine roar, and I felt fear well up inside of me that I had never experienced before, and I squeezed my sister's hand a little tighter.

When we reached the cabin and entered into the safety of our humble home, it felt empty and cold and I was scared. We went directly to our room. There were three rooms in the cabin divided by large pieces of furniture, as partitions. We knelt down by our iron bunk bed and there my sister prayed for the safety of our parents. She hugged me close as she prayed. There was such fervor in her voice; I just knew that God would take care of everything. When Mama and Daddy came in much later, I knew in my heart that it was an answer directly from God. Jesus had answered her prayer. I believed, from that moment on, that whenever anything happens, and it is more than we can handle, that Jesus will answer and take care of everything when we pray for His help.

> *"As for me I will call upon God,*
> *and the Lord shall save me.*
>
> *Evening and morning and noon I*
> *will pray and cry aloud,*
>
> *And He shall hear my voice."*
>
> *(Psalms 55:16 & 17 NKJV)*

Chapter Three

Moving On

"The very character we exhibit in our surroundings is an indication what we will be like in other surroundings."

~Oswald Chambers~

I was about four when we moved from the security of our little cabin on Blueberry Hill, to the little town nestled into the cove of Bartlett, New Hampshire. The mountains loomed on all sides and gave the little town a dimension all its own. Mama had been brought up in a nursing home in Concord, New Hampshire, where her parents lived, so it just seemed like her calling to begin a nursing home of her own. Once Grammie died, Anna, Grampa's second wife, who was Grammie's best friend, from Sweden, which was their homeland, continued to manage the house hold. Anna and Grampa married two years after Grammie's death. She kept the home just as Grammie had done, never moving anything but keeping things as they were during her friend's life. Anna was actually the only grandmother I ever was really close to and had a real relationship with. She was one of God's saints sent to care for another woman's grandchildren, and love them as her own.

"My Grandparents Home"

*Marble mantels gracing the fireplaces with
gold leafed mirrors spreading the walls.*

*Glass doors with porcelain handles
encasing the sun parlor,*

*Where bookshelves in panorama display were
stacked with reading from all walks of life.*

*Oriental rugs stretched across the floor
bordering a corner window seat,*

Padded and cushioned in display with afghan throws.

*Mahogany banisters curved and polished
followed the carpeted staircase,*

*Passing the window seat that sat
beneath stain-glassed windows*

Allowing light to filter into the foyer.

Knickknacks of animal statues and other stately array

Decorated the window casings and mantels.

*Polished silver, braided rugs, fine linen, pewter
napkin holders and strawberry milk –*

Are the memories of my grandparents' home.

*An old piano that let little fingers run
across the ivory in off key tones,*

But were melodious to the ears of a little child.

*Floor lamps, long heavy drapes, beaded
bedspreads and embroidered verses*

Framed over four-poster beds – and

*Listening to tall tales of Grandfather
while lying down for a nap.*

Manicured lawns bordering a crushed stone driveway

*That carried little feet scampering with a
saltshaker after pigeons that homed nearby.*

*For it was the story, "if you could put salt on
the tail of a bird, you could capture it."*

A child can spend hours running after a fantasy

*To skillfully gather a precious treasure
if Grand-father said it was so. . .*

*Latticework that surrounded the
basement entry from the outside*

*And held in the basement toilet room was the
undisturbed web of "Jake," the spider.*

There was no fear of crawly spiders,

*For nurtured was to think of them as a harmless
friend that caught those pesky flies.*

It was so... for Grandfather said.

*Spotless kitchen floors surrounded by white
wooden cabinets and blue marbled counters,*

And this was my mother's home.

*And in this home while crawling
under the booth benches*

That served as the kitchen table setting,

*And rocking in the high backed wicker
rockers that lined the high-rise porch,*

Was where I learned finery at its peak.

*You never went to town without
being dressed like a lady,*

*Even though you walked the stone
curbing above the sidewalk,*

And skipped the steps of door entrances with a hop,

While in your blue cotton checkered dress.

*From the eyes of a child – focuses the
faith from a Grandfather's love-*

He will never let you down-

He will always tell you the truth,

And he will always be there.
But he is human and even a grandfather's life ends,
But our Father in heaven never dies.
He is always there – and He said,
"Suffer the little children to come unto Me,
For of such is the Kingdom of heaven." *
We must become as little children in innocence,
Believing, trusting, walking in faith –
And sometimes when we hop over the stone steps
To the entrances of life, we might trip and fall –
But He is ever able to pick us up and carry us.
Scraped knees, broken hearts and misguided dreams
Can be recreated and restored by our heavenly Father
Because He loves us with a love that went to the cross
And nailed all our mistakes and failures there.
They were cleansed in the blood of Jesus.
Then, one day in the sun-parlor, I was
going to polish Anna's shoes
On the oriental rug.
She was a nurse and had white shoes.
Carefully I took her shoes to the middle
of the rug and placed them there,
Opening the bottle of runny, white shoe
polish, I pulled out the plunger,
And began to spread it across her shoes, not
noticing the dripping specks at first -
Then, the bottle tipped and the runny white
substance flowed all over the beautiful rug.
I ran to find a towel and scrubbed to no avail.
The spot got bigger and then I knew – I
had to confess my deed, my blunder.

That spot was so big and there was no way to cover it.

I went to Grammie Anna and said, "Please kiss me now, because you will never kiss me again."

I took her by the hand and showed her my mistake with tears and a big hurt in my heart.

She gently kissed me again and said the cleaning woman would take care of it.

There was no need to worry – it was forgotten and she thanked me for thinking of her

When we confess our mistakes and sins to Jesus,

He says, "My child don't worry.

I threw your sins in the deepest sea, * and I will help you.

You are my child and I love you. I have gone to prepare a place for you. *

A mansion . . .and

I will come again and receive you unto Myself;

That where I am there you may be also

For the thoughts I have of you are of peace and not evil." *

And the cleaning lady will take care of the mess and you will never see it again,

And that is no tall tale from Grandfather,

But the truth because Jesus said so.

So this was how I came to know how Jesus really is and how much He loves me.

(* *Scriptures: Mark 10:14 NKJV; Micah 7:19 NKJV; John 14:2 NKJV; Jeremiah 29:11 NKJV*)

"Tempting Foods"

At age five the only foods I ate were clean meats as stated in Leviticus 11. I was never offered unclean meats of any kind and never tasted them. My mother was very strict on this point. Although she drank black coffee because she had a heart condition and would have had to take caffeine pills to keep her heart stimulated, she opted to drink black coffee, but my dad only drank Postum, a cereal drink, which I came to enjoy as well.

Bessie & Jennie, lived at the bottom of Blueberry Hill near the spring where we carried our water from and my sister and I would visit them. They would give us coffee with a lot of milk and sugar, to Mama's horror, and white bread lavishly buttered with a generous serving of sugar over it. As I sank my teeth into the sugary mass with great enjoyment, you would hear the crunch of the granules. I would sneak there just to have that cup of temptation.

"Daring the Unthinkable"

I had fast become friends with Joanie, one of the neighbor children. My most prominent memory of our time living there that one year in Bartlett, New Hampshire was when we were waiting for Joanie's dad while he went into the corner store and left his cigar smoldering in the ash tray. Joanie dared me to puff on that cigar and without hesitation I snatched it up and took what I thought was a puff, but the smoke got in my eyes, and the smell was awful, so it was carefully placed back right away as her dad was coming out of the store; thankfully the dare didn't go further. He was none the wiser to what had just taken place.

"Running Away—1952"

I remember being angry with Mama, for whatever the reason was, and I was running away. I was four years old when I packed up a little suitcase—more like a satchel, and went out back of the garage and sat on it. I stayed there until I was sure I had taught Mama a lesson, and when I heard her call, I decided to return back to the house. I don't think she even knew I had run away until she asked what was in my suitcase.

Chapter Four

Physical & Spiritual Eye Sight

*"Now by faith is the substance of things hoped for,
the evidence of things not seen."*
(Hebrews 11:1 NKJV)

Preparing for first grade, at five years old, I was required to take an eye test. Point your three fingers in the direction of the capital letter "E" on the big chart that was held within a certain distance from me with one eye covered. Then cover the other eye and follow the same instructions. I couldn't seem to point my fingers in the right direction. Mama was sure I just didn't understand what the requirement was, but as I sat in the classroom, I could not see the lines on the chalk board that the teacher was drawing. It was soon discovered that I had to be tested for glasses. Mama was near tears realizing I had inherited Daddy's bad eye sight. Her eyes were good and strong, but Daddy had worn glasses since age 4. I remember him telling the story of the first time he saw an airplane in the sky with his new glasses and how excited he was.

I took the trip to Berlin, New Hampshire with daddy annually to get my eyes checked, and for new glasses every year. It seemed like they got stronger every year. My left eye was my bad eye. I even wore a patch over my right eye to make my left eye work, but there was no difference. I overheard the Ophthalmologist tell my Daddy that I was so far-sighted that I couldn't see. In my mind, I thought I should be able to see the peak of a mountain from the ground. This was the same diagnosis my Daddy had and his daddy as well, so I definitely had inherited the bad eye sight. I relied on my right eye to do all the seeing I really needed.

I went to school in a small school, called Pine Tree Memorial, in the town we had moved to, which was Center Conway, New Hampshire. This was where Mama's new nursing home was located. I think Elfie Green, who was Mama's first patient, at the Bartlett Home, before we moved to Center Conway.

"Prayer"

I used to get up very early in the morning and sneak down the stairway from the third floor and sit on the top steps of the first set of stairs peeking through the banister at Mama and Daddy in the kitchen. I wanted to be in on whatever they were doing. I knew I would be shooed back to bed so I tried to be quiet. It was their quiet time together before we all had prayer together. They seemed to know that I was there and always told me, "it was too early for you to be up and get back to bed." I reluctantly would go back to bed. A bit later my sister and I were called to say good bye to Daddy. He would gather us around him as he knelt on one knee, resting his elbow on his other knee, and holding his head in bowed position for prayer. His deep voice left a lasting impact on me. He would pray that we would have a home in heaven and our circle would be unbroken, I believed it was real. It was so real that I wanted it and could see it within my mind.

At five years old, I would look to the heavens and picture Jesus coming any second. As I would swing out on my rope swing, I would sing loudly, "The Old Rugged Cross," and my spiritual eyesight saw Jesus being crucified. I yearned for the home that Daddy prayed about. I believed strongly of Jesus' soon coming, and I was certain that it would be any minute. I would talk to God while looking in the sky, anxiously waiting to see the small dark cloud, the size of a man's fist, (*Great Controversy pg. 640 by E.G. White*) (*also I Kings 18:42-44 speaks of the "cloud small as a man's hand," when Elijah prayed for rain*) coming in the distance knowing as it got closer that it would be Jesus accompanied by many angels, "the number of them was ten thousand times ten thousand and thousands of thousands" of them with a brightness that I would be almost unable to bear. (*see Revelation 5: 11-12 NKJV*)

I started climbing the spindly, Poplar tree out back of the house, just so I could get closer to heaven. I was sure, without a doubt, that the closer I got the quicker I could get there. The sooner I got there, then the sooner I would see Jesus face to face.

How quickly we lose the child like faith, and begin to waver. All those hopes and dreams seem to fade into the distance, and we forget our first love that was once the most important thing in our life, as we take on the world, and the treasures that fade and rust. The sinful nature grasps hold, and Satan has a death grip on our hearts that can only be released by the power of prayer.

"Faith Unlocks the Door"

"Prayer is the key to heaven,
And faith unlocks the door.
Words are so easily spoken,
But Prayer without faith,
Is like a boat without an oar.
Have faith, when you speak to the Master.
That is all He asks you for...."
(*Written by Samuel T. Scott & Robert L. Sands in 1955. Jake Hess brought this song to life in 2012*)

Growing Up in Center Conway

"For I know the plans I have for you, says the Lord.
They are plans for good and not for disaster,
to give you a future and a hope."
(Jeremiah 29:11 NLT)

1953-1962
"The lonely and forgotten"

Growing up in Center Conway, New Hampshire, just five miles from the Maine border into Fryeburg, Maine, was an adventure for me. It was here in this big old farm house that stood on the main road going through the curious little town of Center Conway, that a nursing home, for older folk was born. A place where Mama spent her time and energy caring for and nurturing those who others had cast aside. These folks taught me how to knit and crochet, the love of the piano and so much more. I loved helping.

At eight years old, I washed false teeth, carried wash basins to those who needed to be refreshed, stripped bedding from beds where they had lost control. I listened to stories from Lizzie who told about drowning cats in her childhood, and watching Myna knit with grace and ease; listened to Miss Barnes, eloquently, play the piano with deformed arthritic fingers, and dangerously defied Miss Shapleigh by exploiting myself with the hula hoop, which was such a disgrace in open public! Old Fred never finished breakfast till his dinner tray was before him, and then at suppertime, the dinner tray was taken away to be replaced with the evening meal.

I learned the art of making the perfect bed from Mary. A gate was placed in front of Mary's door and I would slide under the gate to visit Mary and help with making her bed. Mary would wander off at any hour of the day or night, so the gate was for her safety. It was late one night, while I was sleeping in my room on the third floor, when I heard someone, stealthily, climbing the creaking stairs. The bare wooden boards made it seem louder, and eerie. I was frozen to the bed not daring to move. My heart was throbbing so hard that I was sure it would explode in my chest. Finally, I gathered all my courage to go see who it was. My sister was away at school, so the entire third floor with the four bedrooms were mine. I carefully went to the top of the stairway. The bare lightbulb in the center of the ceiling in the hallway glared as I identified Mary, "Mary, what are you doing?" I asked, in a panic. Mary, continuing her trek up the stairway, said, "I heard you crying and I came to see what was wrong." I had not been crying and I tried to convince Mary of this. Mary had the agility of a young girl when she scooted under the gate as she had seen me do so many times. This was her way out to come visit her dear Joyce. Mama came in the nick of time, "Come, Mary," Mama cooed to her, "let's go back to your room." Mary balked at leaving Joyce alone. She was pretty determined that Joyce was her daughter. It took some persuasion on Mama's part to have Mary return to her room. A different gate was installed and I could no longer slide under it or go visit Mary.

I often listened to Mama comfort those who were dying. It was at the bedside of dear Mary, that I watched her breathe her last breaths as she called for me. I took her hand, her fingers clenched around mine, as I stared wide-eyed, and filled with apprehension as she pressed a carved jade ring into my hand, as she breathed her last shuddering breath.

"The DOLLHOUSE"

When we first moved to this antiquated farm house, I would walk the dusty, wooden corridor that led to my doll house. I would pass the curtain-less window graced with spider webs as I made my daily trek from the main house. The main part of the house was affixed to the shed that went through to the barn. At the end of the corridor was an abandoned outhouse. At one era in time this outhouse was the elite three-holler. The reason for it being so special was that it was attached to the shed, and you didn't need to go outdoors to get to it, but now it was dormant and unused, and so this is where I kept my darling babies.

There was my precious Black Mammy doll, her body was stuffed with horse hair. Her hair was also made of horse hair, and it was shedding on one side, showing the black cloth she was made of. I still caressed her as if she were the most beautiful doll. Next to Black Mammy sat Betsey Wetsey, the most modern of my babies. She even had a bottle that was just the right size to press into her rounded stiff lips, and in seconds she would wet her pants, just like a real baby. I would wrap her securely in a little knitted blanket to be sure she was warm. The eldest of the babies, next to Black Mammy was Betty. Betty was the twin to my sister's doll given us one Christmas by Gramma & Grampa Hutchinson. Her hard painted face was artistically designed and her heavy black lashes, on her huge eyes, just intrigued me. When I picked her up, her eyes would pop open, and then when she laid back, they quickly closed and Betty went fast asleep as she dispelled a faint cry that came from her belly. Her wail was so sad, I would pick her up and hug her and her eyes would pop open again, and her gentle cry would stop.

A new baby would arrive every Christmas. One had thick blonde braids, which reminded me of my long strawberry blonde hair and my long pigtails. She was dressed like a Swedish girl making her special, since Swedes were an important part of my family history on Mama's side. It was an important part of the family ancestry and a privilege to have such a baby. There was my dainty glass headed baby, Rosie, that looked like a princess, with her black painted hair and rosy dotted cheeks with her pert red lips. Her black eyes almost came to life with her lashes painted in thin sweeping strokes. Her petite body adorned with bloomer pantaloons under her beige dress, that displayed the tiniest pink roses in a scattered pattern. She was the most mature of my babies. I would sweetly kiss her, and place her carefully in Betty's arms, who was able to hold her securely.

The old outhouse was getting too small to hold all of the babies. Daily I would attend to their needs, with freshly baked mud-pie cakes from the sun, making sure each was properly cleaned and covered each night. I began to worry about what would I do when Christmas came and another baby arrived? How could I care for it in a most fitting fashion?

Slowly I made my way to the kitchen of the main house where Mama was preparing meals for the patients. I was downcast, and pretty sullen. Mama observed that I was sad and asked, "What is wrong?" "Mama," I wailed, "what am I going to do? I have so many babies and there isn't any more room in the outhouse." Mama was so smart and always had a solution for my dilemmas. She gently laid her hand on my shoulder and said very solemnly as she counseled me, "A good mother always makes room for one more." In my heart of hearts, I wanted to be the best mother I could be, so I trudged back to the outhouse and looked the situation over. I incorporated an old paint can as a chair for one of the older babies to sit on, and to hold a younger one. I dusted the old window above the outhouse seats and hung one of my babies up on one of the nails that was sticking out from the wooden slats. It took some imagination and work to organize the children, but I just wanted to be prepared for when Christmas came, so I would have enough room for one more. Certainly I understood how the "Old Woman in the Shoe" felt, in the nursery rhyme, that she had so many children she didn't know what to do!

In relating this little tale of my childhood, I realize the importance, more than ever, of having our hearts ready for when

Jesus comes again, as He has promised that when He returns, He will take us home with Him to have a place that He has prepared for each of us, and there will be plenty of room.

> *"In My Father's house are many rooms if it were not so, I would have told you.*
>
> *I am going there to prepare a place for you.*
>
> *And if I go and prepare a place for you, I will come back and take you with me*
> *That you also may be where I am."*
> (John 14:2 & 3 NIV)

"Panda"

Did you ever have a special stuffed animal, doll or blanket that was important to your life? I had a Panda bear, which I loved. He was black and white checkered with black ears, and was a special stuffed animal in my life. Actually, I think he was the only stuffed animal I ever had. I outgrew sleeping with him, so I placed him in a special place on top of my bureau. When I would enter the room, there was Panda to welcome me in my room, and there he was every morning when I opened my eyes. I just felt special comfort with Panda nearby. Then one day, Mama decided that Panda was too raggedy and looked pretty sad, but not only that, I was in the first grade, so it was time to say good bye to Panda. She didn't think I would miss him, so she threw him away, while I was at school. I came home from school and to my distress, as I entered my room, the first thing I noticed was that Panda was missing.

I was horrified! Oh no! Where did Panda go? I raced downstairs to Mama and told her the terrible news that Panda was missing. It was then she gently confessed that she threw Panda away as she felt that he had lived his life and it was time for him to go since he was pretty sad looking. I was devastated! After my many tears, Mama retrieved Panda from the trash, and we held a suitable funeral for him. He was placed in a box with a comfy little blanket, and the lid put over his ragged body, and off to the wood furnace he went.

As I write this I realize how ragged and worn out we feel with all of life's battles. We fall and hurt ourselves as children and get scars on our knees and elbows. They heal, but we remember what we went through and how we got those scars. We aren't like Panda sitting on the bureau. Jesus is our great Physician. He doesn't throw us away. He retrieves us and gives us hope and strength to continue to live as we give our lives to Him. He helps us to live longer lives, and have a better outlook on life than poor Panda had with me. We never have to worry about what happens to us when we have Jesus near us all the time. He is the One we need to wake up to, and see in our mind each morning. He has promised, in His Word, that He will never "leave us or forsake us." (*see Hebrews 13:5 NKJV*) Panda left a special impact on my life.

"Workers"

The night nurses and day workers that entered my life became family. June was always in her crisp uniform that made a swishing noise as she scurried about in her white shoes. Zelpha, a nurse that often worked nights was loud with a coarse voice. She liked to bake at night to stay awake. Arlene always had a smile mixed with a good sense of humor, and her favorite word for everyone was "dee-ar." She was Mama's best friend, and her two daughters often came over to be with me. Winnie was another one of her nurses that was there during the day, and would trade off times so others could have their days off. Gladys was the cook and a good one. She always had a big smile! She also was the cook at the elementary school, and I saw her frequently there. Her daughter, Roberta, nicknamed Bobbi, was a helper that did a bit of everything. Donna, her little girl, was with her quite often, and she was as cute as a button with her curly blonde hair. Simone, a little French lady, who was very articulate with her house cleaning, came in frequently to clean. Her daughter Mitzi was also at my house often and we were good friends. We were classmates in school.

Mother would sing an old hymn, called "Others," throughout her day, that has come back to mind many times and continues to ring in my ears, "Others, Lord, yes, others, let this my motto be. Help me to live for others, that I might live like Thee." Those words were not appreciated then as they are now.

"Swimming"

Before I learned the thrill of swimming, I used to walk to Conway Lake just one mile from our home. On our way we had to pass by Pete's Pond, where we would burn old tires on the ice, and ice skate after dark in the winter. In the Spring, Pete's Pond was where I would wade in the murky waters, to capture squiggly polliwogs as babies. They looked like raisins trapped in a mush of clouded slime until they developed their tails to swim furiously about.

This particular day, my sister, her friend, Linda, and myself went to spend a good share of the day at the Lake. She was sunbathing with her friend on the beach as I went in the water with my beach ball, wrapping my arms about the ball, and kicking my feet in the water, to propel myself deeper, when whoops, the ball slipped out of my arms, and floated away from my reach. I sank deep into the water, standing on the bottom of the muddy bed, I reached my hand up, until just the tops of my fingertips were above the water's edge. My sister's friend, Linda, saw my fingertips, and raced from the sandy beach to pull me out of the water, as I coughed, spit and spluttered.

We walked back home, apprehensively, as my sister knew Mama would be furious. When Mama learned what happened, she took me back to the lake, immediately, and made me go back in; she didn't want me to be afraid of the water, and from then on I was in swimming classes instructed by Helen Hill. I became an enthusiastic swimmer. Later, I took classes at Camp Lawroweld, in Weld, Maine and once I mastered Swimmers, I entered Junior Lifesaving Class.

From that point on, I would swing off the ropes, that hung from the tree, that fanned over the water. I would swim the dam and under the bridge way, pulling myself over the huge log that blocked the entrance into the dam, daring the waters as I would dare the boys to catch me. I could swim faster and swifter, and with great joy, as they could never keep up.

"Hiking"

Mountain hiking was a passion of my parents and whenever friends were over, they would take us on a hike even on a short trail. This is where I developed a love of the mountain top challenge. The Conway area is in the valley of the White Mountains. I grew to love the surrounding mountains that bordered every side of my existence from Crammore Mountain, where I would ride to the top of the mountain top on the Skimobile (which no longer exists) to see the tremendous view, and pick blueberries in the summer, to riding up Mount Washington to enjoy the adventurous trip, to climbing Mt. Chocoruha, Bear Mountain, Table Talk Mountain, The Loop, and many others that were a challenge to be conquered. I rode on the gondola to Wild Cat Mountain, and experienced the ravines in the notches, from Silver Cascades to Loon and Cannon Mountain, and even to our very own Cathedral Ledge in North Conway, New Hampshire along with a myriad of other trails we climbed as a family.

"My First Kisses"

I was in first grade and my teacher was Mrs. Elsie Masterton at Pine Tree Memorial, about a quarter of a mile from my home, when my first boyfriend, Donny, walked me home in the rain and said he had to tell me a secret, so took me to the far end of the porch and kissed me, then ran off. I can still see, in my mind's eye, his yellow rain jacket as he fled, racing through the raindrops. Mama and my sister were peeking out the window during this encounter and my sister teased mercilessly. I think it was pay-back for all the times I gave her grief. I was in the fifth grade when my second boyfriend, Curtis, kissed me under a street light. I had walked him half-way home after having homemade cookies and milk at my house. We had laughed and giggled over silly things. He stood back and said, "How was that?" My response was, "Wet!" So he wiped his mouth on his sleeve, and kissed me again. "How was that?" he asked again. "Better," I responded. Then satisfied he ran home and I turned and went back to my home just as the street lights came on.

"Memories"

Remembrances of my friend, Linda, and I gathering her sister's wedding gown from the box from where it was stored under the bed, and donning it as if we were brides, then carefully returning it to its box. Linda's mother and older sister, Jeannette, were great cooks and they always had some homemade cookies, cakes or just something yummy to eat.

Linda & I would often meet out in back of the library where an ice skating rink was prepared. The snow mounds from the snow being plowed off made a great opportunity to play "King of the Mountain." We spent hours on ice skates till our toes were nearly frozen. As sweet as these Hallmark memories seem, there was a dark side.

The postmaster who had to be avoided, and squirmed away from, when he would come out from behind the counter and pin you up against the wall with his fingers gleefully playing on the victim of any young girl that entered the post office, and came within his reach. It became a challenge of skillfulness to find ways to escape his advances. I was sent to pick up the mail often, along with others in town, as we did not have mail boxes or mail carriers, so mail was retrieved at the Post Office. Then there was the town pervert that exposed himself in the window, as you passed by on your way to the lake. As we raced by on bicycles, we would shout to each other – "don't look." We were scared, and it made it even worse that he lived next door to the haunted house. Every town has a haunted house that is deserted and run down. It was these times of comradeship that built friendships that would last forever and yet some would be forever lost.

"Religious Convictions

The Conway areas were considered the "dark county" for Adventism. No one knew about Seventh-day Adventist's, and Mama prayed frequently for there to be a church nearby. There was one church, across the street, which was the Methodist Church, and was more like a community church. It was where weddings were held and Vacation Bible School, which I attended. But there was no church that kept the Bible Sabbath. Therefore, we met in a small home, a couple miles away, with an elderly couple, called a "Branch Sabbath School." It was a time of studying the Bible together. There was nothing for children, since I was the only one. But I sparkled with joy when Mrs. Bassett had her clear, glass, gallon, cookie jar filled with hermit cookies, and I was able to have all I wanted.

We later developed a group called a "Branch Sabbath School," in Brownfield, Maine, not far away, in a rented Sunday keeping church. There was a boy and girl that was also part of the group, and sometimes we were invited to their home for dinner. The minister that came once a month was a treat. It was either Pastor Menshousen or Pastor David Shaw. In the meantime, either Mama or Mrs. Grace Howard were the speakers. Mrs. Howard was a high school teacher at White Memorial Seventh-day Adventist Church School in Portland, Maine.

"Living Away From Home"

My sister and I went away to school. We lived in So. Portland with a family from the White Memorial Seventh-day Adventist Church during the week. They were very strict and devoted, but were more arrogant than they were loving, so our time there was often a time of disappointment and sadness. I developed a great deal of resentment because we were treated so unfairly. The year before my sister had lived with an older couple in So. Portland, which were also church members that had been very good to her and she loved them. This family did not resemble the one she had lived with.

My sister would braid my hair, and pull my hair to get my braids tight. I would always be squirming or wriggling, and she would snap, "Stand still," while she tried to get my hair just right. As I think back on this, I am sure she was taking out her frustration of how we were treated, on my hair. She had difficulty with math and for some reason it came easily to me, so I would try to help her with her 10th grade math. I was only a third grader, and I looked forward to school every day, and hated going back to that home after school. My teacher, Mrs. Shaw, was sweet and kind. Her husband, Pastor David Shaw, was one of the ministers that would come to speak in Brownfield, Maine, and visited my parents frequently.

I learned a lot from Mrs. Shaw. Her daughter, Marilyn, and my sister became good friends. Mrs. Grace Howard, in another class room with my sister, was a dear lady, and a friend of our mother. I think she may have realized we were not being treated well, and if she did, nothing was ever said in reference to it.

"Roller Skating with Questionable Company"

I remember one time; we went roller skating. Richard, from our home town, came to roller skate with my sister. We had a fun time! When Mama and Daddy came to pick us up to bring us home for the weekend, I remember very vividly, we had just driven in the driveway, and I blurted out about Richard coming to roller skate with us. My sister slapped her hand over my mouth as I was midway through the my story. Daddy reprimanded her terribly that night. I crawled under the kitchen table and cried because I was the cause of this. I was broken-hearted for her, and even today I can cry over this. In hind sight, this young man was one of the town's questionable young men who preyed on girls and in daddy's defense, he did not want his daughter with such a person. I get it now, but not then.

"Pneumonia"

We didn't go back another year to that school or to that home. My sister went on to Massachusetts to South Lancaster Academy, and I went to live with a family in Rochester, New Hampshire to attend church school there. It was a church school held in the basement of the church, and was a one-room school room for several grades. I was the only one in the fourth grade so I did a lot of fifth grade work. during that time, I was living on a farm with a family of several children. The mother of the house had divorced her husband and married his son. This all had happened before they became Christians.

I was ill most of that school year. I came down with pneumonia, and had to stay at home to get well under my mother's care. Old Dr. Smith came to see me, and I was not to get out of bed as my lungs were so weak. Mother slathered Vicks over my chest, and up around my throat, so I could take in the fumes and be able to breathe better without the constant coughing. She wrapped this nifty pad around my neck and pinned it so it wouldn't slide. Later when I attended Camp Lawroweld, in Weld, Maine, she always packed those same pads in my suitcase. I wondered why and if she thought I was going to be sick. It was not until I was fifteen that I got the shock of my life finding out that those pads were Kotex!

Living Home Again

I returned to Pine Tree Memorial School with my teacher, Mrs. Elizabeth Walker, in the fifth and sixth grade, just a short distance from my house. I was so happy to be back home with my parents. I loved that little school, and I excelled because I had already done fifth grade work in the Church school. This was where I learned, in first and second grade, the art of penmanship under Mrs. Elsie Masterton, who was a stickler for perfection, and I am so thankful today, for her hours of stressing the importance of this. Mrs. Elizabeth Walker was insistent on strict observance for enunciation, spelling words and also current events. I hated current events, but I loved spelling!

"Mama Was So Sick"

Then one day, Mrs. Walker took me upstairs in the office to talk to me. Mama was in the hospital. They didn't know if she would live, so they prepared me to go see her. When I arrived at the hospital, her room was darkened, and Daddy and my sister were standing next to the bed. My teacher took me in. Mama had tubes in her nose and mouth, and couldn't talk. She took my hand and held it, but her pain was so bad that they took me out and I was taken back home. The patients in her nursing home had been taken away. A few days later, Mama returned home.

I learned she had a tubular pregnancy, and they didn't think she would make it through the aborting of the baby. At that time, when all the words had been said, I didn't understand any of it, but I was so thankful she was alright and back home. But all my playmates, Mama's patients, were gone and I would never see them again.

"Pauline"

It was a sunny afternoon, and as I was walking home with my friend, Pauline, she whispered in my ear what a man does to a woman if they are husband and wife. I was in shock! Totally horrified! I emphatically, and quite defensively, told my friend, Pauline, "My father would never do such a thing to my mother." I immediately went to my house and sat on a high stool in the kitchen, while Mama was busy baking, and I informed her of all that Pauline had told me. She calmly answered, "We will talk about this later one day." I was quite sure in my mind that if this were true, she would have said something, because my mother never let me believe a lie. I was never allowed to believe in Santa Claus. He was a man dressed up to make children think he was the one who brought them toys, when it was parents that worked hard to bring them good things.

"Daddy and I in The Woods"

I spent many hours in the woods with Daddy. The woods were his second home. He worked cutting trees and hauling pulp wood. Often he took my sister and I on his trips in the early morning hours to leave off the pulp wood at the paper mill in Berlin, New Hampshire. I remember going with him many times in the woods while he worked. There was one time, in particular, he sent me traipsing, in the deep snow, to get a can of oil for the tractor. I cried all the way to the car, as the snow was waist deep for me, but I did bring the can of oil back to him. He expected me to do as he said without question or whimper. I didn't let him know I had cried.

There was another incident when one of Daddy's workers came to work drunk. That was something daddy never tolerated. He reached down from sitting up on his tractor, and picked this big man up to eye level, and told him, "to either work or get out." Daddy had a voice of authority and when he spoke, you didn't question. This man never came in drunk or drinking again. Daddy was no taller than five foot eight inches, shortest of his brothers, but of broad stature and very strong.

Daddy would take me hunting with him, but he never killed a deer. We would watch them, and he would quietly whisper to me about their beauty, as they would water by a stream. However, I was taught how to use a gun. The first time I fired a shot gun, I landed on my backside with him roaring with laughter. I used to love to target practice with a .22 rifle.

"Entertaining Angels Unaware"

It was a stormy night with thunder and lightning that cut the power out of the area. Daddy was out working in the woods. We heard from neighbors the reports that trees had fallen, and no one could get through the main highway due to fallen trees and limbs. Mama was worried, so she prayed. There came a knock at the door, and two men were looking for a place to stay, out of the severe weather. Mama invited them in, and gave them a room on the second floor. I listened from the top of the third floor landing, in the dark. They noticed her books in her, glassed in, bookcase before entering their room. There were security lights strategically placed in areas of the house that would go on, when the power went out. These men told Mama they were familiar with those books, which were books written by what Adventists know as, "Spirit of Prophesy," then called the "red books" because they were bound in red. They talked for a while longer, then Mama gave them instructions as to where the bathroom, towels and washcloths were located. She assured them she would have breakfast ready for them in the morning as she was sure there would be power back by then, and if not, we had a gas cooking stove. They thanked her and assured her that Daddy was not home due to the roads being closed, because of the intensity of the storm, but also calmed her fears that he was safe. She seemed relieved! In the morning, however, they had gone. Their beds had not been slept in, and there was no evidence that anyone had been there at all. Mama said, she had "entertained angels unaware."

> *"Don't forget to show hospitality to strangers,*
> *for some who have done this have entertained angels*
> *without realizing it."* (Hebrews 13:2 NLT)

"Premonitions"

Mama often had premonitions (which are defined as forebodings, or advanced warnings). It was like something inside her was telling her things in advance, and she would make a statement that would send chills creeping up your spine, and an awakening of your mind that was eerie, I guess it really was holy discernment, but I didn't know that at the time. This particular day, Daddy didn't arrive home on time and she was concerned. Working alone in the woods was always a concern. As the sun began to set, and the twilight ended, she became frantic. I remember her saying aloud, whether to me or to the air, "He has been hurt in the woods." She began to make phone calls, and frantically telling the State Police where his work location was, and that he should have been home. "He has been hurt and I know he has, you must hurry." When Mama was worried or frantic there was no stopping her until someone listened to her. Daddy was found! A tree limb had come down, and hit him on the head, and knocked him out cold. I don't ever remember him being laid up or going to the doctor, although, it may be possible the State Police may have taken him to the hospital to be checked out. He was a strong man with tremendous fortitude. He instilled in my sister and I to work hard by his example. Both of our parents were hard workers and never were the ones that sat around for there was always something to be done.

A quote, often quipped, "Idle hands are the devil's workshop."

"Dreams"

Dreams are forewarnings, or can be just mindless dreams. There was talk that when the Wetmore's dreamt of muddy waters it had a significant meaning. Usually it meant death. But when Mama dreamed something, you can be sure it bordered on her being forewarned, and this particular dream involved a small opening, which was half the size of a regular doorway, in a house where a fire started, and there was no escape. She had no idea what it meant. It bothered her, until one day, she visited her neighbor, Luella, who brought her upstairs where Mama had never been. There she saw the half door opening that had been in her dream, and there was no other way out. She refused to go further, and related the dream to her friend. Mama never went up in that part of her house again. It was several years later that there was a fire, at that home, that seemed to have started near that half-door opening, and if anyone had been in that room there would have been no escape.

> "And it shall come to pass afterward that I will pour out My Spirit on all flesh;
> Your sons and daughters shall prophesy, your old men shall dream dreams,
> your young men shall see visons."
>
> (Joel 2:28 NKJV)

"Gramma and Grampa Wetmore"

My sister was now out of school and working at New England Memorial Sanitarium and Hospital in Stoneham, Massachusetts. (This institution no longer exists). Daddy's mother had died, just three months after Grampa died. It was 1960, and I was twelve years old. Gramma & Grampa Wetmore had lived with us for a year. Grampa loved to garden. We had a plot of land where we had a huge garden down near the river. I used to ride in the back of the wooden wagon that was hitched to the little tractor as we went to check out the garden every morning. His eyesight was bad so he would think the peas hadn't done very well, as I picked them and ate them raw. Gramma had suffered a stroke, and was paralyzed on her right side, and couldn't speak for twenty some odd years. Daddy would pick her up in his arms, and place her gently on the bed, as Grampa prepared her for bed each night—then in the morning, Daddy would pick her up from her bed, after she had been dressed, and put her in her chair for the day. She always had a smile and the kindest eyes, and Grampa loved her dearly. They, eventually, moved back to New York State where she died. All of Daddy's siblings had taken turns to care for them until that time. We had taken many trips out to New York State where Daddy's brother, Don, and sisters, Alta and Ruth lived. The old homestead on Bucktooth Run was always a place reverenced by the family of nine children, one died as a teen from pneumonia. This was the place where they were raised as a Christian family.

I remember taking the 14-hour trip, with my foot in a pie, not daring to move, in the back seat, squished up against my sister, as the car was packed with goodies for Thanksgiving. We played the animal game along the way. She had one side of the road and I had the other. We got points for certain animals or farm equipment we saw along the way. Every so often I would cry out, "How many more miles is it?"

(The following story was written by Alice Wetmore Peterson, my father's youngest sister, about her mother, Grace Wetmore, and her brother, Victor, who died.)

JOYCE A. LEONARD

"The Treasure Box"

"The cold winter days are losing their icy chill and daffodils are pushing brave green tips up the melting snow. Something about this time of year carries me back in thought, to my childhood and to the little house nestled among the evergreen trees in the state of New York where I was born. (10/31/1931) I still envision the freshly laundered white, sheer curtains dancing in the sweet country breeze that wafted in through the open windows. The Spring house cleaning always began in the large upstairs bedroom in the front of the house.

This was the time of year that Mama came upstairs. She had once occupied this bedroom, but when she had taken ill with her first stroke, she and Papa had moved to the room below, where it was more convenient. When we heard the unmistakable shuffle on the steps as she pulled herself along the banister with her good hand, we knew she was coming to look at her "treasure box." After she had rested awhile from her strenuous climb, she customarily delegated one of us to remove the long flat box from its place on the top shelf in the closet. Then she gently and tenderly lifted each article from the container. The room was hushed as she fondly caressed each item and bathed it with her tears.

First to leave the box was the tiny blue Sabbath suit, then came the coloring book and crayons. The pencil box that had belonged to the little first grader followed close behind. Finally, there was the frilly funeral ribbon with shiny gold letters that spelled VICTOR. (1929–1935) When everything has been examined, the box was carefully repacked and returned to the closet shelf, and life resumed as usual.

I was only two when Victor died, and through the years that followed I often wondered how Mama could miss him so much when she still had eight living children to occupy her time and thoughts. But it was not until years later when I had married, and had a family of my own, that I began to realize that one child can never take the place of another. Each one has its own special spot in a mother's heart. I don't know what ever became of the "treasure box." Although, the farm belongs to someone else, but it will always be our home, for that is where the indelible impressions were stamped upon our tender lives.

Sometimes I wonder if God has a "treasure box" of memories. Does He recall tenderly and lovingly the time His faithful children walked and talked with Him and called Him "Father" before death ended the relationship? I am sure He too, looks forward to the resurrection, and the time when the earth is reborn, and all His creation will be fresh and new, when there will be no more sin, no sickness, no death." (see I Corinthians 15:52-54)

"Eloped"

The day my sister eloped at twenty years old, she went to the Town Office, across the road from our home. Mama stood in the kitchen window and pondered about the lights being on so late. My sister had left the house to go to her job in her work skirt, as she worked as a chambermaid in one of the local motels in the North Conway area. But somehow, Mama knew she was across the road getting married. She went across the road and cautiously peered in the window, and sure enough, her instincts were confirmed. She came back in tears! Mama always felt this man wasn't the one for her daughter and she became very angry to the point of violence. When my sister arrived back the next day for her things, Mama tossed my sister's "hope chest" down two flights of stairs at her. I always felt as if I was in the background looking on. Standing in the shadows, always in tears and hiding. I wondered why Mama just didn't let my sister marry the "love of her life." If you look at it in another perspective, our parents thought their children were of a higher calling, and should be with partners that were of good report and Christian standing. What Mama didn't realize is that my sister was re-enacting her own decisions, when Mama and Daddy eloped against her parents' wishes. The old saying still was ringing true, "history repeats itself."

In my mother's case, Daddy was a poor farm boy, and Mama was a woman of higher means, so my grandparents felt that Daddy was not of her caliber. It was later that they said, "he was the best son-in-law they could have ever had." My brother-in-law, at this writing, and my sister have been married for over 50 years. They have stayed together, regardless of the feelings then and raised a family and continue to stay committed to each other.

"Tony"

It was while Daddy was gone to Grandma's funeral that I was left to care for Tony, the old work horse, that Daddy used in the woods to haul logs. My sister wasn't home then, so I would go out to feed and brush him down. I took him out to the field and tied him to a huge log, not realizing that meant work to Tony, so he dragged that old log all around the field until he got entangled in the clothes line. Poor Tony! It was later when Daddy made a lean-to in the woods that he started leaving Tony there so he wouldn't have to haul him from home to the woods every day. One morning, when daddy left for the woods to work, he found Tony laying down on the logging road. Someone had run him to death down in the woods. I never found out if he discovered who did this, but I can bet that if he had, they would have had a thrashing from daddy. He was very upset after learning about it, but it was never spoken of again.

"Driving Tractor Trailer"

Daddy transitioned from working in the woods to driving eighteen wheelers over the road. He was gone sometimes a week or more at a time. It was during this time, when the tractor trailer was parked in the door yard, that my curiosity got the better of me and I decided to get in the truck and check out the gears. I got down on the floor and pushed in the clutch, not knowing that was, what it was and the truck started to roll. I shifted the floor shift and quickly discovered that was not stopping it. I immediately went to the other pedal, which was the brake, and it stopped rolling. When I let off the brake it stayed still, and I scrambled out of the truck before I got caught. It was not too long after that daddy decided I needed to learn how to drive a standard shift, so he got an old beater car for me to learn on in the back field. I tore up the field elated with the sense of freedom it gave me.

"Smoking"

Mama had a friend, Edith, that needed a place for her daughter, Kathy to stay and get well. Mama never allowed anyone to smoke or drink in our home, but for some reason, she allowed this girl to smoke in her room. I used to go into her room, and watch with a fascination, her smoking. I stole a cigarette from her pack one day when she went to the bathroom. I took it to my room and tried to light it by holding it on one end and using a match to light the other end. Remembering how it glowed, when she placed it between her lips, I figured she had to blow out on it to create the glow, I watched carefully in the mirror, to make sure it was done right, but no smoke came out of my mouth as it did hers. However, I was satisfied that I had mastered the art of smoking. ("*Evil conduct is like sport to a fool. . .*" Proverbs 10:23 NKJV)

It was later when walking with some neighborhood boys in town, under the cover of trees by the cemetery, without any interference of parents, or nosey neighbors, I was asked if I smoked, "Oh yes," I replied, as a matter of fact. They seemed a bit shocked and passed me the cigarette they had just lit. I blew out on it, as they laughed with great pleasure and told me I had to suck in on it, as they snickered at my ignorance. They stood waiting for me to choke and cough. I didn't disappoint their expectations. You would have thought that would have discouraged me from any further activity with cigarettes, but instead, I was determined to be the "big shot" with the attitude, "anything you can do, I can do." I continued to steal a cigarette here and there from Kathy's pack of cigarettes, until she was released from my mother's care and returned to her mother's place. Then I continued my habit by stealing a quarter for a pack of cigarettes, which was 24 cents a pack, out of my mother's pocketbook.

> "*The mouth of fools are their ruin; their lips get them into trouble.*" (Proverbs 18:6 NLT)

"A Dare-Devil Challenged"

I was a dare-devil. Dare me and I took on the challenge. We often rode our bicycles to the river, and left them outside of the fenced in pasture, where a bull was kept, and we high-tailed it through the pasture, to the waiting riverbed. When excitement wasn't enough at the dam, we took on the railroad trestle. The boys would climb the dirt banking, and straddle the iron bars to grab hold of a brace on the railroad bridge, and let their body hang until they had stopped swinging in mid-air, then drop to the rushing river below. "Hey Joyce," my friend Carol's big brother, Ricky shouted, "I bet you don't dare to do this," as he made his way to do the daring event. Standing down on the sandy beach, of the riverbed, I took the challenge, and shouted back, "Anything you can do, I can do." I made my way to the top of the trestle, and followed the instructions, carefully grabbing the iron brace, and began swinging. I didn't stop swinging like the boys did so I got a bit nervous. "I can't stop swinging," I cried out, trying not to show fear. "Now what do I do?" I screeched, "Let go," the call came back. I did and the exhilaration was addicting. Carol had said, "If you do it, I will," but she never did, and we all decided to leave, since the day was getting late. Racing back toward home on our bicycles, we went our separate ways. I excitedly went and told my mother what happened. Mama called Lucille, Carol and Ricky's mom and Althea, Bobby's mother. Unknown to me, and probably to the rest, there was an undercurrent there, and by the grace of God we came out of that daring feat with our lives. No one was happy with me because I had told my mother.

> *"The Lord keeps watch over you as you come and go, both now and forever more."*
> *(Psalms 121:8 NLT)*

"Jockey Cap"

When my friends that came to visit or if it was a Sabbath afternoon trek—Jockey Cap was the go-to adventure. It is a huge rock in

Fryeburg, Maine that has a trail to climb. I think if you are in good climbing condition, it takes only about 20 minutes. One place is kind of steep. It has a gorgeous view of the mountain range, at the top. In the big rock are garnet stones. Mama was a rock collector known as a "rock hound." She had chiseled rock, or had Daddy do it from every state they ever traveled through that had a rock quarry, as well as the Herkimer Diamond Mine in Herkimer, New York. We always were intrigued with the little red stones that speckled throughout the top of Jockey Cap. Daddy hauled pails of rock for Mama to sort through from that rock, as well as myself and a few of my friends who were interested in helping with the adventure. A lot of fond memories are connected with that trail and the mere mention of the name, "Jockey Cap."

*The foundations of the wall of the city were adorned with
All kinds of precious stones; . . .. " (Revelation 21:19 NKJV)*

"The In-Between Years"
1960-1964

"If you want to hear God's voice clearly, and you are uncertain, then remain in His presence until He changes that uncertainty. Often much can happen during the waiting for the Lord.

Sometimes He changes pride into humility; doubt into faith and peace...

~Corrie ten Boom~

It was tough with another major change. Since there was no longer a nursing home or a guest home, daddy was driving on road trips with the tractor trailer, and mother started working at the New England Sanitarium & Hospital in Stoneham, Massachusetts. My Uncle Walter, Daddy's brother, was head of Maintenance for the entire facility and my aunt, his wife, Florence, who was also my mother's cousin, was the head switch board operator. My sister became Ward Secretary on one of the floors, and Mama was a floor nurse. We lived in a small apartment on the grounds and I attended the nearby church school. I had a difficult year, socially. I never made any friends there, and I really was not fond of my teacher. She was kind enough, but never left a goodly impression on me.

    I loved to tease and that was the best way to get on my sister's nerves. I didn't care if she yelled at me or threatened to tell. Teasing was part of my nature for whatever reason. If I could irritate her, it seemed like that was my enjoyment! It was an on-going cliché that I was her "rattle-snake pest," and daddy's "bum, bum, bum boy!" I had crawled in bed with her, early one morning, when the incident began. I would hold my breath, and strain until my head felt light-headed, and my face would get red. My sister felt this was not good for me to do, so she would screech, "Joyce stop it!" The more she wanted me to stop the more I did it, until daddy from the other room said, "Here, here, what is going on?" She called back "Joyce won't stop holding her breath." Not quite sure what she was talking about, Daddy asked what she meant. We promptly got out of bed and went to show him. My sister, with her elder sister authority said, "She won't stop." I promptly displayed my action, "like this," I quipped and proceeded to hold my breath and strain. The next thing I remember was coming to from falling backwards on the floor. Daddy's first words were, "I thought you kicked the bucket." That scared me enough to never do that again.

"Colitis Then Baptism"

While in seventh-grade, at twelve years of age, I developed colitis. I had terrible pain in my stomach. It was debilitating and I missed a great amount of school. I had to go on a bland diet and was given charcoal and olive oil in large doses for my stomach to heal that whole year. It was not a year of joy for me.

The happiest day of my life was the beautiful sunny Spring day I was baptized at the Stoneham Seventh-day Adventist Church by Pastor DiMarzo, whom I loved. He was so expressive and my heart thrilled at the thought of being baptized and ready for Jesus coming. After all, this was what I had longed for all my days as a young child......being ready for Jesus. I remember watching the sky as a small child waiting for that dark cloud about the size of a man's hand, appear in the sky and then I would see Jesus face to face. I could hardly wait!

> *"Then the sign of the Son of Man shall appear in heaven,*
> *With great power and with great glory,*

And He will send His angels with a great sound of a trumpet, And they will gather together His elect from the four winds, from one end of the heaven to the other."
(Matthew 24:30-31 NKJV)

(See also Mark 13:26-27; Mark 14:62; Revelation 1:7)

I have no recollection of going under the water in immersion as the Bible teaches, dying to sin, and being raised to newness of life. Mama had made me the most beautiful dress for the occasion. The print was a white background with purple and lavender bouquets of flowers tied with pink ribbons. It was designed with cap sleeves, and had a full skirt that when I twirled around in it, I felt like a princess, absolutely beautiful! I am sure at that moment in time, I was God's little girl basking in the joy of the commitment I had just made. (see Matthew 28:19 NKJV)

"Conway Junior High"

Somehow I passed into eighth grade. I was back home at Junior High in Conway, New Hampshire. I loved French Class! My French teacher, Miss Pinnette, looked like a china doll, with thinly pressed red lips, her short, meticulously arranged, dark hair and dark-framed glasses. She eloquently, enunciated each word from French to English and vice versa. She gave each of us a French name and I was called, "Angelique." Algebra was with Mrs. Elizabeth Gagnon, which was also my home room, and was closely monitored. I liked algebra and did well! She also wore glasses that hung on a cord around her neck. She frequently took them off and they dropped to her chest as she explained a lesson, then she would put them back on again. Mr. Minton was my English teacher. I excelled in English, but I was bored with it as well. We were asked to write a biography. I chose him, since Mama had invited him to supper one Friday evening, and I had learned quite a bit about him. I chose to write about him in poetry form. To my astonishment, I was chosen first to read my writing, and I gingerly began. Only a few lines down, he snatched my paper, and ordered me to sit down.

"My English Teacher's Biography"

It happened in 1930, March eight,
Not too soon and not too late!
The family was Scottish-Irish descent,
Where every woman a lady and every man agent.
This lad, he was brought up by Mrs. Hazen;~
He was ever so good and never
thought of being brazen.
When he was about the age of eight,
They came to visit Maine, another state.
About this time, TV was coming out;
And you could be sure he was
watching it without a doubt!
I think you should know this lad was an only child,
And has a temper far from mild.
When they were done with their stays -
They went back to the "State of Bays."
It has been said he went to Parochial schools,
Where he never thought of breaking the rules.
His first ambition was to be a priest . . .
But he isn't that in the least.
He worked his way through Worcester State,
And studied four years for a teacher's fate.
The description of him in his age he now is,
At height of six feet or just about this;
He weighs about one-sixty –five,
Maybe more, I cannot lie.
He can give you quite a stare,
With his eyes so blue,

JOYCE A. LEONARD

And his combed back brown hair,
Might even frighten you!
He once said poetry he never liked,
But now he seems to have taught us everything except, "Betsy from Pike."
He likes to quote a lot of Shakespeare;
At least that is all we hear.
On the housekeeping slant;
It is one of an unaccomplished talent.
Meatloaf is his favorite food;
At least it can put him in a good mood.
One of his habits is that he smokes till he is blue,
And I might add it is his weakness too.
If you flash a smirk or bat an eye,
Without letting another minute go by,
You are bound to hear,
The famous saying so near,
What's so funny or what are you laughing at?"
Comes out in a stony tone so flat.
Another tone that was sure to come out,
Says he, "two minutes" or about!
I am now at the end of my biography,
Of Mr. Jerome Minton and his geography,
But one more thing I must latch,
Mr. Minton is a batch!
(Written 1961—Joyce Wetmore— age 13 for English Class)
(I received an A- on this paper)

"Skipping school"

Most of my eight grade life at Conway Junior High School was good. This one particular day as it was coming near the end of the school year, I think I had Spring fever. I didn't feel like going to school, so when I arrived at school and got off the bus, I decided I was not going in. My French teacher, Miss Pinnette, however, happened to be watching from the classroom window, and saw me leave the school grounds and head out the gate. When I had not returned for her class, she called my mother. I had spent the day at the river. On my walk away from the school grounds, however, I met two of the town boys walking to school, "Hey, Joyce, where are you going?" I replied with a cocky attitude, "Swimming." In amazement, They came back in a tone of disbelief, "You are, really?" I called over my shoulder as I passed by, "Yeh....I am skipping school today." Pretty intrigued with the thought, they called back, "Do you mind if we come too?" I was feeling like I was in control, and didn't care, so called back again, "Suit yourself," as they ran to catch up.

We walked out of town, and through the covered bridge, and down by the river to spend the day, swimming, laughing, telling jokes, and enjoying the sunshine and warm weather. We swam in our clothes and dried off in the sun. It was getting late in the day and I had a long walk ahead of me so I decided to take the railroad tracks. I had to walk some distance to get to them, and then head for home. I wanted to get there about the time the bus did. The boys went their way and said, "See you tomorrow at school."

I had decided the tracks would be least conspicuous, even though it seemed like it might be longer. As I neared home, I could see someone coming in my direction on the tracks. As I got closer, I could tell it was Mama, and she was carrying a long switch. I kept walking, and so did she. As we met, she told me how my French teacher called, and she switched my legs all the rest of the way till we got off the tracks. Charlie Davidson was there waiting in a station-wagon for us. He was the Town Constable and Mama left me with him, as she continued home. The interrogation began! "Where were you all day?" he demanded.

"At the river," I replied rather sheepishly. "All day?" he questioned as if he didn't believe me, "Yes," I retorted emphatically! "What did you do?" He continued to quiz. "Went swimming," I replied without hesitation. "With who?" He continued to probe, so I gave the names of my accomplices, and I felt justified because they could verify my answers. He looked surprised, then knowingly questioned, "Did you have intercourse?" I thought to myself, "Intercourse?" Continuing to muse, in the few seconds I had, I thought, "I don't know what that is, but it doesn't sound very nice, so in disgust, I answered, "No!" He looked me square in the eye and said, "Do you know what it is?" I didn't want him to think I was stupid, so I answered, quite warily, "Yes." With that he took me home. Mama came out, and met him at the station wagon. He got out and I heard him say, "You have nothing to worry about. She just skipped school."

My dear Aunt Ruth, Daddy's oldest sister, was visiting during this time, and my punishment was being grounded for two weeks. That was no big deal as my Aunt Ruth was there, and I loved being around her.

"The Price of Mischief"

A day of fun
In the warming sun,
With the cup of mischief to be drank,
While teasing and laughing at the riverbank.
What is the price of skipping school?
Showing off and being cool –
Tasting the sweetness of youths' appetite,
Touched with innocence the forbidden bite?
Mischief always carries a price tag,
While learning holds a warning flag,
That obeying the rules never gets caught
Swimming in the river or naught!

Youth lives for the moments cost
Testing the water where others have lost;
Thinking their fate won't be the same –
After all isn't it all just pleasure's game?
"To do mischief is like sport to a fool"
Even if for a moment it seems like it's cool.
The price tag is sometimes hidden inside;
When the heart speaks as your guide.
Don't toss the thoughts out of doing right,
As "out of mind, out of sight"-
For the price maybe more than you want to pay,
And then it will be too late to have a say.
By Joyce Ann Wetmore Leonard (March 13, 2001)
"Doing wrong is fun for a fool, while wise conduct is a pleasure to the wise."
(Proverbs 10:23 NLT)

"Eighth Grade Graduation"

Eighth grade graduation was pretty special. I was the only one with an orchid corsage. Daddy was on an out of state trip with the tractor trailer. He worked for Albee (a trucking company) in Wolfeboro, New Hampshire. Mama was getting me a rosebud corsage, and didn't know daddy had an orchid wired through the company he worked for with the attached note, "Love Daddy." I was so elated!

    I was the envy of the girls. Mama had bought a beautiful white dress for me and I felt like a princess again, just like when I got baptized. Mama had worked hard weeding witch grass for Jim Robertson to have enough money for me to feel like this. She made sure I had underwear and shoes to go with my dress, so that my attire was completely new. This was the end of elementary days, and the beginning of really being grown up. I was thirteen and Mama said I could start babysitting.

Chapter Seven

"The Dark Silence"

"Fret not because of evil doers, don't envy the wicked; for the evil have no future;

their light will be snuffed out."
(Proverbs 24:19 & 20 NLT)

Who is that young girl with stifled screams bearing the brutality of a sexual assault? Raped at thirteen, by the drunken fiancé, of a woman working nights, leaving this young girl to care for her baby that laid in the crib within the next room, as her virginity was exploited by a perpetrator that would never publicly pay for his cruelty, but still there is an account that lays at the judgment seat of God. It was me! A terror I will never forget stands out of the darkness over 50 years later. Blackness, dim lighting, screaming, and obscenities that I can never forget, and this is how it started.

The year was 1961. The television show that depicts revelry were comedies like, "I Love Lucy," or talent shows such as, "The Ed Sullivan Show," with an audience regaling in laughter, accompanied by applause. I was lying on the couch, watching the show with only the lighting, that came from the television set, feeling insecure with the noises coming from the kitchen, as I had heard there were rats under the kitchen cupboards, and there certainly seemed to be something making the pans rattle, in the kitchen, which was the farthest room in the apartment. The first room, entered in this second floor apartment, was the living room, and off from there, was the kitchen to the far right of the living room. A closet was adjacent to the kitchen doorway, and the bathroom next to that. To the left, as you entered the living room, was an archway that went straightway into the bedroom, but in full view of the living room. Just off, to the right of the archway, was a small bedroom. This was the baby's room.

I kept hearing the rattling that came from the kitchen and it made me nervous. Thoughts frantically filled my mind with the stories I had heard of rats eating babies while they slept. I believed that if I stayed there on the couch and kept awake that no rats would pass by me into the baby's room. I feared an attack on the baby. Every so often I would tiptoe to the kitchen doorway and quickly snapped the light on, focusing on the white slatted wooden cupboards, with broom in hand, just in case a rat materialized before me, but once the light was on, the rattling always stopped. I didn't dare to turn my back on the doorway, so I would walk backward to the couch, where I would lie in wait and attempt to focus on the television program once again.

What was the baby's name and how old was it? Those memories have been lost into the shadows of time, and only the paralyzing fear factor remains vivid. Then I heard a different sound. Was it Carol, the baby's mom home early? It sounded like a scuffled thud in the stairwell, that grew louder and closer at each thud. My heart began to beat rapidly, and now I was frozen with fright, that outweighed the uneasiness of the rodents in the kitchen. I didn't even dare to speak. The door creaked open and there stood Carol's fiancé, Ron, with his hair askew and voice slurred, as he said, "So you must be the babysitter?" I immediately sat up on the couch. I could smell the beer on his breath from where I was sitting as he spoke. But strangely the fluttering of my heart stopped as I felt safe because it was someone I knew. I was relieved that someone else was there that might know what to do about the rats in the kitchen!

He said he had to take a "wicked wiss," and excused himself into the bathroom. When he came out, I began to ramble on about my dilemma of the rats, and then made my timely check on the baby. When I came from the child's bedroom, he was standing in front of me so I couldn't pass. He reached down to my face to kiss my lips with his obnoxious breath penetrating my face. I became uncomfortable and quickly turned my face away, to gain relief, with some pleasant air, and to avoid the advance. It seemed it was instantaneous! One minute I was standing there avoiding his breath, and the advances of his roaming hands, and the next I was struggling to get him off me, while he was tearing my clothes from my body.

It is not uncommon for people facing a time of peril or severe trauma to have their mind escape to a place where they are not thinking about what is really happening, but focus on the thing that previously was a problem. My thoughts were anxious for the baby and not for myself, and the rats that could hurt the baby, but then the ravaging worsened. He was doing things I did not want or even knew about. I could see the silhouette of his head and upper body as he moved against me, and I was scared!

It reminded me of the postmaster, Martin. If no one was at the post office, when I went to pick up the mail, he would come out from behind the counter and push himself up against me, and try to kiss me. I would always wriggle myself down, and duck under his arms, and then make a mad dash for the door. This was different --this wasn't trying to run away from a married postmaster who was trying to kiss me. I always managed to get out of Martin's grasp as he would call after me, "Hey, come here! Come here!" Then the next time I had to go to the post office he would always say, "How come you ran off?" I would always say, "Because . . ." leaving my thought open-ended. I had found out from my friends in town that Martin played these same games with them, and they all refused to baby-sit for him and his wife, Charlotte. One friend had baby-sat and Martin took her home and got fresh with her. She was scared to be around him after that. Strange no one dared to tell his wife or our parents. We thought no one would believe us, since he was the postmaster, and had such a good reputation.

This wasn't the post office and there was no door of escape. There was no way to duck the advances of Ron. This wasn't a game for him, and it was worse than any frightening dream I had ever had. He was heavy, very heavy. "Ron, please. ... NO!...NO!...NO!...you are hurting me." It was as if everything turned black and white and no color was allowed in this nightmare. Only now the nightmare was real, and the disturbed cries were screams. I heard my own shrilling screams from my own mouth, only no one could hear them. My cries were muffled, by his big gruff hand, as it was firmly flattened over my mouth. I felt like I couldn't even breathe, not even through my nose. All my air was being depleted, and I felt like I was suffocating. The vivid words continue to ring in my ears to this very day, even when the same tragedy of another being raped is being depicted in a movie. I hear his words, "I'm going to **** you until you DIE...." I waited for death, but the suffocation that took my air caused me to pass out, and there is no recollection of when it all ended. When I came too, he was gone and only the immense sense of filthiness remained. Shame and guilt are two symptoms of a rape victim. Could I have stopped it? Do I dare to tell anyone, and if I do what will they think of me?

I told my mother the next day, after the initial shock of all that took place, and Mama quietly counseled, "We must keep this quiet," she continued, "Your reputation is at stake, and the family will be disgraced." This only made the guilt heavier, and I assumed I could have stopped him somehow. So what comes into play with such a horror of that day? Pregnancy? No, I hadn't advanced into woman hood yet. Town gossip? Yes! Mama feared I would become an easy target for young boys. Silence! The dark treasure of silence, where lurking nightmares only haunt the victim, and never the perpetrator.

There are times today when angry words are spoken, and a rage comes through from someone I love, and the pain begins again. Not like that night, but just as horrible as that night, and the filthiness of the harsh words that have been spoken renew themselves. The pain is there again, and the panic raises its taunting head as I quietly remember, for it is only my nightmare, and no one else knows my horror.

Surely God delivered me from the hand of death that night. And some might ask, "Why would God allow that to even happen to you?" The only answer that comes to mind, is I can now feel someone else's pain who has experienced this horror in, somewhat, the same way. By being able to feel their pain I can minister to their needs with encouragement and sympathy because only one who has walked in the shoes of another, can know how bad the blisters really hurt.

I can recognize the filth of profane language, and understand why God hates it. I can look at the rage of a perpetrator, and see the cycle of abuse and know it firsthand. If I had not been allowed to endure this pain, how could I now love the sinner regardless of the sin? How could I have learned to forgive the unforgivable and love the unlovely?

Only by the experiences of a life that has once endured a pain so deep that it can see beyond the pain, and even though it may bring tears with the remembrance it also brings joy in the victory, which is only sustained by the power and compassion of an all knowing God.

As the sands of time have filtered through my life to an age where I can look back on the battles, waged as stepping stones, that have brought me to where Paul says, "for which I am an ambassador in chains that I may speak boldly as I ought to speak." (*see Ephesians 6:20 NKJV*) I believe, today, as a vessel broken by the chains of experiences in life, that this has brought me to a place of humility, with a willingness to be used, so I may be able to minister to the needs of others, and encourage them to continue, and not allow the enemy to defeat them in their trials, as their characters are being tested, tried and refined by the Potter's fire. A broken vessel gouged with cracks, and scars of wear on the outside, now begin to reflect the beauty from within the smooth lining of glass. It is this refinement that allows me to be able to speak boldly, telling where my victory is gained – only in Jesus, for "*His grace is sufficient. . .*" (*see II Corinthians 12:9 NKJV*)

> "Beloved do not think it strange, concerning
> the fiery trial which is to try you, as though
> some strange thing has happened to you,
>
> but rejoice to the extent that you
> partake in Christ's sufferings,
>
> that when His glory is revealed, that you
> may also be glad with exceeding joy."
>
> (I Peter 4:12 NKJV)

Even this was not learned until much later in life, as I reflect the memories of the past that I will never forget, and I now find that, *"God was guiding me with His eye."* (Psalms 32:8 NKJV)

Chapter Eight

A Rebel's Mischief

".... take note, you have sinned against the Lord;
and be sure your sin will find you out."
(Numbers 32:23 NKJV)

The dare-devil girl, with a glint in her eye, and the curiosity to match, was a recipe for rebellion without thought of consequences, simply compelled the Christian girl into actions that was not conducive to the life her parents brought her up under. That was me at thirteen. I was impulsive, reacting on the feelings, and not relying on the reasoning of the circumstances. I was a rebel!

My friend, Penny, had six brothers and she was the only girl. She came from a poor family, and I always felt drawn to her. We did crazy things that made no sense. We did them just because.... we did! Penny told her mother she was going to my house to play Monopoly, and I told my mother I was going to Penny's house to play Monopoly. Then we would meet and race by either her house or mine and walk or hitch hike to either Fryeburg, Maine, just 4 miles one direction, over the New Hampshire border, or five miles the other direction to Conway.

One day our neighbor, Cassie Davidson, had her old Model A Ford out for a spin, and she stopped to pick us up. Two people could sit in the front and two in the back. I sat in the front, quite intrigued that the speedometer looked like a tape measure and we were going all of 20 miles an hour. Penny sat in the back. Cassie was intent on her driving and very courteously said, "If the wind is too much on you girls, you can put the window up." That was just too much! We had all we could do keep from bolting into laughter and assured her politely, "It is fine, thank you." When we arrived in Conway, just four miles from our town of Center Conway, and got out of her car, thanking her for the ride, we railed in laughter, bending over and holding our stomachs at the thought that the breeze at 20 miles an hour being too much was just too funny. After that good laugh we went on to find mischief.

It was summer and hot out! I don't remember what we did that particular day, but we got away with whatever it was. The game nights worked so well, we continued to use it to get out of the house and find the daring side of life. This time we went to Fryeburg.

It was getting late and we had to get home quickly. We usually walked most of the time but due to the lateness of the day, I was the one who daringly put my thumb out to hitch a ride. The first car to come along was Daddy. That was not good! He not only stopped to pick us up and dropped Penny at her house, but gave us a lecture that beat all lectures. I thought for sure my life was about to end as I knew it. You would have thought that would have ended our escapades. Well, it did end the excuse that we were playing Monopoly. So our tactics went to a higher level.

We decided to go out after dark, when we were supposed to be in bed, and after our folks had gone to bed. I would come down the stairs from the third floor, stopping at each stair to make sure I had not awakened Mama and Daddy with the creaking stair boards. I had to pass by their room to get to the second set of stairs. I would take off my pajamas, and tuck them under the pillow on the cot that was on our screened in porch. I had clothing on under my pajamas, and only wore the pajamas as a safety in case Mama decided to see what the creaking stairs were. I could say I was going to the bathroom, but she would wait till I was on my way back up the stairs before she would fall back to sleep.

Once I made it to the porch, I would race to Penny's, a little over a quarter mile away, past the little elementary school house, and the cemetery was across the road from the school. There was no street lights. Because of the cemetery, I was on one side of the road running, and Penny was on the other, and neither of us knew the other was there. I got to her house and no Penny! I took a small stone and threw it up to her bedroom window. It smashed through the window pane. It was a matter of a few minutes, and her mother came out on their porch. I hid behind the big Maple tree in the front yard. "Penelope," her mother shouted angrily. No answer! "Penelope," she shouted again with a sharper tone. No answer! This next time she demanded, "Penelope, are you out there?" Just a couple feet from me, Penny came back with a defeated tone, "Yeh, I'm coming." Her mother was now shouting angrily with demanding questioning, "What do you think you are doing?" Penny answered, kind of irritated, "I was meeting Joyce." Her mother retorted in disgust, "Joyce is home in bed, and that is where you are going right now."

I could have touched Penny, as she went by me, but I stayed quiet. Once she was in her house, I raced back home, never stopping, not even to catch my breath, till I was safely on the front porch. Going by the cemetery at night was the worst fear of all—then the ritual of getting my pajamas back on and sneaking back over the stairs. That adventure was thwarted! Yet, the spark of adventure became a greater challenge to be attempted.

I could never go anywhere or do anything the other kids did–dances, movies, dating. I was fourteen now and I was always looking to fit in and show I wasn't so different after all. I was allowed in the eighth grade to participate in square dancing that was promoted in the school. I loved it, and I was good at it! Spinning around and locking arms with various partners, going forward and back again, listening to the calls from the dance coordinator gave me a thrill and I wanted more.

Mama took me to my first movie, "The Ten Commandments," at the drive-in theatre. She had her Bible in hand and followed along with the movie making sure that it was accurate, because if it was not, she certainly would tell me the difference. I loved the movie and it stayed within my mind for some time. The second movie was one she allowed me to see with some friends, "One Hundred and One Dalmatians." I actually went to a movie theatre for that and it was really exciting to be allowed to go, but dating was out of the question.

Penny and I decided, somehow, to get out again. We went to Fryeburg and met up with some guys that evidently were out looking for a "sweet young thing" and we fit the bill. They asked our age and we said, "seventeen and eighteen." We were thirteen and fourteen! We went off in a car with them, and forgot about the time. They said they had to stop and "see a man about a horse." They pulled into a rundown house that looked empty and like no one was home. They got out and went out back. Penny and I sat in the car wondering why they would stop here when it didn't look like anyone was home, but then they went out back so we thought perhaps they knew the people and they had another entrance out back. But where did they keep the horses? They finally returned and we continued to ride around, but no mention was made of the horses.

They drove to Conway, back over the Maine—New Hampshire border and we continued to ride around. They stopped and picked up some beer. We refused it! They were telling jokes and heading back for Fryeburg. We had to pass by my house, and there was Mama out on the side of the road stopping cars looking for me. We didn't even slow down as I squealed, "That's my Mother looking for me!" I think that was when they fully realized we were not the ages we said. And maybe they knew anyway and just didn't care until now.

My hair was long and flying in the wind as the car windows were down. That was a dead giveaway—the chase was on. The young men began to question us as to our age again, and now were scared out of their wits. Daddy was gaining and they pulled over and tossed their booze out the door. Daddy caught up to us and we got out of their car. I was sure he would kill me before I could ever make it home again. He barked at the young men, "Do you know how old these girls are?" I don't remember their answers as I was in Daddy's car. Penny and I were shaking, knowing our sins had certainly found us out. Daddy took hold of the jacket I had on, and shook me so hard it ripped apart. Penny and I were banned from seeing each other again for a very long time. I don't think we ever reconnected.

I took Home Study Institute courses for the ninth grade. I was an avid reader, and spent most of the time at the library reading. I loved to read biographies of Florence Nightingale, Walter Reed, Pocahontas, Henry Wadsworth Longfellow, and many others. They were my get-away! Then Mark Twain's stories with Tom Sawyer and Huck Finn just excelled within me the adventurous spirit I already had. Daddy was good with math and Mama was good with English and History. I excelled in those areas.

Alyce became a part of my life. It was the hope of her mother, Gladys, and my mother that she and my sister would connect, but instead she and I connected. She was a few years older than me, but that did not matter, since I had a sister six and a half years older than myself. We became close friends. Alyce had a car and what I didn't know about driving, she taught me. The stunts we pulled were a step up from what Penny and I did, and the rebel in me, still lived for mischief. Alyce and I continued to walk the path over "fools hill."

"He who walks with wise men will be wise,
But the companion of fools will be destroyed."
(Proverbs 13:19 NKJV)

Chapter Nine

Hormones Gone Crazy

"When I was a child, I used to speak as a child, think like a child, reason like a child; when I be came a man (woman) I did away with childish things." (I Corinthians 13:11 NKJV)

My sister was quite young when she made the transition into womanhood and I was in my teens. I clearly remember the horrific day that I was totally unprepared for. I was playing the game, much like tennis, called badminton, with one of my friends on the lawn where the net was installed at my home. In the midst of the game, I excused myself racing into the house to the upstairs bathroom to discover blood on my underwear. I was certain the badminton birdie, as it was called, had hit me there, and must have injured myself somehow. I screamed at the top of my lungs, "Mama, come quickly, I have been hurt." She came bounding over the stairs bursting into the bathroom and discovered that I had not been hurt, but had just entered the transition of becoming a young woman.

She passed me the nifty pad that used to be used around my neck when I had pneumonia. She told me I had to wear pads for a week between my legs, which was attached to this belt that had metal clips that were used to pull the ties through to hold it in place. I would have to go through every twenty-eight days.

How could she have overlooked telling me about this crucial event and pretend it was no big deal? I was not just in horror, I was mortified! When I returned to play badminton, which by now I wasn't in much of a mood to play, I explained it to my friend, who seemed to know all about it, as she had already started this. How come she didn't tell me? It seemed like this had been a deep dark secret that everyone knew but me.

I used to go into my sister's room and hop in bed with her, but every so often she would go in her closet, and take out this little brown paper bag, and go to the bathroom. There was an odd odor that accompanied her. One day, I decided to check out what was in that bag in the closet, so when no one was around I snuck in her closet and found the little brown bag tucked in the corner. I carefully opened the little brown bag and saw nothing of great interest to me. What was her big secret? Why on earth did she make it so secretive? Well, now I knew!

That evening when Daddy had come home for supper, Mama said at the supper table, of all places, "Joyce has just become a young woman!" I was totally in disbelief that she would announce this to Daddy, of all people. Why should he know? Why not open the window and just tell the neighborhood if you are going to go this far! Daddy's response was, "Oh," in his booming, base voice, but with no other comment or look of surprise. I went to bed in tears that night.

Twenty-eight days later, I didn't have that "thing" appear again and was so relieved. In fact, it was fifty-six days later and I still did not have it. I was so happy and felt that maybe I had escaped this doom. Then Mama came to me with this remedy called, "Lydia Pinkham's Elixir." I heard Daddy say, "There is a baby in every bottle." Again I was traumatized! Now of all things, Daddy wants me to take this terrible liquid because he wants me to have a baby! I held back the burning tears that were ready to escape. Was there really a baby in that bottle? I wasn't ready for that. Obediently I took two tablespoons of it, and on the following day I had "the curse" again. It was my understanding, that meant I was not pregnant. I was thankful for that!

I don't believe Mama realized all that was going through my mind as she seemed as happy as I was that I had that "curse" back, so she didn't want me to have that baby either, much to my relief. It was months later, I realized that Lydia Pinkham's was helpful in regulating a menstrual cycle. That cleared up that misunderstanding and I was grateful.

Chapter Ten

Contentions-Prickly Communication

"For rebellion is as the sin of witchcraft, and stubbornness is as iniquity and idolatry."

(I Samuel 15:23 NKJV)

Regretfully, Mama and I had a time when we didn't connect. It was a hot summer day and I was on the third floor where my bedroom was located with the window open. The hot breeze made the third floor even warmer than it already was, but I was there to smoke. The phone rang and Mama called to me, that the phone call was for me. I believe it was Alyce! Leaving my cigarette burning, in the make-shift ashtray stationed on the open windowsill, I went to answer the phone on the second floor, which was at the bottom of the third-floor stairway. Not many homes had a private line, but had a party line. We acquired a private line when my mother had the nursing home, but before that we had the party line, which meant you had to wait for whoever was on the line to get off before you could make your call. You were also careful as to what you said so it wouldn't be repeated. Often you picked up the phone discreetly to hear if anyone may be talking, and if it was important you would ask the ones on the line if you could use it to make your call. Then there were times you were just nosey and would listen quietly. Sometimes you didn't care if they knew you wanted the line, so you would slam the phone down hoping they would end their conversation!

I answered the phone and Mama began ascending the third floor stairs saying, "It must be unbearably hot up here, why would you want to stay up stairs when it is so hot?" Quickly, I put Alyce off and went to reroute Mama from finding my burning cigarette. "Mama, no, don't go up there, it is fine." I panicked! Boy, if that wasn't a dead give-away that just made her pursue it further. And she did, discovering my guilty pleasure. I was on her heels, trying to get ahead of her to get rid of the cigarette, but never managed to cover my sin. Mama had not been well, but adrenalin took over as she dragged me down over two flights of stairs by my long braided hair to the kitchen, where she proceeded to get the Fels-Napthar bar of soap, known for its stain removing power, and tried to shove it in my mouth. I clamped my mouth shut and she bit my hand. I yelped! As soon as my mouth opened the soap was plunged in. She made sure I had a good dose of it. Then she gave me some juice to drink to get the taste out, which I spit at her.

Daddy was away and she told me he would deal with me when he got home. I knew it wasn't going to be pretty. It came time to face the music. Daddy was home. As I sat listening to his lecture that he never smoked, my mother never smoked, my sister never smoked, my grandparents never smoked.... (and probably no one in my entire ancestry ever smoked) so "whatever had possessed me to take up this filthy habit?" He pointedly asked me, "Why are you smoking?" Defiantly I answered, "Because I want to."

As soon as the words escaped my lips, his thick, broad hand, back-handed my mouth with such force, my jaw was knocked out of place. It was only a matter of seconds that Mama knew what had happened, and immediately she drove me to the hospital at high speed. The doctor asked, "What happened?" Tearfully, and with as little wording as possible, I lied, explaining I had been on a skate board and took a bad fall. (Skate-boarding began in 1958 and was called sidewalk surfing.) Mama stood close by, but soon they made her leave the room. I was questioned time and time again and my answer remained the same, as soon as I was able to talk more clearly. After a while, I was released under her care.

When I returned home, I was tucked in the mahogany spool bed on the second floor, in the old room where Kathy stayed, the girl Mama had cared for, and where I was introduced to smoking. How ironic! Daddy came to my bedside and knelt beside the bed in tears. He had a little tiger stuffed animal, he put beside me. He asked for my forgiveness. Those tears, hurt worse than the hard hand across my face. I couldn't stand to see daddy cry. I couldn't bear to see the pain in his eyes. Anger made me defiant and harshness turned me into a demon, but tears from my daddy's eyes melted my cold heart, and hurt far worse than anything he could have ever done. I didn't go to sleep right away, I just cried about everything.

"Baby Gene"

It was September 1963 that death shattered the sunshine of our existence. Aunt Alta's baby boy, 18 months old, was tragically, and accidentally killed by his Daddy. (Aunt Alta was one of Daddy's younger sisters.) Baby Gene had crawled out into the tall grass where Uncle Howard was digging with his back hoe, to create a pond in their back yard. He had not seen baby Gene until he lifted the bucket and he was there in it. When we heard the news, we immediately packed up and left for New York State. It was a critical time when family was needed for emotional support. A time that will be etched in my memory forever. One of Gene's sister's went out to pick buttercups and daisies for her baby brother, and brought them in, and gently laid them on top of the clear cover over the casket.

His funeral was held in their home in Bliss, New York. Aunt Alta in her tremendous grief, went to the casket, and without warning, flipped the cover off her baby boys casket, screaming, "I want to hold him one more time." Strong arms held her back as emotional pain seared through her soul. She was engulfed in an agony only God Himself understands and only He can comfort. It was this time of grief that filtered in through the sunshine, and made its way into a darkness that is buried in tears; that can never be redeemed until the day when baby Gene will be laid in Aunt Alta's faithful arms, when Jesus calls the dead from their graves. For the Bible states, "the dead know nothing," (see *Ecclesiastes 9:5-6 NKJV*) and "the dead in Christ will raise first," (see I *Thessalonians 4:15-18 NKJV*.)

"Alyce"

Alyce was pregnant! She had met Edward, (who was nicknamed "Hughy,") at a bowling alley, while she and her girlfriend had been bowling. One thing led to another, when he and his friend gave them a ride and that was the start of their love affair. She worked at the local telephone office as a switch board operator. She never knew he was married until she went through his wallet one night while he was sleeping. She found out, way too late, that the father of her baby was already married with several children.

Mama was the one who accepted Alyce with her pregnancy and said, "Everyone is entitled to a mistake." It was considered shameful to be pregnant out of wedlock. People tended to look down on the one who was pregnant rather than the one who helped make that a reality.

"Freddie"

I met Freddie through Alyce. He was Edward's younger brother. I didn't know he was married either. We met for the first time at a little café on the outskirts of Conway one evening. It was pretty awkward for me since I didn't date but once or twice, so I wasn't sure how to act, but I liked him! He smoked, and so I could smoke when I was with him. The episode with daddy didn't stop my rebellion.

I would sneak off to meet with Freddie double dating with Alyce and Eddie. He was older but that didn't matter to me. Then came a weekend that Dave, from Bath, Maine, was coming to see me and Steve from Stoneham, Massachusetts was coming that same week end and then Freddie. I gave a lame excuse to the first two and stuck with Freddie from Auburn, Maine.

After many secret meetings, I decided that I didn't want to sneak around to see him anymore and wanted him to meet my parents. I asked him to come to the house. He chose a Friday evening, which was the beginning of the Sabbath hours, from Friday night sundown to Saturday night sundown we honored the Sabbath, as the Bible clearly states, "the evening and the morning were the first day." (see *Genesis 1:5b NKJV*) Man changed it to be from midnight to midnight for the convenience of man's rules. The Sabbath hours were kept by God's rules. (see *Exodus 20:8-12 NKJV*)

Freddie visited me on Friday evening by sitting in the living room in a rocking chair and me in another rocking chair eating popcorn, and listening to hymn records from seven to nine o'clock. Daddy never came in to speak to him, but stayed in the kitchen, and at nine o'clock he called out, "This is the time we go to bed around here." How embarrassing for me was that! It was a blatant hint to leave if there ever was one! So obediently, Freddie got up to leave. Mama saw him to the door and shook his hand but I was not allowed on the porch or to go outside the door with him. Daddy made sure I knew how he felt with his statement that boomed and bounced off the kitchen walls, "He seems fine as far as the world goes, but you are not of the world and you will never see him again." Within myself, the rebel, I immediately thought, "That is what you think!"

"Pills and A White Horse"

I became very depressed thinking that everything I did was wrong and Mama and Daddy didn't understand me. I couldn't do this and I couldn't do that. I wasn't allowed to make my own choices or make my own mistakes, but live under what I felt was a dictatorship. What was the point of living? I might as well end life as I know it—I would be better off! At fifteen years old, I decided pills would be the best way to end it, and I would just go to sleep and never wake up. I used to listen to the popular song "Running Bear." This was a song about a young Indian brave who loved an Indian maiden, Little White Dove, from two tribes that were in conflict with each other. These two, who were so in love, were forbidden to see each other. They decided to meet in the raging river and die together. This song was by Johnny Preston in 1959. I had that song racing through my mind, thinking about not being able to even see Freddie. I felt I was in love with him.

Was it aspirin or something Mama had in the medicine cabinet, I don't remember, but I took the entire bottle. I fell asleep! Mama came in search of what I was doing up on the third floor, in that hot room, and found the empty pill bottle. She literally once again dragged me down over the stairs to the second floor and into the bathroom. I could hear her screaming in tears as she raced down the second set of stairs. She returned with a disgusting concoction she forced down my throat, that made me puke till I was sure I would die, from throwing up, which wasn't the way I wanted to go. Then everything became dark.

The next thing I remember was waking up, to see daddy sitting in the rocker next to my bed as I was coming out of a dream of being on this beautiful white horse and riding into the ocean. It was so beautiful and so much fun just riding, feeling the wind flow through my hair, I wanted it to go on forever, but I never did go deep into the ocean water so that it covered that beautiful horse and I. It just seemed, we were riding endlessly, and going nowhere. I awoke! Daddy had tears in his eyes. He was waiting for his little girl to wake up. Did I know it then? No! Did I know he prayed for me to wake up? No! Did I understand his pain? No! I was too involved with my own pain. I was too selfish to see his or to even think about what he may be going through.

I had written many poems in a time of recognition of my pets, forgiveness from my mother, safety for my dad's travels, the love I had for my step-grandmother and my sister's first baby, Anna. But the following was an ode to death.

JOYCE A. LEONARD

"Sweet Death"

If I could die a natural death, without pain or sorrow-
I would give up all my tomorrows
Knowing the next thing I would hear,
Is the voice of Jesus falling on my ear?
If I could die with faith and love lying in my heart -
From this world I would gladly depart,
Knowing next I would be encumbered
in the Savior's arms,
Hearing His voice like the Bible psalms.
If I could die with the assurance of His Word
With this my heart would be stirred,
And I would know and feel His love for me,
Knowing this love would eternally be.
If I could die for my Savior now -
All of my life I would endow,
For the next thing I would see,
Is the Redeemer coming and meeting me.
If I could die today. . ...
And forget the troubles for which I pray,
And see tomorrow as the new dawn,
Breaking forth as a young fawn;
If I could die in the arms of the Savior's love,
As pure and simple as the morning dove-
How sweet and lovely death would be,
If only sweet death would happen to me.
(Written by Joyce Ann Wetmore—
February 27, 1964—age 16)

Chapter Eleven

Sweet Sixteen

"Discipline your children, and they will give you peace;

they will bring you the delights you desire." (Proverbs 29:17 NIV)

"Birthday Party"

The layout of the outer limits beyond the main house consisted of a large shed that was like a board-walk around an empty dirt area that held wood or was used for storing farm equipment. As you made your trek about the area at one end was where the outhouse was located, and where my doll house now laid dormant. Overhead this area, which we had a stairway to enter this part of the house, and this was used as an extra living space, for games, and family time, which acted as a big living room. It was also a place for storage, but this was where I had my "sweet sixteen" party. I invited several friends from town that were my age. We played 45 RPM phonograph records, while we danced and played board games. No one quite knew how to act and were pretty sullen at first. In fact, it wouldn't have been a party at all if it hadn't been for Daddy. He got everyone moving with his teasing, contagious laughter, and his idea of dancing. He twisted his body this way and that getting everyone to laugh. This got them to get into the mood to dance. Lucky was my birthday present. He was a German Shepherd puppy that I could tuck inside my jacket. He became my protector and my pal.

We always had cats and canaries, which the canaries were actually my sisters. They had been given to her from the people she stayed with while she was away at school. Mama would throw a shoe at the cats if she caught them staring at the birds, and they quickly learned that was not acceptable, at least not in the house. Those birds were off limits! Our cat, Mittens was particularly special. He was black and gray tiger striped with white paws that dictated his name. Mama would put Cheerios on the edge of the kitchen table, and he would take his paw, carefully curling each Cheerio in his paw one at a time and eat it. He was pretty fascinating to watch!

"Pepper"

Daddy had cut down a tree finding two baby raccoons in it. He brought them home. I got one and my cousin, Donna, got the other. She named hers "Salt" so mine was "Pepper." I had tonsillitis, at the time, so Pepper would lay on the pillow beside me so I could feed him from a bottle when he was hungry. He grew to be quite big. We had to build a wire pen out in back of the old, unused, outhouse for him. As he got older, he only allowed me and Mama to come near him. He and Lucky were great friends, and I would take walks with them to the lake.

Pepper would be curled over my shoulders and I would have Lucky by the collar. Daddy used to get pretty upset with Pepper, because he was like a pack-rat and liked things that were shiny. He often ran off and hid Daddy's belt with the shiny buckle, silverware, a watch, or whatever would glisten. He also liked to wash his food. He would sit on the drain board of our white ceramic sink, and wash his little hands and his food over and over. This annoyed Daddy! One day, Mama decided Pepper had to be where he could roam. I was away this particular day, when some friends of Mama's came from the upper part of Maine to visit. They had a lot of land, and they were sure Pepper would be happy. When I came home, Pepper was gone, and a piece of my heart was gone too. I guess Pepper wasn't happy either, because he ran away from them and never returned.

"Nurse's Aide"

I ended back at New England Memorial Hospital and Sanitarium (no longer in existence) with my Aunt Florence and Uncle Walter and their son, my cousin Everett. I was able to take my Nurse's Aide Course there, and became very infatuated with Biffen, who was taking the same course to become an Orderly. The song "Pretty Woman" was the rage and he would sing that to me. Of course, I felt I was his one and only since I never saw him with anyone else, but I was fickle. As infatuated as I was with Biffen, there was a young man, Steve, I had eyes for on the hospital floor I worked on. He was a patient, and I had been assigned to care for him. He seemed pretty interested in me as well. Daddy used to say, "One day you will get your heart broken, like you have broken the hearts of others." I would laugh and think no more of it. I was the youngest to ever take the Nurse's Aide Course, and older men took advantage of my ignorance of certain things. I enjoyed the work of caring for the sick. I grew up doing this, as it was second nature for me.

"Tonsillectomy"

In the Fall, we moved for a time to West Bath, Maine in a small rented house. Mama worked at the Brunswick Mill Outlet, while I had a tonsillectomy at Parkview Hospital. Mama worked wherever she could to help make ends meet. I had a difficult time with healing after the surgery. It seemed like every time I was sick, I was very sick, and I took longer than other people to recuperate. The little girl that shared the hospital room with me also had a tonsillectomy, and she was eating right away. It took me a couple weeks of soft foods and sucking on ice before I was able to eat a regular diet.

"The Kuykendalls"

Josephine Kuykendall was a medical secretary at Parkview Hospital and Milton, her husband, was the contractor that built the hospital. It was under their direction and abilities that the hospital came into existence. Mama and Daddy went with them when the land was surveyed before the erection of the building. My parents and the Kuykendall's had been friends for a number of years. In fact, they had stood up with my parents when they eloped, as their witnesses. So they knew me from the day I was born. They had gone to Hawaii to be missionaries for five years; and returned to work in Maine under the direction of a God-given dream that Josephine had. She was called "Jo" by those who knew her and I called her, "Mama Jo," and I called Milton, "Daddy K." They became my second set of parents. Eventually, I came to live with them, while I attended the new school, which again was built under Milton's direction, and is today, Pine Tree Academy in Freeport, Maine.

"Pine Tree Academy"

I was fifteen years old when I entered the tenth grade at PTA, and Ronald Rodgers was our teacher. He was a wonderful man! It was another one room class room. I made a lot of friends here. It was quite possibly the happiest year of my life. I learned a lot from Mama Jo starting with nutrition, faithfulness in tithing, and preparation for Sabbath among other things. My Dad had always said, "Never trample on the edges of the Sabbath." That always stuck in my mind—perhaps because he said it so often, also that God answers prayer. It was here I sang in the choir, and went to perform in singing groups, that inspired my love for music even greater. As a little girl, Mama wanted me to learn the violin, and the same as my sister, but neither of us enjoyed it simply because we did not have the right teacher. My teacher was of German decent, and he was difficult to understand. So I just gave up! My real passion was for the piano.

While going to Pine Tree, I worked after school in the cafeteria at the hospital with several others from school. It was to help pay for my tuition to go to church school. The mother of one of the boys that attended school with me was head of the food preparation. She taught me how to put together salads for the patients, and serve. She was a lovely woman and I loved her!

There were three of us left in the kitchen, this one night, to finish up pots and pans. It was Bob, Phil, and myself. We were horsing around and spraying water at each other, chasing each other around, and eating the desserts that Malcolm, the baker, used to squirrel away for us once he had left for the night. Bob doused me good with some water. I ladled some water in a big tin cup and ran after him. He raced through the boiler room door, my arm was outstretched with the dipper of water ready to throw at him. As he went through the boiler room door, my arm was first to go through, when he slammed the door shut on my arm. Quickly, he opened the door at my scream! We called a truce and returned to finish the pots and pans amid grins and giggles.

I was wiping a huge pot when suddenly I couldn't use my arm. I didn't want to complain and be a sissy in front of these guys, so I bore it as long as I could, then began to complain. At first they teased me, saying I was just trying to get out of doing the dishes, until they looked at my arm and concluded I needed to see the nurse on the floor. My arm was turning purple and swelling. After an ex-ray, the doctor diagnosed that I had crushed the muscle in my arm. I didn't tattle on the boys, but took the blame so they wouldn't lose their job, but I had chocolates and cards every day for two weeks from them.

It took all that time to get my muscle to work again in my right arm with therapy. I had to stay in the hospital for that entire two weeks. It was during this time that David from Bath took an interest in me. He sent me cards as well. He was a little older, and I felt flattered, but I really wasn't as certain of my interest in him as his was in me. I was allowed to date him and we later took a trip to Bailey's Island, and climbed the rocks, watched the ocean waves slap against the rocks spraying its mist and enjoying the breeze of the salty ocean air. He bought me a little wishing well that I kept for many years. On our way back to Mama Jo's I asked him to pull over and close his eyes. He did and I kissed him! Then we continued to Mama Jo's. No comment was made. I think I put him in shock! He kept pursuing me for some time, even after I was out of school for the year. He came to visit me in New Hampshire. My mother felt he was definitely the one for me!

"Bath Seventh-Day Adventist Church"

I attended here weekly for over a year. Mama Jo used to say, "Even if you only have a quarter, never let the offering plate pass without putting something in it." Daddy K was Church Treasurer and Mama Jo was the Sabbath School teacher, Prayer Ministry Leader, Health and Temperance Leader, which were the callings of her ministry within the church. They held these positons for years. They were dedicated to service. She conducted many nutritional classes, which I attended and helped with.

Fellowship dinners were plentiful, because Mama Jo brought enough for everyone in case someone couldn't bring anything. She felt no one should go away hungry. If there were left overs, they were divided among those who had little and sent home with them. It was always a time of fun on Saturday night. Closing the Sabbath hours with popcorn, fruit salad and homemade cookies, which Daddy K made as his specialty. This went along with Saturday night game night. Daddy K was as good of a cook as Mama Jo. He was also a professional bread maker to add to his accomplishments. Many people were invited over to their home where it overlooked the ocean on Rossmore Road in Brunswick. They had large picture windows that overlooked their property, and the sunsets were glorious. They had several acres of land that later were sub-divided and other homes were built. Daddy K was the contractor that built these beautiful homes. Mama Jo and I used to get up early in the morning and take walks before school. They housed another girl, Marsha, and she usually went home in Bath on the weekends, and some times during the week. They paid for her schooling. We became like sisters, and later when I left, she stayed and helped them with the upkeep of their home, for room and board. We never connected later on in life. They did have one daughter, who visited from time to time. I always felt she resented me and the time I had with her parents. She and Marsha became close, but I never did. However, during the time I had with them "the Kuykendall's" home was some of the happiest times I had ever had.

"Happy Birthday Sweet Sixteen"

In Nineteen forty-eight was seen
A baby girl, all neat and clean,
She gave her parents joy unseen
And answered the prayers of a sister.
Happy Birthday, Joyce Ann.
We would beat up the band
If we could and be so glad
That a baby girl was not banned
From the pleasure of our company.
Happy Birthday daughter dear,
Accept our congratulations so mere.
We love having you near us this day,
And hope always to keep the wolves at bay,
From that sixteen-year-old daughter so dear
Happy Birthday, Sweet Sixteen!
Daddy and I are sincere in our love for you,
And hope always on us you will lean,
As our love for you is true
And may the skies for you always be blue.
May the sun shine all day, Happy Birthday

JOYCE A. LEONARD

And let's have it a day of play
Or whatever you say
Wish to do this memorable day,
Happy Birthday Sweet Sixteen!
(It was signed "Mama" one corner "Dad" the other).
February 23, 1964
(My mother, Priscilla H. Wetmore wrote this poem in commemoration of my sixteen years of life.)

Chapter Twelve

Defiance - Manipulation - Deception

> *"Now no chastening seems to be joyful for the present, but painful, nevertheless, afterward it yields the peaceable fruit of righteousness to those who have been trained by it." (Hebrews 12:11 NKJV)*

Rebellion had stirred in my heart to the point of no matter what my parents said or did, I would not obey their rules, and so they resorted to harsh punishment. Daddy got a little over zealous with the Bible verse, "He who spares his rod, hates his son (daughter, my addition,) but he who loves him, disciplines him (her, my addition) promptly." (Proverbs 13:24 NKJV).

I am sure they must have been beside themselves and wondered, "What can we do? What can we do?" I would not listen! I was going to see Freddie no matter what the consequences were. I was going to do things my way—I was going to smoke. My heart had gotten hard and cold. Daddy resorted to spankings that bordered beatings. I refused to cry! No matter how hard the razor strap stung across the back of my legs, and at times managed to land on my derriere, I refused to show remorse! And I know today that frustration must have grown so deep within him that he was at his "wits end." *(see Psalms 107:27 b NKJV)* In one of his lectures out behind the barn, he asked me if he had to horse whip me into submission? I pictured the event in my mind, and clearly my sheepish "no!" showed some sort of remorse to him. But I didn't really listen clearly enough to realize he did mean business. Excluding any horse whipping that he tried to reach my mind with, I took his threats with a grain of salt and would test him to his limit.

A few years' prior, the root of this rebellious stage reared its ugly head as I hung over the back of the car seat leaning near his ear as he drove, snapping bubble gum, blowing bubbles and popping it in his ear was a great joke. (There were no seat belts then). He had warned me that if I continued to do that I would have to get out and walk. I pushed the joke until I had gone beyond the boundary and the car stopped. I was made to get out, and Daddy drove away. I was in dismay! He actually left me here to walk. I don't know how long I was left to walk, but it seemed like a long time. When Daddy returned to get me, I sat back in the seat, and didn't continue to aggravate him again. The joke was over!

But somehow this was different. I tested his patience and pushed him way beyond his tolerance level, which was unacceptable to him and there was no compromise. Daddy was ready to take me to the barn again, as I had defied him once more, and was going to meet Freddie. I told him so, as I was not just rebellious but brazen. Alyce, Ed and Fred came knocking at the door, pounding loudly, and threatening Daddy that he was going to "regret it" if he laid a hand on me. Mama went to the door and I do not know what was said from there.

It was later we went to court, and from my understanding certain unknown neighbors had made complaints that they felt I was being abused. I was taken out of their care at age 17. It was in the Spring of 1965, that I was placed in a foster home. I was not allowed to see my parents or my sister. (Unknown to me my mother was pregnant.)

"Foster Care"

I only remember bits and pieces of this experience. I was told by a counselor, sometimes when something is so traumatic, our memory of that trauma shuts down, for it is too painful to bring up. The following are the memories I do have:

I was allowed to smoke, but only the cigarettes that were placed on the table in a bowl, and only smoked during certain times, that they allowed me have them. I would iron for hours for rich people. I ironed men's boxer under shorts and lady's bras, learning how to make creases in the right places in such a uniform way that it was very professionally done. It had to be perfect or it was redone until it was. I never saw the money; it was given to the foster caretakers. I was the oldest of the children there. They considered me a child, and treated me like one, yet, used me as a maid or however else they saw fit. I attended church with them on Sunday, and sometimes the pastor of their church would come to their house late in the evening. They had a mind controlling ritual, of some sort, over me. I remember the candles, and being on my knees, but I cannot remember anything beyond that, and each event was held in the same manner. I was scared, and wept continually, and often uncontrollably.

"Awakened Horror"

The sun was streaming in my room as I awakened. I instantly became aware of someone lying next to me, running their hand over my body, reaching into the secret places that were not for his hand to touch. The soft tones of the voice gently murmuring, "not to be upset, he would make me feel good." I turned and looked at him, in disbelief and sheer terror! I began having hallucinating visions of family members protruding from the walls. "Joyce this is wrong," my father was scolding, as his head poked in and out of the air in one corner of the room. My sister was in the other corner coming through the walls, laughing, "Look at you. You were never any good anyway."

I frantically began to answer the torments, and it became obvious to the molester lying next to me. The molester kept trying to soothe my outbursts of tears and anguish with gentle luring touches to my body. In a lunge, I bolted out of the bed, screaming, crouching in a far corner of the room, shaking like a scared rabbit.

The department that was responsible for me being there, sent someone to rescue me from the situation. It seemed like hours, and it may have been until this little white haired lady came in, and spoke with a soft voice. She was taking me out of there to a safe place. It was under her soothing direction that I was able to find some sort of solace and I went quietly with her. I was exhausted! She said she was taking me to a hospital, where I would be safe and cared for, until they found another home for me. I rode in the backseat next to her in a police cruiser, while she talked to me about my stay with my foster parents learning the bits and pieces of my life, the past few months I was there. She assured me that I would be placed elsewhere as soon as they found a home for me, and I would never have to go through such an ordeal again. I trusted her!

It was sometime later I learned that the cigarettes on the table I was allowed to smoke were filled with opium. The effects of opium can cause drowsiness, confusion, withdrawing socially, depression and or suicidal thoughts, which also induce hallucinations if overdosed. I was left vulnerable to be under their control.

> "Not everyone who says to Me, 'Lord, Lord,'
> shall enter the kingdom of heaven,
>
> but he who does the will of My Father in heaven.
>
> Many will say to Me in that day,
>
> 'Lord, Lord,' have we not prophesied in Your name,
>
> cast out demons in Your name?'
>
> And then I will declare to them,
>
> 'I never knew you, depart from Me,
>
> you who practice lawlessness."
>
> (Matthew 7:21-23 NKJV)

Chapter Thirteen

"*Demons of the Mind*"

*"For where envy and self-seeking exist,
confusion and every evil thing are there."*
(James 3:16 NKJV)

The walls were naked. They were white washed in emptiness. The echoing silence screamed from within, vibrating to the bone of one's imagination. I entered a heavy, ominous, front door, and waited in a hallway that permeated with an impersonal chill that would be my destiny. Behind the doors, jingled keys, with each repeated slamming door, fake smiles, nodding heads and terror!

"We have to leave you here for a few days, my dear, until we find another home for you," cooed, Joyce's caseworker, who had ridden in the cruiser next to her that transported them to a Mental Institution. "You've had a nervous breakdown, dear, and they will take good care of you," she continued without waiting for either question or answer. It was as if she never expected one.

I was ushered into the Day Room of Ward 2 by a heavyset nurse. "Everyone is placed here when they first arrive," a girl a little older than myself spoke as I approached her. She had straight orange, blonde hair with black roots. It was coarse like hay and her lipstick was shocking red, plastered on her thick lips. Her voice was as coarse as her hair and when she smiled a prominent front tooth was missing. "Wanna cigarette?" she asked, in her gruff voice, shoving the pack at me. Without answering, I grabbed one.

I had a flashback of how I used to have to wait at the foster home to do a good deed, before I was allowed one of the cigarettes in the bowl on the table, while ironing for my keep there. I didn't realize they were paid by the State to house me. There were huge baskets of ironing to be done for wealthy customers. I ironed every clothing item, pressed to perfection and hung without a spot or wrinkle waiting to be picked up. I labored for hours for that one cigarette on the table. Cigarettes that were laced with opium that caused so many affects that brought me here under the control of those hallucinations. The strange visits held in candlelight was a vague blur, and only now were these incidents being revealed for what had really happened. My mind snapped back to the present dismal surroundings. I hesitantly reached for the cigarette being offered. "You have to go over to that wall, next to the cage to light up at that little square box, and when they see you there, they will turn it on long enough for you to get your light. We aren't allowed lighters or matches," she explained. After lighting my cigarette and inhaling deeply, I returned to the section of the room where my new friends were seated. "I'm Carrie and this is Pam and Katrina. We are card partners. We will let you join us." I sat in the straight wooden chair that was around the square table that was just right for a game of cards. I actually found myself laughing, as I became involved in the card game and then focusing my attention on the sad stories of the lives of these young women and what fate had dealt them.

Then the reality of my own circumstances set in as I glanced around the room. It was a huge room with approximately 20-30 women of various ages milling around. Some were rocking in rockers with intensity while staring off into space as if playing a game to see how fast the rocker could rock and skip into different positions. Others, were pacing, smoking, pacing some more, talking to themselves, screaming, laughing, crying and every so often, one would come up to my face, look blankly into my eyes and stare, as if looking past my soul, then they would walk away and continue obliviously in their own world, locked in an imprisoned mind, medicated into silence, and tormented by the demons of their fears. It was written on their faces and reflected in their eyes.

"Chow time, girls," the heavy-set nurse, named Janice called out from the cage. She emerged long enough to lead the way to the cafeteria from the Day Room, unlocking doors as we came to them. We walked in single file to our destination, marching around the perimeter of a room lined with cots. There were three lines of about 10 cots in each line. "This is where we sleep," Carrie whispered, as she turned her head back toward me marching behind her, long enough to tell me, "They will assign you your cot tonight," she continued to whisper as we methodically scuffled to the chow hall.

Chow hall was in a huge kitchen area, cafeteria style. The nice thing about the cafeteria, was you could see the sunlight. The Day Room, as well as the sleeping quarters, were covered with bushes from the outside against the mesh wire and barred windows, keeping the sunlight out or the lighting dim enough to keep lights on inside during the day. You ate what was placed in your plate and there were no seconds. The food was tasteless. You ate only to get rid of the hunger. There was no want for more. It sure didn't compare with Mama's mashed potatoes, gravy, garden beans and hamburgers.

All the nurses and attendants were dressed in white starched uniforms. They kept their distance from everyone. When it was med time, they just called you to the cage and slipped you the little colorful pills or the chalky drink in a paper medicine dispenser with creased edges. Everyone seemed to obediently take the meds without hassle or question.

"Here you go Joyce," a thin, blonde, sweet faced nurse, passed me my new clothing. "Strip, pass me your clothes, and after you shower, put these on. This is your cubbyhole for your clothes and personal belongings," she finished and walked away. The closet area was cubicles in uniform size, and each cubbyhole held only personal belongings, which was the gray garb she passed me along with deodorant, soap, toothbrush, and a comb and brush, for my long soft, light reddish-brown hair.

I stood outside the shower room naked, wondering if I should wait or go in as there were others already in there. I was feeling quite uncomfortable, when a woman with long dark hair, also naked, walked up to me and poked her finger into my left nipple and remarked, "That nipple is funny," she laughed, "It points downward like it's inverted." I was astonished by her brazen gesture, and looked down at my breasts as if I had seen them for the first time. "What was wrong with this woman?" I thought. Now I really felt uncomfortable. "Well, get to it, *****, take your shower. Let's see what you've got!" This woman was scaring me with her vulgarity and aggressiveness. It was Carrie, who came to my rescue, "Leave her alone, she's mine!" And the other woman, Lisa, backed off. I was grateful to Carrie for putting Lisa in her place. I wondered though about the impact of Carrie's words and what they meant. Bedtime was another story. And I don't mean a bedtime story out of Uncle Arthur's Bedtime story books either!

Lights went out at 10:00 p.m. and the only lighting was the light that filtered in from the cage under the closed doorway. The room was completely locked between the Day Room and hallway, which led to the cafeteria, and maybe the outside, as nurses and attendants walked through during all hours of the night. You could hear the jingling of their keys and the squeak of their rubber soled shoes on the polished floors as they walked. Nights were the worst! Dreamers woke screaming! Whimpers broke the silence! Occasionally, nurses would come in and shine a flashlight in someone's face. This was a scary time, as I learned, it usually meant someone was taking their own life. I consoled myself with thoughts that I would only be here until they found me another home, and that should be soon.

One day just became another without distinction into the next. I kept remembering the words of my social worker and I would ask the nurses to contact her to come visit or even telephone me, but she never came to visit or even telephoned. It was like the outside world had forgotten me. I decided my new friends were more than demented. Carrie went about giving graphic detail explaining how she blew her mother's brains out, and she was going to get her kids back once she got out of there. After listening to her tales, I decided to keep to myself and not get any more familiar. That became difficult for it was sometimes the choice between two evils, the staff or the patients. Katrina was into ear piercing. "Do you want me to pierce your ears?" she asked. "How are you going to do that," I quizzed. "I can get the nurse to let me use a needle to make a hole and then you just leave the thread in," she answered, as a matter-of-fact. I agreed to the procedure as it seemed it would make her happy, and I might gain some comradeship if I went through with it. It was almost like an initiation. Katrina returned with the needle. She had an olive complexion, and almost coal black hair that fell to her shoulders in natural waves. She was a little on the heavy side, and always so depressed over her boyfriend leaving her. My heart had great compassion for her, and I tried to keep a positive outlook for Katrina. There was no ice to numb the pain, but it hurt only for a minute or two. I wore the thread in the holes that were left in my ears as an open reminder of the fraternity I was now a part of. I would religiously keep the holes opened by twisting it back and forth till it hit the knot at the end and then reverse the action again.

Whispers and wailings were reverberating through the Day Room, and I went to Carrie, and asked perplexed! "What happened?" "Lisa killed herself." Carrie's crass language spewed from her mouth as she directed obscenities toward "the cage." I stood stunned! "But how?" I gasped in a coarse whisper! Carrie looked at me in disbelief. "Oh, you are so dumb! It's quite easy," she explained. "Stuff a sock in your mouth to cut off all your air," she continued, "then cover your head until you suffocate," she concluded. "It's better than living in this hell hole," she added as a final description.

I felt overwhelmed and commented out loud, "I'm so glad they are looking for a home for me and I won't be here much longer." Carrie broke out in a guffaw of laughter, "Do you really think they are looking for a home for you, you ignorant *****? You aren't getting out of here until you are of age, and even then, it won't be easy." She walked away shaking her head in laughter at my ignorance.

I became sullen and instantly depressed. I went to the cage and complained to the nurse that I didn't feel good, so they allowed me to go to my cot. It seemed within moments, but was really hours later, Mama and Daddy stood next to my cot. I was remembering when I, myself had attempted to take my own life while I still lived at home. My parents wouldn't let me see Freddie, my boyfriend, not of my faith and six years my senior. He wasn't good enough for me, under their rules, and Mama had threatened to place me in a convent to keep me away from him, and others like him. Anger whelmed up inside me as I looked into mother's face, questioning her in bitterness, "Is this what you wanted for me?" My words spewed like venom. "Does it make you happy that I am here?" I continued. "I have nothing to say to you." Resentment dripped from my lips with malignant spite. Mama burst into tears, while Daddy, quickly, ushered Mama out of the room, following the attendant, who opened the doors for them to leave. I could hear Mama's tearful wails with her sobbing echoing through the corridor outside of the locked room. Anger filled me along with a deep bitterness that left me in severe depression. My tears burned, with screams echoing my own voice back to me.

I was placed in the "time out room" with padded walls and flooring thick enough to bounce on, creating a barrier that no one could get hurt or your screams heard. And it was there I lay, within the heavy thickness, smothering in my own thoughts, as the stillness penetrated my insides, my tears emptying back into my own soul. I was broken!

Depression was a black pit. A hole I couldn't climb out of. It was twenty-four hours later, believing that no one cared, that I entered back into the society of my surroundings and became a model patient in every respect. I attended the round circle sessions during the day, when you talked out your problems among each other, trying to find answers for your life and how to make right choices. It seemed absurd to even think about talking with some of these people. They were crazy! Really crazy! They had suffered from the demons that were far worse than what I had experienced. They had no hope and they were going to wither and die just like the fruit on branches that are never watered. But this was a process of willingness to participate. The thing that counted most on the little log books that was held in account behind the cage. . . was participation.

"School"

It was time for school to begin and the high school was just across the street, in the triangle intersection, outside of the high chain link fence, that surrounded the grounds of the institution. I was required, by law, to attend school. I was enrolled and transferred to Ward I, known as "Open Ward." I could now walk in and out of the Ward during certain hours of the day, go to the campus canteen for coffee or soda breaks and socialize with other patients that were also on an "open ward." It was a sunny afternoon as I was walking around the park that circled the paved walkway among shade trees and benches, when a car came through slowly. It pulled up beside me and called my name softly. I looked. It was Daddy, and he had a small package he tossed through the open car window, calling, "This is for you." Then he drove away.

 I caught the package, which held a pack of Marlboro cigarettes. The very things he had thrashed me for was over my smoking. The very reason, he had used the razor strap on me for my disobedience. The one thing he detested and had never done in his life. . . Smoke! The one thing that had caused me so much physical anguish at his hand. And here after all of this, he had bought me a pack of cigarettes, and with it were a pair of ear rings. I had never been allowed to wear jewelry. It was sinful! It was of the world, and I was "not of the world," in their words. It was an adornment and calling attention to self. I was cautioned to always stay focused on Jesus. Jewelry called attention to oneself. But here in my hand were, white laced metal earrings that dangled an amber stone at the bottom. I clutched them in my hand and caressed them to my face. Daddy really understood and loved me after all. Oh! how I ached to have him hold me, and tell me that he accepted me just the way I was, and how I wanted to go home. If I could only go home!

Lost in my thoughts, I wandered to an empty corner at the backside of one of the brick buildings, and sat in tears, holding my treasures. I didn't realize I was in the backside of the dormitory, where the attendants rented rooms to live on campus. A tall, heavy built black man, dressed in white uniform came by on his way to his room and spotted me crying, huddled in the corner. He came over to console me. He gently reached down and took me by the shoulders and helped me up. I stuffed my earrings in my pocket and opened my new pack of cigarettes as I unlocked my story to this attendant.

He lit my cigarette, and suggested I come to his room where I could talk more freely. I followed him over the stairway that entered into a second-floor dorm with many doors facing the corridor. He unlocked one door and invited me in. As soon as the door was shut, I felt immediately uneasy. "Maybe I better go," I stammered. "Relax!" he said calmly, as he locked the door behind him. He began to get undressed as I stood nervously in the corner of the room. I was thinking, "Oh God," when someone began pounding on the door. "Hey Mick, open up! Open up now!" the voice demanded. He pulled his pants back on quickly and went to the door. There stood Dennis, his colleague, my first cousin, which I knew vaguely. "What's up, man?" Mick questioned. "That's my cousin, you got there. Leave her alone." Dick stood in a stance ready to fight. "Hey, man, I didn't know. Take her on outta here. Sorry about that, man. No hard feelings, huh?" Mick sputtered. Dennis grabbed my hand and led me out, hurrying along, I had to skip to keep up as he scolded, "Don't go near here again, I'm warning you." As we hurried down the stairway, Dennis looked at me, admonishing again, "Don't wander over in this area again, understand?" I gratefully and sheepishly nodded my head and without a word ran back to where was more familiar. I heard Dennis call out, "I can't always be around to save your butt, so you have to stay away." I glanced back as I ran calling out, "Thanks," and kept running.

School started, and it was hard from day one. I was in the 11th grade and loved school, but this was different. I was accompanied by an attendant to the school grounds, and allowed to come back on my own. It was the other kids whispering that made school unbearable. "She's the crazy girl," I heard some girls whispering, "Yeah, she's the one that lives in the mental institution." I heard all the remarks, even the ones that they tried not to say too loud, "She doesn't look crazy, but you can't really tell."

It never got easier to go to school. Even the teachers didn't have any concern or compassion. Chemistry class was the worst! I just couldn't understand the concept. As hard as I tried, it just didn't make sense, and every time I raised my hand for help, the teacher ignored me. I had no friends to help me or to confide in, so I did the best I could which was bad. There was a major test coming and I dreaded the day. I looked over the test paper and there was just no way I could decipher any of what the answers would be, so I sat there without writing out one solution, while everyone was busy filling out their formulas. I turned my paper over and slunk down in my chair, holding my head on my hand propped by my elbow. I vowed that this would be the last class I would ever attend there. That was on Friday!

They decided at the Institution that I should have as much of a normal life as possible, so I should be allowed to attend the dance coming on Saturday night. Some of the nursing staff had gotten together and bought me a new skirt and blouse for the occasion. The heavy set nurse, named Janice, gave me a pin of synthetic diamonds at the top of the "J."

My hair was brushed till it shined, falling like silk around my shoulders. Tonight I was being allowed to go to my first school dance. I had until 11 o'clock, my curfew time to be back. They sent me with a male attendant to the party. He would drop me off and pick me back up later. I got in his car, and when we rounded the corner, he turned the opposite direction of the school. "Hey, where are we going?" I frantically questioned. "I thought you might like a joy ride with your new freedom," he quipped. It was a warm night and that didn't seem like a bad idea, I thought to myself! I wasn't too interested in the dance. After all who would want to dance with a "crazy girl?" This was a nice looking, blonde guy and it would be more like a pretend date. It wasn't in my plan to return to the hospital that night. This was my night to run away, so a short ride might be fun as long as it wasn't too long. It was just a short distance up the street, when he pulled into a cemetery. He put the car in park and a queasy feeling hit the pit of my stomach. "Now what?" I thought. He unzipped the fly of his pants and looked at me and said, "Suck it baby." I stared at him, in horrified disbelief, stuttering, "No! No! No! I can't. Please. I can't." He grabbed me by the hair of my head and shoved my face onto his penis. He lifted his butt off the seat, thrusting his hard penis deeper into my throat, while his hand was still holding me by the hair of my head, pushing my face deeper into his crotch. It was a nightmare! The urine smell combined with the perspiration made me choke as if I were about to vomit when he ejaculated into my mouth. He sat back in satisfaction for a moment, pushing me away. "Not bad, baby! Not bad!" He spoke with the satisfaction of a Cheshire cat that had just swallowed the canary, "We'll do this again," he instructed. "It will be our little secret." he quipped as I spit and spit again, wiping my mouth on the sleeve of my blouse, red faced and tear stained. I vowed one day – one day he would get his, but there was nothing I could do now, because I was at his mercy. He dropped me off at the back entrance of the school. Thank God, everyone was inside! He drove off and I ran the other way, as if the devil was chasing me. I flew like the wind and had no idea where I was going. A huge, gray stoned, Catholic Cathedral, on the main street of town, seemed to be my only refuge. I went to the door, which was unlocked. I entered quietly, slipping into a small room that had nothing in it but a seat. It was quiet and I felt secure. I prayed! I had not prayed in a long time. I didn't think God would listen to me anymore. Desperately, I cried softly, "God, if You are here, please, hear me."

I felt dirty and repulsive! How could God protect me when I was so filthy, inside and out. No one could love me. Who would love a crazy girl? How long I was there, I cannot tell you to this day. I slept sitting up and ready for flight. Have you ever been hidden under the shadow of God's wings? I went out in the broad daylight into the five and dime store and stole hair dye for my hair. On my way back to the church, two Marine soldiers approached me and began a conversation, "So where are you going?" they asked as they came up from behind me. I looked at them and a peace fell over me, and I willingly without reservation told them my story. They listened, without condemnation or judgment, of any sort, and escorted me to the apartment of one of the nurses from the Institution; the thin, blonde nurse with the sweet smile took me in.

She dyed my hair a dark auburn color and cut a few inches off to give me a different appearance. I fell asleep on the couch that night while the two Marines and the nurse talked and laughed. Everything they talked about was just a blur and there was no sense to anything. While they talked, it seemed like there were bright lights left on, as it was very bright even as I slept! The next day, the nurse reported that an APB was out for me and Pam also. Pam had run away too! The two Marines left, and at the end of the day, Pam arrived with them at the apartment. Pam had thin, penciled eyebrows, her eyes were dark brown, and she had long brown hair, she wore pulled back away from her face. It pronounced her features of high cheekbones and a thin pointed facial appearance. She had a nice laugh and spoke with confidence.

Almost two nights later, the Marines took Pam and I in their car under the cover of darkness to a phone booth outside the city limits. They made a phone call to my parents. It was suspected that the phone may be tapped, yet it was a chance they had to take to get me out of the area. Daddy answered, "Mr. Wetmore?" the Marine questioned. "Yas!" Daddy answered in a wary tone. "I have your daughter and another girl from the Institution. They need your assistance in being taken out of the State."

Daddy questioned without surprise, "Is she safe right now?" The Marine assured him that I was fine and made arrangements quickly where to meet. Within a few hours we were on a dark dirt road that went nowhere, and there was Daddy waiting for us in his old beat up, green 1957 Ford wagon with wood grain panels.

Daddy had arranged blankets and mats in the back with the seats down and Pam and I climbed in the back and snuggled under the cover of the blankets keeping very still until daddy pulled into the driveway of "home" a few hours later. I slept that night in my own bed on the third floor. My old bedroom was so comfortable, but it seemed foreign. It was as if I were in some never-ending dream. A dream that had become a nightmare. I learned Lucky, my German Shepherd dog, had died. After I left home, he had laid on my bed and refused food and water. He died of a broken heart. Mama was quiet, yet had that determined look on her face. She hugged me, but never spoke a word. The hug said it all! That same night, my dear cousin, Jim showed up. Jimmy was home on Christmas break from college. He came to visit his Uncle Stan & Aunt Priscilla before heading home to New York State without any known reason. He and I had been close growing up as kids and often visited with my parents, his aunt and uncle. Daddy had helped Jimmy out of some scrapes, like being broke down and fixing his car for him several times. Jimmy was good for a road trip! In no time arrangements were made to take us girls to New York State. New York was the one state that they didn't continue searching for someone who had run away. It was a safe state!

As I reflect back on the Marines that assisted me with their calm demeanor, their gentleness, yet, strong assurance, that always made me wonder if God sent angels in human form to assist and make a way of escape where there seemed to be no way. I also remember the brightness of their presence as I slept, and their ability to know where to go and how to get there. The reasoning of their coming up to me as I exited the store with the hair dye, and then keeping me close between them as a covering until I reached the apartment. I look forward to the day when I will be shown how God, in His mercy kept me under the shadow of His wings.

It was getting colder, and weather was changing fast. As we traveled through Vermont, taking the longest route and the most remote, when it began to snow. The roads were slick! Other vehicles were having a difficult time making a steep hill. Jim rolled backwards and turned around deciding that he should go another route that was fifty miles longer, but probably safer. He picked up speed to save time. Pam and I were laughing and joking about our get-away and how we had fooled the staff at the hospital when Jim came up on a sharp curve faster than he should have. "Swoosh!" In a split instant, the car spun around in the road and with the expertise of a stuntman, his old 1955 Plymouth was buried in a heap of soft fallen snow. "Wow! That was neat," I squealed, dizzy from the whirl and amazed that it was so quiet. We sat there a few minutes stunned at what had just happened! Jim was much more serious about it all, and decided he had to go for help after trying to brush snow out from under the tires with his hands. He wasn't gone long, when a truck had come by and was equipped with a set of chains. He pulled us out of our predicament in short order. The man refused any money for his Samaritan's deed. Clearly God was guiding us! It was late, in fact, the very wee hours of the morning when we arrived safely at Uncle Don's home, who was Jim's dad's. Safe at last!

"I will instruct you and teach you in the way you should go; I will guide you with My eye."

(Psalms 32:8 NKJV)

JOYCE A. LEONARD

"My Sleepless Wake"

In total silence of a lonely room
Where emptiness lies in quiet groans;
I lie awake in wonder of fearful doom,
Of what lies beyond the darkening moans.
As tears fall silent from my face,
I hunger for strength to embrace.
I dream of the days that have long past;
Transfigured by the years that didn't last.
As silence continues in the night hours' grace.
I think of Dad in agony's pace
I feel his eyes upon my face,
I hear his voice heavy and grim,
As it haunts me deep within.
Thoughts wander in memories with visions untold;
They caress the stillness growing cold;
Distasteful voices in hatred's throng,
Carries my heart in dreams where I belong.
An angel touches my brow
Soothing the fears that enter now.
I feel helpless to the tears that surge within.
I am weak to the battle of raging sin.
Dreams melt into the times of past
And I stay alone in horror fast.
I yearn for the magic of sleep
Where time stands still and hopes keep.
(Written by Joyce Wetmore—17 years old—1965)

Chapter Fourteen

Cherry Creek

The Lord shall preserve you from all evil. He shall preserve your soul.

The Lord shall preserve your going out and your coming in from this time forth and even forever more. (Psalms 121:7 & 8 NKJV)

Pam and I were guests, after our escape, at Uncle Don and Aunt Fern's home in Salamanca, NY, which is within the Seneca Indian Reservation in Cattaraugus County. Cousin Janice, Jimmy's oldest sister, was having her difficulties with her husband, Reggie, who was from the reservation. He enjoyed his alcoholic beverages, and was often out drinking at the bars. They shared living space at my aunt & uncles', her parents' home, with their two boys. Janice's life was often in chaos and uncertainty. Jim and I, with Pam tagging along, would be out doing detective work, looking for Reggie. Pam became a conquest for Reggie, therefore, she never returned to Aunt Fern & Uncle Don's. Reggie began threatening bodily harm to Janice, and the police became involved. Reggie was arrested! It was suspected that since Pam was involved with him, and after his arrest, she fled to parts unknown. She was never seen again. I went to Aunt Ruth's in Cherry Creek, as there was not enough room in the house for everyone to be comfortable.

Aunt Ruth and Uncle Maurice lived on Leon Road in Chautauqua County not far from the Pennsylvania border. This is where the little town of Cherry Creek was located. They were friends with the Amish. Uncle Maurice would shoe their horses for them. Sometimes late in the night you would hear them having horse and buggy races, galloping at break-neck speed through the dark of night. It was so authentic and reminded me of books I had read.

Aunt Ruth and I were best friends. She was my go-to when I needed advice. I was told by Aunt Ruth how happy Mama was that I was there with her, and now she seemed to be able to rest easy. I took on the job, across the road from Aunt Ruth and Uncle Maurice, caring for their disabled neighbor, Rose, who was disabled from brain aneurysms and needed home care. She was paralyzed on her left side and could only make groaning noises as she was unable to speak. Her fifteen-year-old son, that was of no help, and her husband could be pretty crude. They abused her mentally, at times, with their attitude. Many times she was left uncared for and needed someone to make her meals, dress her, help her to her chair, and go to the bathroom. Her husband worked and her son was in school. I seemed to fit the need, and had the capabilities, since I had been trained in nurse's aide work. They provided a room for me on the second floor. Her son's room was also on the second floor. There was a bathroom upstairs as well as downstairs. I came to love Rose and felt so badly for her. I called her Ma, and I wrote the following poem as a tribute to her life.

A JOURNEY OF TRIALS STRENGTHENED THROUGH FAITH

"I Called Her Ma"

First impression is pity of hearts.
Second glance, love imparts,
Although quiet in simple array,
Upon her head was a silver crown mixed with gray;
Time passed her slowly with affectionate taste,
And her history of kindness was traced,
Within the lines of her pleasant face.
For her eyes twinkled as the evening star,
And I called her Ma.
Through the miles of her years
Often passed into many tears,
Something troubled within her heart.
Something that words cannot impart;
For in the awkward grace of her mishap,
She lived within herself as a tattered map,
Yet her eyes twinkled as the evening star,
And I called her Ma.
Around each curve where life bends,
She had drawn many friends,
Some stain of grief had been engraved,
Producing the way, she behaved;
But, as I looked into her face,
And tried to read her troubled pace,
I could only see eyes that twinkled as the evening star,
And I called her Ma.
(Written by Joyce Wetmore—December 28, 1965)

"My Brother"

Stanley Marlon Wetmore was born December 24, 1965 and I had written a poem of his birth. It was strange to have a brother after so many years. I was almost 18 now, and I wanted to see him.

"A Letter to My Brother's Birth"

Born this day, the day before Christmas -
My baby brother is born.
A thousand miles away am I,
But my love goes out to the brother I adore.
Many tears fell as I began to cry,
And not being able to understand why.
My darling brother, when years progress,
So you may be able to read this address,
To yourself and know that it was
written especially for you.
On the day you were born and brought here new
During the hours of every waking day,
And through the slumbers of the night,
For your happiness forever more I will pray
And peace for your heart aright.
If I could bestow the gift of all gifts upon you,
I would give you understanding and
happiness for all time's sake.
I wish for you to be the boy who
kisses the morning dew,
The boy who climbs trees and swims in the lake;
To have freedom within your soul,
Then one day you will reach your goal,
And within your dreams, my baby
brother, this will not depart,
But will be determined within your heart.
Written by Joyce A. Wetmore – December 24, 1965

I had made contact with Alyce again, and Freddie wanted me to come and I questioned what I should do? I had saved up a lot of money – almost $200. He wanted me to come to Maine to marry him. I talked it over with Aunt Ruth. It was getting difficult to care for Rose. Her husband was demanding and her son was hateful to his mother. I was always dodging their advances in one form or another. I finally moved back to Aunt Ruth's and we would discuss late into the night what I should do. I saved $200 within a few short months, but since I made contact with Freddie, I asked him to send money ti buy a bus ticket and luggage for my trip to Maine. He sent me $100. I never let on about the money I had. Aunt Ruth said to me to be careful how I spent it. Uncle Maurice used to tease us saying we acted like a couple of school girls laughing and giggling in the night, as I slept with her and Uncle slept in the cot next to her bed. We put him to sleep with our chatter!

When I turned eighteen, I bought a travel trunk that held all my belongings and Aunt Ruth and Uncle Maurice took me to the nearest Greyhound bus station in Tannersville, New York for my ride to Maine. I now reached the age where no one could say anything about where I went or what I could do. After many hugs and kisses of a time that bonded us forever, I left to be with the man I loved more than anyone else, the man I was going to marry.

Chapter Fifteen

A Broken Heart – And No Where to Go...

"After you have suffered a little while, the God of grace, who called you to His eternal glory in Christ, will himself perfect, confirm, strengthen and establish you. (I Peter 5:10 NASB)

I felt every bump in the road, as I laid back in the Greyhound bus seat, trying to catch a nap as I thought of Freddie and what it would be like to see him again. I remembered when he first told me, while I still lived at home, that he was married and had a little boy. I was devastated! I was in love with him and had a desire to be with him, but he belonged to someone else. I was thinking back on that time, and how he reassured me that he was not in love with his wife, Henrietta. They didn't get along, but how he loved his little boy, Harvey.

Even though I knew I should not be with him back then, he was always in the background of my thoughts. The "if only" thoughts we have. So having him want me, and willing to send for me, I imagined he must have divorced his wife by now, since he wanted me to come and be with him. I was apprehensive, excited, uncertain, but anticipating the living happily ever after with the man I loved. Words just could not express all my hopes and dreams, that had died, were now renewed.

I was dressed to the hilt, with thick make-up, lacy black tights, well-fitting teal blue jumper with a pale yellow blouse under it. I did not fit the picture of what I had been. Things had changed for me. My hair was still long and I would roll it in huge rollers to create waves around my face. Fred met me at the bus station in Portland, Maine with his brother Edward and my best friend, Alyce. They were, somewhat taken back with my makeup and Fred asked me to wash my face, and I did. We arrived at Eddie's Diner, (now known as the Village Inn) where we had a good meal, and then Freddie took me to our apartment on Hampshire Street. I asked him the obvious question — "When are we getting married?" In my mind it was going to happen right away, but no one else seemed to be thinking the way I was. It was a furnished three room apartment, with a bedroom, living room, kitchen and full bath. However, the bed needed sheets and pillows. There were no dishes or cookware or groceries. There went a good portion of my $200! Edward and Alyce went their way and Fred and I went shopping. I bought the needed items and we returned to the third floor apartment. He answered my question with, "In a couple of weeks." I was a bit disturbed with that, but willing to wait. I really had no choice. He and I would be living together in this little apartment. I fanaticized a beautiful wedding!

He went right to bed, while I went to the bathroom and donned my flannel pajamas and quilted bathrobe as winter in Maine was as cold as Upper New York State. I was appalled at the condition of his boxer shorts and thought, "I must buy him some new underwear." I laid next to him on the bed. He had fallen asleep instantly, and began snoring so loudly, that I got up on my knees, bent over his face watching him breathe and snort, thinking he would die any minute. My mind was in a whirl thinking, "I had traveled all this way and now he was going to die on me." I was next to tears as I spent most of that first night listening to him breathe, and praying that he would not die.

He awakened, alive and well and left for work that morning in the white van that belonged to the newspaper company he worked for. He used the van for the newspaper deliveries throughout the surrounding towns to different variety stores. While he was gone, I found out that the second floor apartment was available so moved our things to that one, as the top floor was pretty cramped and I liked the windows on the second floor, as well as it had a back porch area with a place to store things. I didn't have much to store but my hopes were high.

After a week had gone by, I applied for nurse's aide work and I was immediately hired at the local hospital. I began the 3-11 shift. It was about a half hour walk one way. I walked to work from our apartment to the adjoining city across the bridge and up the hill to Central Maine General Hospital. I began work on T-3. Freddie would meet me after eleven p.m. on my return to the apartment at the end of Hampshire Street.

It was a sunny day, I was alone in the apartment deep in thought, when Henrietta, Freddie's wife, burst through the door without knocking, stroller in hand toting baby Harvey. Two of her cousins were close behind. She informed me that she and Freddie were still married and pointed out that this was "their son." Freddie didn't come back that night, as he was out drinking. The only thing I could really say to her was, "This is my apartment, get out!" She did, slamming the door so hard, it nearly came off its hinges, which I am sure loosened it up for Freddie when he later ripped the door off its hinges, since I had locked him out! And the tears started, and flowed night after night.

"So Freddie, when are you getting a divorce and how come you hadn't gotten it before you sent for me?" There was always an excuse, and I believed every one of them, "I don't have the money," he would exclaim, "She won't sign the papers," he would protest! "I am afraid she will keep my son from me," he would cry out. And the excuses continued!

I went to meet his grand-parents, Pop and Gram. They were pleasant and hospitable but a little odd at times. Their two sons, who had mental challenges, lived with them. They accepted me without reservations. I would frequent their home as that seemed to be Freddie's go-to place. Then one day, he said he wanted me to meet his mother and father! I later learned that Pop and Gram were the grandparents of his wife, Henrietta! I was still that naïve girl from Center Conway that everyone seemed to have the tendency to take advantage of, and I would believe everything anyone told me because . . .. I did!

When you are not used to being lied to, or led to believe in lies, you expect everyone to be honest. The shocker comes when you find out they are a bunch of liars but you *still* believe them because you want to believe the best in people. Somewhere in the midst of all of this, my friend Alyce, came to live with me and in a short period of time, all chaos unfolded on Hampshire Street. What happened and what stories were disclosed is not clear to me today, but our friendship took a beating at the hands of those around us and, once again, I believed the wrong people. The words came back to haunt me that Mama used to say, "You seem to trust the enemies around you before those who have your best interests at heart." I did and I have regretted it to this day. Thankfully my dear friend, Alyce, never held it against me.

"Freddie's Parents"

I finally met Freddie's parents, Dorothy and Omar. They lived on Hamden St. It was a three mile walk one way from where we were. His mother was kind. She sat in a wheel chair with one leg. She had lost the other leg to gangrene from her diabetic condition. Her oldest daughter, June, faithfully cared for her other foot daily to make sure there was no onset of the nasty disease to take the other leg or even a toe! Ma, Freddie's mother, had a very deep, crackly voice, probably from her years of smoking. They lived in a small house, which had a small entry way as you entered their home, which they called the porch. It was cluttered with boxes and plants, along with some unknown things stacked high, before you went through the glass paneled door into the kitchen. The black iron wood, cook stove graced most of the kitchen. Ma sat in her wheelchair at the head of a small red-glazed top, kitchen table held up by metal legs. It was stationed between two medium-sized windows that over looked their driveway in front of their street. She would wistfully gaze out the dusty windows into the outside world, dreaming of the fantasy of living a more comfortable life, although she never complained. Beyond the table in the far corner was a small refrigerator. The white porcelain kitchen sink, located next to the refrigerator, had metal faucets protruding from its high porcelain back, displaying the piping underneath the sink. A make-shift wooden side board was attached to it with a single cupboard over it for the few dishes that were there. Just under the sink that had no cabinet, sat a pail used by his father to urinate in until it needed to be emptied.

Off to the left of the kitchen was a full room divided only by a partial wall that the stove was against. In that room was a cot nearest the kitchen sink and this was where father slept. "Father" was a title of respect, that in my eyes, he did not deserve. Beside his bed was a dark green painted chair that held his six-ounce glass of beer, that he had before going to bed, and first thing in the morning, when he awoke, he drank beer again. There was a dresser that supported the back side of the wall that held both of their clothing. At the other end of the room was where Ma slept. Her single sized bed was next to a window, and she had a small nightstand next to it. Her baby picture hung on the wall. There were no other pictures or wall dressings of any kind.

Off from the kitchen, to the left as you entered, was a small room that had a black iron pail with a make shift toilet seat, which was where one went to relieve themselves. There was no wash basin, tub, shower or towels. Toilet tissue hung on a nail on the wall. Beyond that was the shed where his father made his home brew. There was a small black wood stove there, used during the cold months. The round tin chimney was piped out through the wall to the outside. A wooden work bench, that was never used, laced with cobwebs and housed by spiders, had been erected from the dirt floor. Father's crock was always full of his mixture of his home brew poison to drink as he needed. I called it "rot gut!"

Father was a small man in stature. He had a beard, a fiendish grin, grimy hands with long fingernails and dancing blue eyes. He had a heckling laugh that chilled your imagination. His snickering began when Ma would beg him for the bedpan, until she was near tears, waiting for him to come to her rescue. He would chide and ignore her until she came to that point. Her temper gave way, on one occasion, when he had made her wait so long, that when he was near enough, heckling in her face, she hit him with her doubled fist, and the force of the blow left a knot on her upper arm that almost knocked father out. I never witnessed the event, but it was told with an applaud of her victory!

Saturday nights father played "Jigs and Reels" on the electric, mahogany radio that was on a shelf, between the windows, in the kitchen. He would dance about the kitchen, like a drunken, giggling fool, until he passed out. Ed & Freddie were often there with Ed's family coaxing him on to dance and laugh. This really enhanced his antics to a greater level. He would come at me with those dirty fingers as if to touch me, and I would escape by jumping up on the sideboard screaming at Freddie to, "get his father away from me or I would kill him." Freddie would laughingly demand, "Father, leave her alone." This was often the week end attraction, to visit Father and Ma, as if it were a glorified spectacle that they could not miss. Friday and Saturday nights were drinking nights, and one day went into the next.

One particular night Daddy came by, looking for me, while everyone was there with all the beer bottles strewn over the table. He wanted to take me home. Oh no, I wouldn't go! I didn't want to hear, "I told you so." I would rather live in the filth of the world than to go back to any possible rebuke of my parents.

I really didn't know that daddy was masquerading as Jesus and coming to my rescue. Jesus is a gentleman and He will never force anyone to come. You have to go willingly. I hadn't lived through enough pain, yet, and I was determined that I could "fix" the brokenness. I was still bitter and angry at Mama and Daddy or was it God? How many times did Daddy walk away in tears that no one saw, but never gave up? How many times did he hang his head in his hands and cry for his little girl? Only heaven knows, but all tears will be wiped away. And Mama... she left the porch light on day and night, to light my way should I want to come home. But I wasn't ready yet!

> "And God will wipe every tear from their eyes...."
> (Revelation 7:17, Rev. 21:4 NKJV)

"Working at the Hospital"

I loved my job at the hospital. I was given more and more opportunities to learn, and greater responsibilities to go higher within the nursing career. I was paying Freddie's support payments of twenty dollars a week to Henrietta, so she wouldn't throw him in jail, as well as paying the rent. We had moved to High Street, which is today the parking lot at the hospital. We had a second floor apartment behind the hospital, and easy access for me to walk to work. Fred was not working. Every day, he would leave to look for a job, but always came back drunk. He did find a job in the Mill that lasted two days. He caught his shirt sleeve in the conveyer belt and that was the end of that.

Since I worked nights, I slept days and usually got up around 4 p.m. to make our supper. We had a diet of macaroni and butter seven days a week. It was cheap and it got us by. This particular afternoon I decided to go ask the bartender at the Ponderosa Café (no longer in existence) to trust me for a pack of cigarettes until I got paid. (oh, yes, I was still smoking!) I walked down over the hill and there in one of the booths was Freddie sitting with two women and eating an Italian sandwich. Strangely enough the women didn't bother me as much as what he was eating! I had nothing but the same old macaroni to eat that I faithfully prepared every night for us. He had no worries about the next meal. so I decided to stay and drink with him. It was getting late in the evening when he emphatically said, "Joyce, you can't drink anymore because you have to go to work."

It was at that moment, the same as when Daddy said I couldn't see him anymore—the same reoccurring thought came back, "That's what you think." And that was when I lost my job at the hospital. I later regretted staying and drinking with him, it was a grave mistake. It cost me a job that I loved, the loss of the apartment, and any independence I had established at that point. Perhaps if I had not let my anger overrule, and the rebellious spirit take over me, I may have run back home and begged for Mama & Daddy's forgiveness, instead I decided to walk in my own willful way.

> "Don't sin by letting anger control you.
> Think about it overnight and remain silent."
> (Psalms 4:4 NLT)

"Moving in with His Parents"

I woke up with a hangover. Fred told me to have another drink, and that it would knock it out of me. I tried it, but one day and night became a solid week of being drunk. We lived in his 1954 Plymouth. The only thing I can remember, at that time, is hunger, filth and puke. Fred went to his parents and they consented to take us in, so we moved in with them. I scrubbed the back shed, and the cobwebs and spiders disappeared. The dirt floor was cleared of cigarette butts and debris that was unfit to live in. A cot was put in the corner, and the wood stove was used on the chilly nights as it was the Spring of 1966. We had a side entrance to the back shed so, if we came in late at night, we wouldn't disturb his parents.

    I had fully made up my mind I was not going back to do any work until he got a job and kept it for a while. I took care of Ma and I know she appreciated it. Yellow was her favorite color, so I bought her a bedspread and matching curtain for her window, with big yellow flowers parading the spread on her bed and dancing on her curtain. Father complained that I used too much water to do the dishes and clean the house, "it cost money you know," he would quip. I ignored him as much as possible. He would wander out to pick bottles, by the side of the road, since recycling in Maine brought in two cents per bottle or can. It gave him enough for his fix, for the day, to buy his next bottle of beer.

While sitting at the table with Ma, one Spring morning, Father was out in the yard sitting on a kitchen chair with his feet in a bucket of water. His legs were black up to his knees and I said to Ma, "Father forgot to take his socks off!" She laughed till tears came, while gasping, "Those ain't socks, that's dirt!" Wide-eyed with disbelief, I exclaimed, "You're kidding!" Ma religiously took her PTA bath, (I will leave this to one's imagination), as she called it, every day, when I would bring her a basin of water, a clean towel and washcloth. I did laundry next door, at her daughter June's place, which was the next street over, but connected by a path out back of Ma's house that continued over a little hill to the next street over. Their property had once been owned by Ma & Father, but was sub-divided, giving June and her family a nice plot of land to have a house for their six children. This was always a point of contention between June and her sister Dot. Dot never seemed to feel that her sister deserved this gesture and that June owed it to her mother to care for her diabetic condition. I listened to both sides and tried to stay as neutral as possible.

"'Freddie's Parents"

At one-time father did work for the city, as a laborer. His birth records had been destroyed and he was brought up by his grandmother, Lillian Robinson. It was determined that he was born approximately 1904. There is no record of his month and day. So this would make him about sixty-two at this point in time. Ma's maiden name was Buckley. She was born on May 7, 1907. She had one sister, Grace and a brother John.

Father had crafted braces for his son Omer's club feet, but was never able to have it patterned. At some era of time, the braces he crafted became the wealth of another by copying his idea. This was never rectified. Ma & Father had 11 children. (June 1926-2007,) (Omer 1927-1939,) (Edith 1929-2008,) (Edward 1930-2013), (Betty 1932-2004), (Dorothy 1934-2019) Those still living, John B. 1938, Fred B. 1942. There were three that were adopted. They live out of state and the family did reach out to them late in life. Fred, however, was the last child kept at home, so he was considered the youngest. Omer was killed, at age twelve by drunk driver while he was walking beside the road. I do not know the details of the entire story. It was not talked about.

"The Bottle of Vodka"

June used to get irritated that Rene and Freddie would go out in the garage and drink. She knew there was a liquor bottle out there somewhere. I knew it was kept up over the door of the garage opening, tucked into an opening between the studs. I carefully climbed up the side ladder and retrieved it. I dumped the clear liquid out in the sink, replaced it with water and put the bottle back. June and I laughed at the thought of Rene and Freddie getting the bottle to have a drink.

June had gone to Beano and I was doing laundry. I came in the house, in time, to hear Rene call to his neighbor, out the kitchen window, in French, to come over and have a nip with him. She hurried through the field, and came in and sat in June's rocker next to the sink sideboard. Rene got two glasses from the upper cupboard, and then set them up pouring just the right amount from the Vodka bottle. "Hey, Joyce," he called to me, "do you want a little nip?" I was about to split a gut from laughing inside and hurrying down the basement stairs to the washer, I declined, "No, no, I don't want any, thanks anyway!" I came back up to see him adding water to the clear liquid he just poured. Mrs. C. tasted it and commented in her broken English accent, "Rene, I tink you added too much water." He tasted his and decided his needed more vodka as well, so he added some more of the clear liquid from the Vodka bottle. I couldn't take it anymore, so I fled from the house, and almost rolled down the pathway laughing. I got inside Freddie's parents' house and exploded my secret to Ma. Father was out on his trek for empty bottles so he wasn't in on the secret. We sat together laughing over it, when Rene came storming into Ma's little house cursing up a storm over, "those kids!" He thought his kids had done the deed, and was pretty upset that he was made a fool of in front of Mrs. C. I never told him the difference and neither did Ma. Since he wouldn't want

June to know, the kids were never reprimanded for the deed they never knew anything about.

"Trying to Teach Freddie A Lesson"

Another weekend had arrived and true to Freddie's predictable behavior, he had gone to the Golden Dome Café, (no longer in existence) down by the Androscoggin River front. The Café hung over the side of the river and apartments in the building were up over it. There was a diner next door attached to the same building where many staggered next door to eat and sober up before heading home. This was where all the locals and run of the mill lush bums headed for a weekend of hootin' tootin' howlin' ragtime dancing and drinking! This was my first stop. I walked in, to see him sitting next to his estranged wife, Henrietta. She was laughing and tossing her long black curls back as he flirtatiously whispered in her ear, "Cut it out, Freddie," she would laugh! I sat down next to Larson across from them. Larson was Lori's husband and Lori was June's oldest daughter. Larson ordered a glass of milk for me, since I was now pregnant. Freddie grabbed at Henrietta's blouse, reaching for her breasts while playing with her hair. She pretended disgust as she pushed his hand aside and gave him a sly grin. Larson looked at me and asked, "How can you stand that?" I couldn't answer, but threw the darted looks of an evil eye across the table at them. Freddie's drunken stupor kept him from noticing any look of disdain. Larson answered his own question with reasoning another question, "You know he is drunk?" Henrietta's boyfriend, arrived and she took off with him.

Freddie's little game with Henrietta ended, and he turned into a monster, that had been defeated. He went to the men's room. I thought I would teach him a lesson for treating me so badly, so I took his 1954 black Plymouth Barracuda, and headed out. Around and around I went through the outskirts of the city limits trying to find my way back to his parent's place. I was not familiar with the back roads. It had begun to rain and it took me forever to find the little knob on the dash to put the wipers on. I worried about getting back to his parents before he did because

I didn't know what his reaction would be. I prayed, "Lord please help me to find my way back." (I hadn't forgotten that if I needed help, God was the Source of help, even though I lived the life of a heathen). As I rounded the lake, and finally got my bearings, I knew where I was, so I turned right onto Center Street and found my way back to Hamden St. I drove in next door to his sister's driveway on Nysquina Street, and parked the car there, leaving the keys in it. I hurried down the path that connected the two places, and entered the shed by the side entrance trying not to awaken Father and Ma.

In the stillness of the early morning hours, I thought I heard a motor running. I sat up on the cot and looked out the thin paned window of the shed. I saw Freddie get out of a taxi, get in his car and drive way. It was Sunday night before I saw him again. I know the Lord "heard the voice of my weeping." (*see Psalms 6:8 NKJV*)

"Laughter Followed by Tears"

Freddie had begun working with his brother, Ed, on construction with Owen Taylor Construction Company. (No longer in business). Ed was a heavy-equipment operator, and pretty much known to be the best around. It was a Friday night, so Fred was back at the Golden Dome Café. He had given me money to keep for him, so he wouldn't spend it all. I tucked it in my shoe, because I never carried a purse. He was too drunk to drive, so I drove us to his parents' house. The State Police officer, Oliver Dore, pulled me over. Ollie knew Fred, personally. He asked for my license and registration. I passed him the registration and told him I did not have a license. When he raised his eyebrows at me, I said, "He is too drunk to drive." He flashed his light over on Fred, who was sitting with is head hanging down and slurring his words. Ollie passed the registration back to me and said, "I will follow you home." Once we were in the driveway and getting out of the car, he turned and went on his way. When we got into the back shed and preparing for bed, Fred asked for his money, which I gave him.

A JOURNEY OF TRIALS STRENGTHENED THROUGH FAITH

Then the accusations began. "Where is the rest of the money?" he barked at me. "I gave it all to you," I cried, in alarm, as he was in my face with his lip curled in a snarl. "There is money missing," he glared at me while cursing under his breath through clenched teeth. I tried to reason with him, looking at him in disbelief, "I have been nowhere else, but with you the whole time. Look there is nothing more in my shoe." I frantically was justifying my actions, while showing him my socks and shoes.

I was sitting on the cot, but as I looked back up at him, his left-handed fist clipped me in the jaw, and knocked me back onto the cot. My teeth clicked together at the blow. I reeled with a stunned dizziness, and tried to get back up, when the blow came again and sent me convulsing backwards. I again tried to regain my position, and for the third time I went down. My head was whirling so hard; I could hear him, but it sounded like he was far away yelling at someone else. He wasn't waiting for me to come up and meet his fist anymore, he came down at me ready to rip me from one end to another, as he reached for me, I curled my knees to my chest, and as he came down at me I feared I would be beaten to death. Somehow I was able to have presence of mind to use both of my feet as a springboard aimed at his stomach. With every ounce of strength, I had left, I kicked, sending him sailing backwards, and falling into the wood stove, whacking his head. It knocked him out long enough for me to make my escape. I staggered out of the shed, into the night, scrambling to find my way to his sisters, when I passed out in the driveway of their home.

Rene, June's husband, had been out drinking, as well, and upon returning home, he pulled into his driveway, where I was laying on the ground in front of his garage doors. When he got out of his old Edsel, he heard my groaning. I could hear him screaming, "Joyce are you okay? Oh God! I don't think she is breathing. I think she is dead!" He thought he had run over me. I vaguely felt him scoop me up in his arms, and carried me in the house crying out to June in his pet French name for her, "Petite Bout, Petite Bout." June met him at the door, Rene was in a frenzy and confessed, "Oh Bout," (he would call her this when he thought he was in trouble) "I think I ran over her." June surveyed my face and said, "No, she has been beaten." And in her next breath she asked, "Where is Fred?" They laid me gently in one of the beds, that had fresh sheets, and tucked me in there with Jean, their daughter, to keep an eye on me, making sure I would be alright the remainder of the night. Rene went next door to find Fred.

As I drifted in and out of consciousness, I heard him say, "It is all dark over there; the car is gone." He continued, "I don't think we should upset Ma." June affirmed his decision and said, "It's just as well, we will deal with this later." The next morning when the sun came up shining and temperatures were climbing, the snow patches that were scattered here and there were the only evidence left that winter had been there not long ago. After a warm bath and breakfast, I was able to feel like I could talk and through my swollen lips and black eyes I related the story. June was furious! While I was still relating the perils of the night, Fred returned.

He sat outside in the yard laying on the horn for someone to come out. I think he thought I would appear. June scuffled her way to the doorway in her slippers and robe, with her blonde hair all in disarray and a scowl embedded on her face, while toting her cigarette between her fingers, and using it as her pointer, as she met Fred from the porch railing. He sat in his car with the window down. She demanded emphatically, "Get the **** out of here." She gave a lengthy stare waiting for him to defy her command. There was silence. She pointedly asked him, "Don't you think you have done enough damage?" Her voice was crisp and sharp. Just as she was about to open her mouth to continue her chastisement, I interrupted her, as I came out onto the porch. Begging June, I said, "Please, let me talk to him. "She disgustedly answered me with, "I hope he's worth it."

Cindy, June's youngest daughter, wanted to brush my hair. I sat in the rocker while she lovingly combed and brushed my long silky hair, as if to heal my brokenness. Later in the day, Jeannie was at the front door looking out the window. "There is a stranger here," she said warily. "A man is coming to the door," she warned. June was sitting in her favorite chair smoking. Nothing ever seemed to rattle her, too much, as she calmly answered, "Well, invite him in." It was Daddy. He asked for me, and was escorted to the living room where Cindy was still combing my hair. When I looked up at him, he asked, "What happened to you?" It was as if he were asking a stranger a general question. He was cold and distant. I lied to him saying I had fallen down the cellar stairs taking laundry down and hit my chin on the cement. No one said anything differently. Light conversation was made and I went to hug him, but he never hugged me back. He left shortly after that. As he was pulling out of the driveway, I looked at June and asked if she had called him. She said she was as shocked as I was to see him show up on her doorstep. My tears fell like rain, and the hurt inside seemed almost too much to bear.

I learned that he had been told by Father that there had been some problems, but exactly what was said I don't know. We were not to go back to Fathers again to live. June would not have Fred there, so we left and went to Lori and Larson's. Fred had said, once again, he was, "sorry and this would never happen again." I believed him. . .. because after all he was drinking and didn't know what he was doing. He didn't mean to. At least that was what I wanted to believe. I was pregnant for my first child, but did not know I was pregnant until later.

"Saved by The Unseen Hand"

Lori and Larson lived in a third floor apartment on Goff St. and this was our next place to live. I helped by babysitting. I enjoyed knitting, so I knit two matching sweaters for their boys, nicknamed "Peanut" and "Love Bug." The blue and white designed sweaters came out quite nice. It was another Friday night, and the hunt was on to find Freddie. There he was, with the familiar crowd at the Golden Dome, laughing and pounding their fists on the table with belly rolling guffaws! It had been a night to measure one's private part laid out on the table. The laughter was deafening! When I discovered the nature of their regality, I was pretty disgusted and flabbergasted that he would do such a thing. He was angry with me that I interrupted his party time, so he stormed out and did not want me with him. As he was taking off in the car, I jumped in, while the car was still moving. He drove into Lori and Larson's driveway, and pushed me out of the car on the ground. I got up and began pounding on his car, while he began backing out of the driveway, with me still attached to it. I lost my grip, and fell to the ground, and as I laid on the ground, I heard the engine roar. I realized he was returning full speed back into the driveway, and I still could not move. I was certain at this point that I was going to die there. The pain that was searing through my abdomen became unbearable, and any movement made it far worse, paralyzing me! I heard the tires squeal, and knew he couldn't stop in time. The angels had to have taken over, for when I opened my eyes, the tires were next to my head. He again put it in reverse, and left the driveway without checking to see if I was alright. The neighbor on the second floor heard the squeal, and came running to see what was going on. He carried me to the third floor!

From there Larson took me to the hospital. He left the hospital to go look for Fred, and brought him to see me. In his drunken condition, he laughingly tried to get in bed with me, acting like an idiot! The nurses quickly ushered him out, and called security to show him to the door. Larson's thought was to shock him into the reality of what he had done to me. It was a senseless situation! *"Before they call, I will answer: and while they are yet speaking, I will hear."* (Isaiah 65:24 NKJV) I believe I was saved by the His mighty *"right hand of His righteousness."* (see Isaiah 41:10 NKJV)

"Marines"

Freddie had joined the Marines, but before he was inducted in the service, he had gone to Bangor, for some unknown reason., a town more than 50 miles away from his hometown. He was driving while drunk, and drove down a one-way street the wrong direction. He was stopped, and since he was intoxicated, he was arrested, and put in jail for 30 days. The recruiting officer took me to the jail there to visit him. On our trip to Bangor, I unfolded the story of my involvement with Fred. When we arrived at the jail, I was allowed in to visit. He had lost so much weight, he was down to a 28 waist, and looked pretty haggard. The Marine officer brought me back home and later Freddie received an, "Undesirable Discharge" paper in the mail.

"The Baby Shower"

Fred had asked me to take a walk with him on a cold night "to talk" is what he said. We didn't talk about much. I thought he was going to tell me he was leaving me. He didn't seem to be making much sense, so I insisted on returning to the apartment, because I was cold. I saw some people in the living room when I got back inside the apartment, but paid no attention because I was so annoyed with Freddie's senseless talk. He had not come upstairs with me. I decided to go in the living room, and I sat next to June. I never noticed the table with all the gifts on it, and I curiously asked, "So what is going on? How come everyone is here?" They all yelled, "Surprise!" And even though I had not recognized what was happening, it truly was a wonderful "surprise."

"The Love of Dance"

The fun thing at the Golden Dome was dancing. Ralph, the bartender and proprietor, knew all his customers. He was a fun-loving guy that was just a joy to be around, and made you feel like you were important. I loved the atmosphere, and became drugged by it. Freddie was a good dancer, especially when it came to being spun around the dance floor. He could do the polka like no one else and was a sought after partner for anyone who wanted to dance. Larson's sister, Ellie, we affectionately called "Big Bertha" loved dancing. "The Beer Barrel Polka" was a common polka dance, and Freddie could pick her up off her feet and swing her around with ease, while everyone would clap and stomp their feet as the dance floor cleared for their performance. When he twirled me around the floor, I felt like the queen of the dance floor, as I am sure every other woman he twirled felt the same. The music was intoxicating, and I was addicted.

Since the "Beer Barrel Polka" was the only dance that Fred really liked to do and was good at, and if I wanted to dance anything else, Jimmy was the only one I was allowed to dance with. I never knew why, but I would search out Jimmy to dance whenever we went there, as I loved dancing the fast dances. There were others that he seemed to trust, Bootie being one of them. He and Bootie worked together. Bootie and I never got a long much, but tolerated each other. Fred was working for Lewiston Crushed Stone driving a cement truck. June's husband, Rene got him the job. He later began working with his brother, Ed, as heavy equipment operator. There were many more nights of dancing between the Golden Dome Cafe, Ponderosa Café, Little Casino and the Manoir. (none of these establishments have been in existence for some time.)

I was known for "dirty dancing," and enjoyed being a show off, because I could out-dance any female around. I knew I was good! This particular night, at the Ponderosa, I was dancing with Fred, when five girls attacked me, and held me down, pounding on me, and pulling my hair out by the handfuls.

Eddie's wife, Louise, jumped in, and belted them with her pocketbook. She pounded on them until they scattered and left. I was fighting for all I was worth, and would have had a better chance if I had not had so many to deal with. Evidently, they were aware of this. The only reasoning for this attack was they didn't like my dancing!

"Jealousy"

Freddie was very jealous, and I could not glance in the direction of anyone of his friends without him getting very angry and accusatory. I had been out searching the bar rooms one evening, and went into the Golden Dome deciding to sit it out, and wait for him to appear. While sitting at a table nursing a beer, a friend,

Buck, came in, who dated Henrietta, Freddie's wife. Buck saw me immediately, and sat down with me. We began talking, and he could make me laugh! The waitress, Lizzie, came rushing to our table exclaiming worriedly, "Freddie just walked in." I said, "I don't care—what is the big deal?" I guess Lizzie knew him better than I did as he unexpectedly, without warning, grabbed Buck by the back of his shirt, and hauled him to the fire exit that hung over the back of the Café. He was going to throw him over the fire escape. I pleaded for him to leave Buck alone. The more I intervened for Buck the angrier Freddie became, and looking at me with disgust, he cocked his head in the direction of Buck, "You care about him?" Instinctively, I knew if I tried to reason any further with him, he would let him fall to the cement below, which was equivalent to two stories high. I said, nonchalantly, "Naw, I don't care about him, drop him if you want to." Perspiration was beaded on Buck's forehead, as he looked at me in disbelief. With that, Freddie relented by draping him over the iron railing, and turned on his heel and headed for the front door. I ran after him, leaving Buck to fend for himself.

"At The Ponderosa"

At the Ponderosa, Fred wanted to get rid of me. Unknown to me he was seeing this red-headed babe, Sandy. He called a cab to take me home, and paid the driver to drive me around. (I am sure it was to keep me occupied). I became aware when we passed by the apartment twice. I had asked the driver, "When are you taking me home?" He calmly answered, "When I get around to it." At the next red light, when he stopped, I jumped out, and walked back to the Ponderosa. Fred was in a booth sitting nearest to the wall. The woman, that was with him, was on the outside. I tapped her on the shoulder. She turned and looked up. Without a word or hesitation, I drove my fist into her mouth, loosening her teeth, and breaking the skin on my knuckles. Fred was so angry at me! We walked out of there, and took the railroad trestle back to the adjoining city, in an argumentative fit of rage. It was well past midnight! It was only a miracle that we got across without incident, as we crossed the Falls between the Twin cities. I later crossed that trestle alone. Looking at it today, it is hard to believe that I attempted such a feat. I believe angels were walking with me!

"The Spectacle"

This particular weekend was rumored that there was going to be a rare event at the Sportsman Lodge off on a back road. There was a show with "Christy," the transvestite from Boston. Fred was determined we were going to go witness this phenomenon. Sure enough, the crowd was pressed together with people standing on their tables to get a better view of this man made into a woman. She had long metal strands attached to the nipples of her breasts, accompanied by balls of fire, which she began swinging around and around so fast that it left a blur of a continuous ring of fire.

This was part of her show, like a circus spectacle. Everyone applauded and hooted with laughter as they pushed and shoved to get a closer view. It was rumored that she would take individuals to an upper room for a hefty price to have an encounter with her. When we left that night, Christy was embedded in our minds. It is difficult to comprehend that today this seems to be a way of life that many males and females choose. They feel they are trapped in a body they do not want. I believe God created them perfectly the way they were to be at birth, but Satan has deluded their thinking.

"Make The World Go Away"

There were those bar room drinking nights that Freddie and I swayed to the music, as I linked my arms over his shoulders, and clasped my hands around his neck, as he held me close to himself by pulling me in at the waist, as we swayed in slow waltz fashion. The song that was ours, was crooned over the juke box by Eddie Arnold, "Make the world go away. Take it off my shoulders. Say the things you used to say, and make the world go away." Those nights, kept me connected to him. Those were the nights when he whispered the sweet nothings in my ear and made the "world go away."

There will come a day, when this world will melt in fervent heat, and the One who loves us most will wipe those tears from our eyes, (see Revelation 21:4) and this world will literally be wiped away, and made new by the Creator of life, the one who will hold us close to Himself, and we will feel safe forevermore. The great spectacle will be when He comes to get us with tens of thousands of angels, in a glorious production, never before witnessed by human eyes, and every knee will bow, calling Him, Lord of lords and King of kings. Don't miss being part of the first resurrection! (*see Romans 14:11,* and *Isaiah 45:23 NKJV*)

Chapter Sixteen

Tammy Marie - My Baby Girl

*"Behold children are a heritage of the Lord,
the fruit of the womb is their reward."*
(Psalms 127:3 NKJV)

Dot, Freddie's sister, felt I should see Dr. Frederick Lidstone for my very first internal to see if I was pregnant, and how far along I was. Since I didn't understand the procedure of an internal, it was a humiliating experience. I sat in the waiting room while the receptionist called the nurse to come for me. In the examining room, the nurse told me to remove all my clothing, while she pulled the curtain around me and gave me a johnnie to put on. I thought to myself, "they can't mean my bra and underwear so I won't take those off," feeling confident that would not be necessary. I cautiously came out from behind the curtain and stepped onto the stool to sit on the examining table. The nurse had me lay back and place my feet in these metal stirrups, then covered me with a sheet. Dr. Lidstone entered the room and prepared by donning a pair of silicone gloves and opening the sheet that had been placed over me, he discovered my underwear was still on, in disgust he abruptly admonished the nurse, "This patient is not ready." The nurse was surprised that I had not followed her instructions and repeated that this was necessary. So I returned behind the curtain and finished my part of taking the rest of my clothing off and returned to the table, feeling quite naked and scared. My knees shook uncontrollably! I could not hold them still as they kept shaking together, while the doctor was trying to examine me. Dr. Lidstone, was not sensitive to my feelings and had the nurse hold my knees apart while he placed his gloved fingers into my vagina and moved them about. He, quite emphatically, exclaimed, "You are three months pregnant. You can make an appointment for next month."

On my next visit, the following month, Dr. Lidstone took me into his office, peered over his glasses and stated with confidence, "I have a nice family that would like to adopt a baby, and since you are not married, this would be a good way to get rid of this problem." I was immediately angry at the suggestion that he would even think that I would consider doing such a thing, and I answered curtly, "That is not an option for me, and I will no longer be retaining your services." The following month, I made an appointment with his colleague, Dr. Theodore Sanford, who continued to care for me during the remainder of my pregnancy.

"15 Pleasant St."

Fifteen Pleasant St. was another furnished three room apartment, but on the first floor this time. My neighbor, Vi, short for Viola, lived across the hall from me with her five children and became my close friend. We often left our doors open to walk freely from my apartment to hers, and so forth. The third apartment over was Dawn's and her door would be open as well. It was a sunny day, in March and my baby was two weeks late. We all had stayed up late into the night playing Canasta, eating chips and whatever else was my fancy waiting for the "time of arrival." Today, I baby-sat Dot's kids, as there was no school. Everyone in the building checked in before leaving asking if I was alright. I told each one that I was fine, and when the last one left, I picked up the broom and went to sweep the living room floor, when a gush of liquid came from between my legs. My water broke! There was no phone to call anyone, so I instructed the oldest child, Mark, to go to the phone booth just around the corner from the apartment and call the number I wrote down on a piece of paper. I explained to him to tell whoever answered to come right away. He ran off and did as I asked. It wasn't long when, Larry from the next street over, appeared. He was one of Freddie's drinking buddies. He had a distinct gruffness to his voice that always ended with a guttural hack sound as if his throat was full of phlegm. As he came in, I squealed in disbelief, "Larry, I think my water broke," searching for answers from him. He looked bewildered and said, "Joyce, I never had a kid. I don't know what to do." I looked at him in bewilderment myself and said, "Well, neither have I." He immediately answered while hurrying off, "I will go call an ambulance."

It wasn't long when Larry returned and said he would stay with the kids until Dot came to pick them up and that the ambulance was on its way. I saw the ambulance pull up out front of the long walkway and I grabbed my suitcase, and hurried out to meet the two attendants walking toward me. They were wheeling a stretcher along rapidly, and in seconds I was on it, as they swept me off my feet and strapped me on it as they began their assessment of my condition. I protested, "I can walk." They were not listening.

I was on my way to Central Maine General Hospital, with sirens blaring. When I arrived at the hospital, they placed me in a room and darkened it, by closing the blinds. The nurse had come in to check on me and make sure I had dilated enough for delivery. I laid in the bed quietly wondering where Fred could be, knowing he was out drinking somewhere. There was no way to get a hold of him or even know where anyone would begin to look for him. I felt like I had to have a bowel movement, and here I was with the side rails enclosed about me with a belly so big I could barely move; I had to get to the bathroom, so I inched my way to the bottom of the bed, and cautiously slid off the end of the bed, and made my way to the bathroom. I felt like I must be constipated, and if I could only have this bowel movement I would feel much better. Nothing! I reluctantly went back to the bed, and using the chair I was able to hike myself back on to the end of the bed and squirm back in position.

The nurse kept coming in to check on me throughout the evening until she came and wheeled me into the delivery room where Dr. Sanford was waiting. He smiled at me as he calmly exclaimed, "You are going to have your baby now," and began preparing for the delivery. I had just glanced at the large clock high up on the wall, it was 1:25 a.m. As soon as I looked at the clock, I turned and saw the blade of knife gleaming in Dr. Sanford's hand and I believe I passed out. When I came to several hours later, I vaguely remember a baby being laid on my chest, but now there wasn't one. When the nurse appeared, I anxiously asked, "What did I have? Can I see my baby now?

The nurse calmly smiled while opening the blinds to let some sunlight in, "You had a baby girl, and you will have to wait until you see the doctor first." She methodically went about freshening up my bed then silently left the room and left me in wonderment.

It was a beautiful Spring day—March 30, 1967. I had gotten out of bed and was gazing out the window wistfully wondering where Freddie was, and how much I wanted to be back in my apartment and wondered if my parents would come see me? As the thoughts crowded my mind, Dr. Lichtner came in to my room. I had returned to my bed, and he stood close to the bedside, taking my hand. He was the children's physician, and he had just examined my baby girl. He slowly began his questioning. "Did you go through any trauma while carrying her?" I answered, quickly and affirmatively, "Oh yes!" Then I, apprehensively, asked, "Why? Can I see my baby now?" Hesitantly he answered, "No, no not yet, she is in the incubator and is very blue! The umbilical cord was wrapped around her neck when she was born and she suffered trauma at birth." He kindly continued to question, "What happened during your pregnancy?" I turned my head away from his searching eyes and did not respond. The tears silently rolled down my cheeks remembering all I went through carrying the child I wanted so much. I never told him, and he quietly left the room.

A couple days later, Henrietta, Freddie's wife burst into my hospital room in a huff demanding her support money for her son. And where was Freddie? I thought "And I am supposed to know?" Anger crept through my veins as I angrily shouted at her to, "GET OUT!" I continued in a fit of rage, "I just had a baby, just leave me alone." Henrietta turned on her heel spewing her vile threats that she was going to have him arrested and thrown in jail if she didn't get her money?

It was several hours later when Freddie arrived drunk and staggering. He bent over me, slopping a wet, beer-ridden kiss on my mouth saying that he was going to pass out pink cigars to everyone! Eight days later, I got to see my baby girl, and I named her Tammy Marie. On the day I was able to come home, Tammy was placed in my arms while I was seated in the back of a cab to be taken home to 15 Pleasant St in Auburn, Maine, which was Tammy's first home. My dearest friend and neighbor, Viola, was there to welcome me, and I thank God for her.

"Baby Blue"

Baby Blue, tucked inside of me,
The punches came wild and free,
You were sheltered only by my cocoon.
I added your life to the baby boom.
I was too young to really understand.
The damage done by daddy's hand,
For the life within my womb,
Could easily have become a tomb.
Now as I look back on time past,
Contemplating the mystery revealed at last.
The secret is out, my Baby Blue—
I had always wanted to tell you too!
You were given less chance than most,

A JOURNEY OF TRIALS STRENGTHENED THROUGH FAITH

For your breath and air were little to boast.
I stayed out of fear and fought in fright;
You see, I wanted you with all my might.
I thought your life would change daddy dear;
Help him to realize life was more than beer.
I didn't know I was playing a dangerous game
I thought the demons I could tame.
Baby Blue has grown to a woman long ago.
I have kept the secret others didn't know.
I played with life and lost,
While he won the prize at my cost.
But someday you'll know, my Baby Blue,
That I have always loved you and God does too!

(Written in memory of my daughter Tammy Marie's birth in 1996 while remembering past trials that should never have happened. Those times will be etched forever in my mind on the tombstone of life.)

(By Joyce A. Wetmore Robinson Leonard)

Chapter Seventeen

From Pleasant St. to Main St. to Roak St.

"A good man, out of good treasure of his heart brings forth good;

and an evil man out of evil treasure out of his heart brings forth evil.

For out of the abundance of the heart his mouth speaks." (Luke 6:45 NKJV)

Mama came to see Tammy while Daddy stayed in the car. He was ashamed of me for having a baby out of wedlock. He did not want to see her or me. Mama hurried to give me a quick hug and adoringly held her grand baby briefly. She took a picture of Tammy and me through the window as she left. I felt a new closeness to Mama I had never felt before. Tammy was born March 30, 1967, which is just a couple years younger than Stanley, my brother, born December 24, 1965. I did not see him until he was almost three years old. I was so fanatical over how Tammy looked to show her off. I meticulously ironed her little dresses and made sure she was clean at all times. I never nursed her because Tom thought that was ugly and wouldn't allow me to do that. I had so much breast milk, it ran out of me like a faucet. I cried not knowing what to do. Dr. Sanford was a dear doctor. He gave me medication to dry up my milk. That was such a relief!

Having a baby was far more than I ever wanted to do again. I stated out loud, "I am not going through that again!" I had wanted to be pregnant, the first time, as I felt a baby would bring some sense of joy to Freddie since he could not have his son, but that was it! I assumed my baby bearing days were over. There was almost seven years between my sister and I, and eighteen between my brother and I, so I was sure that you didn't get pregnant unless you wanted to be.

Fred continued his drunken sprees, and I never knew where he was or when he would be back. Vi taught me how to care for an infant. I went to work, just as soon as I was able, and she babysat for me. This particular day, while I was stewing over where he was, as he said he was just going up to Eith's (pronounced IKE'S) Bakery on Hampshire Street, which was around the corner from our apartment. It had been a couple hours and he had not returned so I knew well enough he was somewhere drinking.

A motorcyclist was getting ready to leave out front, at the end of the walkway. "Hey Mister," I yelled. "I need a ride over town, can you take me?" I continued to call out to him as I kept racing toward his motorcycle expecting there would be no problem. "Sure hop on," he called back. He never questioned who I was or why, but sped off and we were in Lewiston in no time. He dropped me off at the mouth of Lisbon Street. I jumped off waving "thanks," and walked as fast as I could as I began my search. I would often try to sneak in the Manoir. There was a bouncer at the door, they called "Babe," who was actually the owner. He was a huge guy and pretty hard to sneak past, but on occasion I would manage when enough people entered at the same time. I wasn't of age to be in those places as drinking age was twenty-one and I was nineteen. When I got in there, they would bring me a Pine Tree float, which was a glass of water with ice and a toothpick. Go figure! This was done as a courtesy to Fred as he was a frequent customer so they accommodated me when he allowed it. No, he wasn't there, nor at the Circle Canadian or Duke's Café, or the Ponderosa, or even the Knotty Pine Cafe. The Golden Dome Café was going under new management so it wasn't the hot place to go anymore. I found him at the Little Casino. This was a hole in the wall dive, that as you descended into a basement to enter the establishment. There were go-go dancers in the cage. There was Fred, and seemed pretty interested in the go-go dancers in the cage, so I inquired with the owner if he needed anymore. He said he would try me out for a while and see how I did. But once I started to enter one of the cages, Fred made such a commotion I didn't get to strut my stuff! Oh no, but he could watch those who did!

"Crabs"

I came home from work, six weeks after having Tammy, to find Fred in the bath tub trying to get rid of crabs. I think he thought he could soak them off. "Where did those come from?" I shrieked. "I got them from the toilet seat at the bar," he sheepishly explained! I believed every word and admonished him, that he should stay out of those bathrooms at the bars. I read on the label of a bottle of head lice shampoo that Dawn had recently used when I fixed her hair and discovered her head lice. This supposedly helped with eliminating crabs as well. It had turpentine as an ingredient. I had some turpentine from painting the kitchen in the apartment, so I told him to put that on himself, and it should kill the crabs. Well, it almost took his skin off! He swelled up in that area, terribly, and got all red. He was in extreme pain. He soaked in lukewarm water to relieve the pain. I went to the drug store and got medication to get rid of his crabs.

Later I checked Dawn's apartment, while she was gone, to inspect her toilet seat, as I didn't quite believe he had gotten them in the bar room. My suspicions were not verified, only that Dawn had a filthy toilet, so I assumed that it could have been a possibility. Later, Vi told me he couldn't have acquired them from a toilet seat, but from another human. And still I didn't get the picture! A doctor told me later that to acquire crabs it had to come from a moist, warm area, usually another human, but it was possible to get them from bedding, and I didn't learn this until long after the fact.

"Auburn Heel—Lancing My Ears"

I started work at Auburn Heel (no longer in existence) in the Lown Building (now vacant) on Minot Avenue. It was not far for me to walk. I was nailing heels on a machine that required speed and rhythm to make piece work. I was doing quite well for a couple weeks until I nailed my index finger on my right hand. My boss sped me off to the emergency room to have it taken care of. I didn't work any longer at that job, but while waiting for my finger and nail to heal, I took on babysitting for my neighbor's baby boy, Todd. He was fair-haired and such a good baby. I cared for him from 3 months to 9 months old! I continued to babysit for Freddie's sister, Dot's kids. My ears began to hurt, unbearably, and I laid on the couch in tears with the pain. I finally had some time off from babysitting and walked to Lewiston to Dr. Flanders office. I did not have an appointment, however, the nurse went and spoke to him and in a few moments came back and took me into his office. He lanced both of my ears with this incredibly long pointed pick that I felt in my eye balls and in my throat at the same time. He had me tip my head sideways and the amount of fluid, that rushed out into a stainless steel pan, astounded me. I could hear so well it seemed like the sound of the traffic was on high volume. I could barely stand to hear so much noise. I will always be grateful for that doctor. He was getting ready to transfer his practice to another district, and only by the grace of God, he took me in and never charged me anything for what he did. I have never had trouble with my ears since and I have always had very acute hearing.

> *"But I will restore your health and heal your wounds, declares the Lord, because you are called an outcast, Zion, for whom no one cares."* (Jeremiah 30:17 NIV)

"Another Waiting Day and Night"

I don't know what I would have done without Vi in those days. She cared for Tammy like her own. The hunt for Freddie was continuous—I searched for him because if I didn't, he would have spent all the money that he worked for before he got home. There would have been nothing to take care of the family unit. This night was really late when he left for Eith's Bakery again. (This establishment no longer exists) He said he was visiting Shorty. Hours passed and he didn't come home, so I let Vi know I was going to find him just up around the corner. I climbed the narrow stairway, going up over the rear of the bakery from the outside to Shorty's alcove apartment, and found the door that entered Shorty's was padlocked from the outside, but I could hear noises inside. I knocked at the door and a boy's voice answered. I asked where Shorty was and he said that Shorty and Fred left together and he didn't know where they were. I questioned, "Do you know you are locked in?" He answered quietly, "Yes!" I didn't respond, I just left. That short conversation and the remembrance of that night still haunts me today. Why was he there, as Shorty had no children? Why was he padlocked in? What was happening that I was oblivious to? What damage was left on this child's life that I couldn't imagine? And then the days Shorty would come to my apartment and, literally, seemed like he was asking my permission for Freddie to go with him, and he always came bearing a gift of some sort, or something I needed for the household. I do recall sitting across from Shorty and Fred while in the Knotty Pine Café. I had come in looking for Freddie while they were drinking. I began drinking as well. I looked Shorty in the eye and told him, as a matter of fact, "You are queerer than a three-dollar bill." He laughed and nothing more was said. I really did not realize the implications of my statement and my thoughts only remain a speculation.

Today, in the Gay world, it is different compared to how it was once considered in my day. The word "gay" meant someone's name or someone that was very happy. The word "queer" was something odd, unusual or strange. Homosexual was a word I didn't know or understand what it meant. I know many homosexuals today, and I have a respect for their life, even though I feel that this is a lifestyle that is against what the Creator wants them to be in, yet, they are still God's children. In that given time frame, homosexuality was a place of darkness, and using the lower passion of this lifestyle was a place of defilement. *(See Romans 1:26-32 NKJV)* I was not educated on these matters, for if I had been, perhaps I could have saved this boy from something that may have altered his life forever.

"Coping"

Deny! Deny! Deny! That was Freddie's way to get around anything that you did not catch him red-handed at. Questions always remained unanswered and so I continued to believe his lies. We got behind in our rent, and the landlady was so upset with us that she tried to throw us out, but I had learned that she legally had to give a written notice to have us evicted. We then had 30 days to stay, regardless, and then she would have to write another notice for another 30 days. During this time frame we did not have to pay any rent, and I played that as long as I could until I found another place to live. Our landlady did not want to write such a notice, until I pointedly showed her that it was required by law.

"177 Main St"

I was fortunate enough to find another first floor apartment with three rooms. As one entered the apartment, which was a basement apartment, it had a combined kitchen and living room that followed into a bedroom as one archway connected into another. The bathroom was off the bedroom. Freddie and his friend, Gil, came in drunk, laughing, hooting and hollering. Tammy was on our bed sleeping— "Quiet!" I demanded angrily, "Tammy is asleep." Freddie always was so dramatic when he was drinking. He would give a performance as if I was to be feared when I spoke, which was all an act and done as if it were all a big joke. A faint knock came at the door. I opened it to find little Harvey, Freddie's son, standing there asking for "Daddy." When I turned to Fred, Henrietta barged through the door screaming at Gil, her boyfriend. He got up from the table, staggering his way to the living room in an attempt to get away from her advances.

She was close behind him, cursing and screaming as she pushed and shoved him until he lost his balance, landing on the bed, on top of Tammy. That did it! I immediately lunged at her, pushing her with such force she fell to the floor. I did my own cursing at her. She grabbed hold of my pants, to pull them down, while I in turn, yanked her blouse, popping all the buttons like popcorn. She clenched hold of her blouse holding it together and fled the apartment. Little Harvey obediently trotted behind her as they left. I was so angry, I let loose on Freddie and Gil, while rescuing my baby girl. They retreated out the door, off to the unknown, and Freddie's acting was over.

"The Lobster"

Our stay at the Main Street apartment in Auburn, only lasted three months. It was here I was introduced to a live lobster! Fred thought it would be funny to bring one home to me. He brought the paper bag in and said he had something for me. When I peered into the bag, I screamed. This was his is que to take it and run after me, with its claws opening and closing, threatening to pinch me. I ran to the bathroom and slammed the door shut, refusing to come out until that dreadful thing was gone or I was going to kill him and the huge bug! I had no idea that it was an unclean scavenger, which I had never eaten, and which was cooked alive in boiling water. That was not happening in my apartment, and neither would I ever eat such a horrid creature! (*See Leviticus Chapter 11 in any version*)

"Hit and Run"

We often purchased Italian sandwiches at "Pop's Place," (no longer in existence) just down the street from our apartment. They were the best around and the cheapest. Fred had sent me to get some, while he watched Tammy with his buddy, Gil. They were not drunk at this point in time. While crossing the street to get to the other side where the store was located, a car came out of nowhere, and in the nick of time, I made it to the sidewalk before it bounced off the curbing. It was a deliberate attack to hit me. It was Henrietta. I got the Italians, and headed back to the apartment a little shaken, and watching for her to come with another attempt. She came barreling out of a side alley, and again attempted to hit me. It was a narrow escape for me, as she was going to get restitution for embarrassing her when I tore her blouse. I never encountered her actions in this way again.

"Lisbon St Brawl"

It was another night of searching for Freddie. Vi kept Tammy for the night, while I went out bound and determined to find him, which I did and then managed to get him out of the bar-room. We didn't have any form of transportation, other than our feet, so we walked everywhere we went. On our walk back to our Main Street apartment from Lewiston, another drunk was following us, and making sexual comments, and innuendos as we walked. Fred was teetering back and forth as he walked and seemed oblivious to the comments. I was livid! I was disgusted with Freddie, and enraged that he was so oblivious to this drunk behind us. I was infuriated that this man wouldn't shut up! I stopped, while Fred continued to saunter on down the walkway. Turning to this man, I screamed at him, "What is your problem?" He laughed at me! Impulsively, I grabbed hold of his shirt around his neck and began clobbering him with my pocketbook. We went around and around in the middle of the street, as I continued to beat on him with my pocketbook. He pulled away from my grasp and fled. I turned to Fred, who was now leaning on the nearby light pole to steady himself. I angrily commanded, "We are going back to the police station and report this guy," and we did. Fred followed me as I fumed all the way, walking as fast as my short legs allowed. I made out a police report, and later was required to go to court and make a statement. He was put in jail for 30 days. I learned then that he was a former boxer and his hands were considered lethal weapons.

"Always a Battle"

The Circle Canadian (no longer in existence) was a private club, and also a place of interest for Freddie. Only members that knew where the buzzer was located could get in. The button was high above the door, and if you were not tall enough to reach it you could not enter, and once you pushed the button, the door was unlocked from the inside so you could get in, then once inside it would lock behind you. I stood at the entrance, and as soon as someone came by that I knew, I asked them to ring the buzzer so I could go in. Tammy was less than a year old, and I had her in a stroller. When I entered, the bartender behind the opened cubicle, shouted, "You cannot come in here with a baby, you have to leave." I glared back at him, as I made my way into the back room where the pool table was located, daring his authority with, "Make me." I could hear Freddie's laughter and no one tried to stop me. I spent the evening there until he left with me.

"The Move to Roak St."

Dawn's parents came to my rescue. They were God's angels, on earth, caring for the needs of others. They had custody of Dawn's five girls, and they gave them a good home. For some unknown reason they felt they needed to help me with my unsettled situation, and I accepted their help.

I didn't have any furniture so they supplied bureaus, table, chairs and a bed. They also found an apartment for me on 90 Roak St., about a mile or so from where we lived on Main St. They hired movers to take the furniture and my meager belongings to the new apartment, and they paid the first month's rent. I had a place for my little family to live comfortably. Fred was amazed at their generosity.

The day we moved, Fred was working on Lisbon St. in Lewiston, with Owen Taylor Construction Co., putting in drainage pipe for the city. I was walking back and forth between the two apartments, getting things settled, when I reached our new apartment, one of the movers for the company was the guy that had spent 30 days in jail. As I left to walk back to Main St., the truck came at high speed down over the hill, accelerating full throttle and veering my direction. Once again I escaped being hit, by diving into some hedges along the way, until I felt the way was clear before continuing. I reported this to Dawn's dad and there were no further problems. He had that man fired from his job. I worried that he might come back, later on down the road, to find me, but he never did. God had His hand over me!

> *"You are my hiding place; You shall preserve me from trouble."*
>
> *(Psalms 32:7 NKJV)*

Chapter Eighteen

Roak Street

"God is just; He will pay back trouble to those who trouble you and give relief to you who are troubled." (2 Thessalonians 1:6 & 7 NIV)

I was so happy to have a five room apartment with bathroom and shower on the second floor at 90 Roak Street, within the city, in a quiet neighborhood, near a school. I didn't know I was pregnant again. I didn't want any more children and so there was no reason, in my mind, for me to be pregnant.

Eva was a wonderful neighbor who lived downstairs. She was a divorced, single parent with two boys, Peter and Sidney. Her ex-husband came to visit, and sometimes spent the night with her and the boys. She was a brittle diabetic, but very active within her home, and caring for her two boys. We became very close friends.

Our landlady, Mary LaBozzo, lived in the main house that had four apartments attached to it. She was Italian and spoke her mind, quite bluntly. She also liked her wine and liquor, but only drank discreetly. The neighbors who lived on the second floor next door to my apartment kept to themselves, but were always cordial. Above me was Mrs. Myles, who was a widowed, Canadian French lady. She wore a bandana on her head, and had a pet rabbit that was her companion. Her eyes bulged and grew wider as she spoke, which commanded attention, and spoke with authority, yet she had great compassion. I loved her! I was truly blessed to be able to live here.

"Dawn Babysitting"

Dawn frequently walked from my former apartment on Pleasant St., to visit. I had acquired another job in the Lown building at New England Counter as a piece worker molding counters on a machine. I had Dawn babysit for me. I was still very particular with Tammy. Vi had allowed her to have an Oreo cookie one day, and when I came to pick Tammy up after work, and found her face plastered with chocolate cookie, I went into a tizzy because she was dirty! Vi had laughed at my horror, seeing Tammy with a dirty face. This day, when I arrived home with Tammy under Dawn's care, I heard Tammy crying. I opened the closed bedroom door, and found the rail down on the crib, with Tammy wedged between the railing and the mattress with a very heavy dirty diaper on her. I quickly changed her diaper, and got her cleaned up. I went to the bathroom to discover, after rinsing the dirty one in the toilet, that the diaper pail did not have one dirty diaper in it from the entire day! "So where are Tammy's dirty diapers," I quizzed Dawn. She deliberately lied, "Oh, I washed them," she quipped. I didn't have a washing machine, so diapers had to washed by hand in the shower on a scrub board, as there was no bathtub. I knew for sure she had not done that. Pampers had just started to make an appearance, but only those who could financially afford them were the ones who bought them. I called Dawn on her lie, and she added another lie to it. I was infuriated by her carelessness, and in a blind rage, I bounded from the two steps, that exited from the bathroom into the kitchen, leaping onto a kitchen chair, onto the table in the dining room, and flung myself down on top of Dawn. She was sitting in a chair on the other side of the table. This all took place so quickly, she didn't have time to get out of her chair before I knocked her off it, with the force of my lunge. I put my hands around her throat and shook her head, banging it on the floor, close to the Larkin desk, Mrs. LaBozzo had given me. My neighbor across the road walked into the chaos. Bud was

Henrietta's uncle and also had become a good friend. He picked me up off Dawn, and told her to leave, which she did. She never babysat for me again. She had also eaten all the baby custards I had on the cupboard shelf for Tammy. Fortunately for her, by the time I recognized this, she wasn't anywhere near.

"Tammy's First Christmas—1967"

"I am going to go buy you a Christmas gift," Freddie announced, as he sweetly kissed me before going out the door at 3 p.m. on Christmas Eve. He stood teetering in front of me, in his drunken stupor, moments before he made the announcement.

There were no gifts under the tree for our baby girl of almost 9 months. There was no gift to me from my husband. I had placed a gift of aftershave beneath the tree, which I wrapped with used Christmas paper and a bandanna along with a homemade Christmas card that rested in the tree unopened. I looked at him pretty skeptical, "Freddie, I don't think there are any stores open now!" He gave me one of those crushed looks, as if his intentions were not honorable and that he would lie to me. "I'll surprise you," he insisted, "I will be back with the best gift money can buy before you know it!"

I had just laid Tammy in the crib after playing with her, and having tea with Mrs. Myles. Tammy was fed, and I held her close squeezing her hard. I loved my baby girl, beyond what words could express. It was six thirty, and the dishes were done, and the bare wood floors were washed. Seven thirty and I straightened the tinsel out on the tree, and cleaned the bathroom. Eight-thirty, Tammy was sleeping soundly. Nine-thirty and I could hear the church bells in the distance peeling out, "Silent Night." The loneliness of the music was so intensifying it penetrated my very soul. My tears fell quietly then turned into heart-broken sobs. The realization set in of how alone I really was on Christmas Eve.

From my second story window I could see the traffic on the main street, and each time a headlight caught my eye, I hurried thinking it was my Freddie coming home. There were families coming together with their children, dreaming of candy and presents, while parents were busily wrapping gifts for their children for the "big morning surprise." It was eleven thirty and still no Freddie. The lights were blinking on the tree. The bare gaping branches that held the tinsel, and the homemade paper chains, with the half dozen bobbles, that spelled out Christmas cheer. I nestled on the cot that served as a couch, hugging a pillow, and blanket like an insecure child. I could feel the movement of my unborn baby, and I wept uncontrollably. Freddie never came home that night.

"Christmas Pain"

Where do you go when pain hits you so hard you can't bear it? There is no morphine to dull it or take it away, and you feel like a wild caged animal, with no escape for the emotions you feel. It overtakes you in a fury of frenzy, and all you can do is scream till you can't speak, cry till you sleep out of exhaustion, and all that is left is silence, deafening silence, that tortures the mind. Then in panoramic view all the past words that were spoken and believed, all the smiles you trusted, all the hopes, you held on to for dear life, were ripped from you as if you were just a manikin standing void of all feelings. Your life seems to have been used to scrape the mud off the feet of others, while they walked on past you and left you groveling in the dust, and words hurt. When they are said with hope, and feeling, you believe them, and then they are thrown back in your face as the wind slaps a rag hanging from a line. The sting hurts and it is meant to. How much can human life take of abuse before they become worthless to society and withers in a mental breakdown, or dies from the mental pain becoming so great that it overtakes the physical body and the grave becomes its only source of comfort? This is the pain I felt as I looked out at the Christmas lights blinking at the homes of others that seem to twinkle and laugh. They sent out the message of warmth and cheer on a darkened path in the night hours.

So Long Ago....

That night, so long ago didn't have Christmas lights glowing with a message of cheer. The Savior of the world was born in a barn with the stench of animal waste, and the musty smell of hay mingled in the air. The only glow was in the sky. A silent star beaming bright, "O Star of wonder, star of night, star of royal beauty bright." That was the only Christmas Light, the Light of the world was born to give hope to the dying soul flung in sin, and left to die in a helpless, hopeless condition. The King of the Universe lowered Himself from the courts of heaven embedded with gold, and silver, and every imaginable glitter of riches that the human mind can put together. Yet, it still cannot fathom the depth that Jesus stooped to be born in the humblest form, without gratitude or praise, other than a few lowly shepherds that came to pay homage, and kings from the Orient following that brilliant star to see for themselves, as they had studied in the Scriptures, and found that the Christ child was being born. These men of wealth knelt in the sawdust and the hay, with animals baying, tails switching, and the strong urine and feces smell, to pay homage to a baby they knew to be the Star of Bethlehem, the Rose of Sharon, yes, God in the flesh!

And Now....

A loveless home, an absent spouse, the death of a dream ended in bitterness, making Christmas lights a mockery. Christmas lights represented all through my life, a family time of togetherness, and love as the major ingredient. Jesus is Love! He is the main ingredient for love. As I reflect on His life and the abuse, rejection, and dishonor He endured, I have no right to feel sorry for myself. He loved His enemies, and while He was preparing to come here and die, He saw me. I was His enemy, living in a sinful condition. The Bible says there is no reward in loving those who love you, but to love those who hate you brings a reward of the greatest love. (*see Luke 6:32-33 NKJV*) It makes life no easier when you stumble in the darkness, and fret over the evil all around. "Fret not yourselves of evil doers." (*Psalms 37:7 NKJV*)

The only consolation is to remember that those who want to be like Him, and travel the road of sacrifice in obedience to the Commandments of God, will one day be rewarded as they sought after Him diligently, and this is His promise to the faithful. (see Hebrews 11:6 NKJV) He will pick you up as you stumble in the darkness, and endure the pain that is dealt in this sinful world. The only morphine are His precious promises. We hold fast to them by faith, grasping them in the darkness, when the Christmas lights fail to glimmer in the night, and while deep in our hearts we know that the Love of God, Jesus Christ in the flesh, makes the Christmas season, and giving of one's life to the service of others, is the true meaning of what the Christmas lights and the Star of Bethlehem are all about.

"Listen"

Listen, you can hear the angels sing.

Listen, quietly, you can hear love ring.

Sadness combined with joy brings forth the beauty of the season.

Christmas trees and lovely carols have a beckoning gleam for some reason.

Listen, you can feel hope come to life like a candle glowing.

Peace and good will to all men! Radiance and grace flowing.

No distinction of race, color or creed;

Miracles fulfilled that meet every need.

Listen, you can feel the spirit of care.

Listen, the stars are whispering the silent night prayer.

I can feel these things deep within my heart;

In silence I pray, that this peace will not depart.
So if this season should leave you lonely and blue,
Listen, and you will hear Christmas joy, too!
(Joyce A. Wetmore 1965)

"The Mica Mines"

We often went to Freddie's sister, Dot, to visit. He would go off in a radio room with his brother-in-law, Sam. This summer day, we walked out back of their house, on the Hatch Rd. to the Mica mines that are on the back side of the Garfield Rd., and where the Army Rifle Range is located. It seemed to have a sinister effect on those who visited the mines. The quarry has a sixty-foot drop, and was shaped like a large three-sided barrel of ledge, with an opening that extended as high as the ledge itself, to go into the water. It was rumored that cars had been shoved over, and dropped so far that there was no retrieving them. It was considered a bottomless pit.

In the heat of summer, sometimes adventurous young people would go swimming there, but today, Dot's oldest boys, were ready for a joke, which they challenged me to take the 60-foot jump. I was in my swimsuit and up for a swim, so standing at the top edge of the ledge, I took the plunge sailing at such force that it almost took my breath away. I could feel the cool water vapors before I even hit the water. The force was so great, as I rapidly spiraled downward, and riveting deep into the recesses of the cold water, that my bathing suit was stripped from the force of the projection. I was able to retrieve it as I began frantically pushing my way upward, keeping my focus on the gleam of light through the waters, and frantically working toward the top. When I finally reached the top, I breathlessly broke through the water barrier to air, grasping my suit and quickly pulled it on. I didn't try it again, but gained the applause of those on-looking at my dare-devil action. Later I had nightmares that Tammy was at the mica mines edge of the ledge., where I had jumped. I was always running to save her in my dream. I never went back there again!

Six Months of Sobriety

Freddie quit drinking! I thought my life had finally turned around. It was October 28, 1967 when we married. Mama and Daddy came and picked us up and brought us back to my childhood home in New Hampshire for the wedding. I had a brand new dress Mama bought. It was a sleeveless, "A" styled white dress with silver threads weaved through it. I had a blue light-weight knee length coat to go over it. Mama gave me the wedding band that Grandpa Hutchinson, her father, had given his wife, Emma. Inside was engraved W.C.H—E.O.H. Initials for Willis Chandler Hutchinson to Emma Ovitie (Berquist) Hutchinson. I was honored. Something old, something new, something borrowed, (a lace handkerchief,) and something blue. Mama and Daddy stood up with us at our ceremony, with the Justice of the Peace, in Brownfield, Maine, across from the church we had rented as a small Sabbath-keeping group. We went back to the house and Arlene, Mama's best friend, along with close neighbors Luella, and Gertrude had prepared a huge dinner, displayed with many gifts from town neighbors. I felt so blessed!

"Marriage"

Marriage was first given by God in the Garden of Eden. In (*Genesis 2:24 NKJV*) it says, "*Therefore a man shall leave his father and mother and be joined to his wife, and they shall become as one flesh.*" I took this seriously. My parents were faithful to each other, and I expected that all couples were, and the only provision for divorce was unfaithfulness. The marriage vows repeated were "for better or for worse, in sickness, and in health until death....." And daddy always said to me, "when you make your bed, remember you have to lie in it." I never quite understood the saying other than the fact that once you have made the commitment to a situation, it is up to you to follow through with your decision. There was no turning back! God is strict in what He says and so was Daddy.

Freddie had given me a diamond ring not too long before we were married. It was a pawn shop special. It was a fairly large diamond, of what I considered large, with two small teardrop diamonds on either side. It had cost him $200 at the Pawn Shop, so I am sure that by today's standards it was an expensive ring. I knew when I looked at it, it was a signature of his love for me, and our love was forever. Daddy gave us a 1949 Ford pick-up truck for Freddie to get back and forth to work. It was old, but ran beautifully, and we were pretty happy with it. All was well with the world! I still smoked, but never was I allowed to smoke even on the property, while at Mama and Daddy's, but Fred could. It was okay with me. Mama and I were on good terms, and even better so was Daddy and I.

"Hungry"

We were hungry! I gave Tammy whatever food we had. There was no money to buy food and we didn't have any communication with anyone to let them know we needed food. It was six thirty p.m., and we went to bed so we wouldn't think about food. We moved from the bedroom to the living room to sleep, as it was cold and we needed to conserve on heat. We heated our apartment with a little oil pot-burner stove. It was about 9:00 p.m. when a knock came at the door and I got up to answer it. It was the Pastor of the Auburn Seventh-day Adventist Church, John Williamson, and an elder, Kenneth Lee, at the door. Their first question was, "Joyce, are you hungry?" When I answered emphatically, "Yes!" the story unfolded. Your mother called, Pastor Williamson began, adamant that you needed food, and she could not eat until you got some food. It seemed, while Mama and Daddy were beginning to eat supper, a vision came on Mama that I was hungry. She immediately called the church. Within a few hours, members put together enough food for me, and for my unborn baby. I had enough food for my baby for the next three months. Pastor Williamson prayed with us there in my kitchen. This was Freddie's first introduction to a pastor praying, and praying for him! We ate that night before going back to bed.

"Baby JUDY Rose"

I knew I was pregnant, and I certainly didn't want to be! I had recognized some of the same symptoms I had when I was pregnant for Tammy. I didn't have money or insurance, but made the appointment anyway with a different doctor, Dr. Geraldine Lynn. When I arrived at her office, I stated, "I think I am pregnant." She looked at me rather disgustedly, and sarcastically asked, "What was your first clue?" My belly was protruding, and it was definitely a pregnant belly. She did a preliminary exam, and said I was seven months pregnant, after questioning me about certain dates of my period. Another appointment was made for the following month.

It was about a week or so later, since Pastor Williamson had been at the apartment and had given me the church phone number along with the food, so I could contact him if I needed. Freddie had just left for work and I hurried to the bathroom. I began to urinate, and as I continued to sit there for quite some time without any let up, I knew something was wrong! I placed a towel between my legs, and went down the stairs to Eva's apartment. She told me my water had broken and I should get to the hospital. I went in to Mrs. LaBozzo's, as I still did not have a phone and neither did Eva. I called Pastor Williamson, and he came right away, and took me to one of the local hospitals. He left me there at the emergency room, then he took Tammy to my friend Vi, who now lived on the third floor on Blake St in Lewiston. He then returned to the hospital to see how I was doing. It was determined at the hospital, that I would not have the baby just yet as it could be dangerous at this juncture, so Pastor Williamson brought me back home to be on bed rest for at least 6 weeks, but within two weeks I began having contractions around 4 a.m.

Freddie was snoring. I hesitated to wake him, but I knew what contractions were and I was sure this was it! I awakened Freddie and told him I thought it was time. He methodically got up, dressed and went down to the truck. I thought he was starting it up to warm it up, since it was a very cold February morning, but off he went down over the hill. I kept watch out the window for his return, thinking he must have needed gas, and was going after that first, but in about a half hour he finally returned. He had forgotten me! He came in, with irritation in his voice and said, "Well, are you ready?" My response was, "Ahh, yes, just waiting for you!" He drove me to the hospital without conversation and dropped me off and went on to work. I stayed there and had Judy Rose, my second child. I believe Eva contacted Pastor Williamson, who in turn contacted Mama.

Delivery

Judy's birth was dry and painful. All the fluids had run out of me before birth, so when I started to deliver, it was as if someone had lit a match and placed it at the birthing canal. I screamed! Dr. Lynn had no compassion. She slapped me on the butt and said, "Shut up!" I wanted to cry! Nurses had attempted to give me a drip of chloroform anesthesia in what looked like a strainer over my face, that made me so sick that I wanted to vomit, so I pushed it away. I tried to watch Judy's birth in a small mirror strategically placed for the event, but I was in so much pain, that I couldn't focus, nor could I see with my poor eyesight without glasses. It was approximately seven twenty a.m. that my second baby girl was born. I was taken to a room and left there. I got out of bed, with no one around, to use the bathroom. Just as I was about to sit on the toilet, something fell from inside me. It was a big blob that fell to the floor, and I panicked, thinking, "Oh no, there was another baby in there and now it is dead!" I frantically rang the buzzer for the nurse. In no time she arrived, and assessed the scene, while listening to my wail! She calmly gathered the blob on the floor with a towel, and projecting a very matter-of-fact attitude said, "Oh, that is just the after birth!" I still was not understanding the ins and outs of being pregnant and having a baby. My thought process was, "After birth! What is after birth?" I was too worn out to ask more or find out anything else.

Judy was 4lbs and 2 oz. and 18 inches long. She was placed in the incubator. Mama came to visit with Arlene. They went to the window to admire Judy, noticing she was the only girl among several boys. They came back expounding that this was a "sign of war!" Fred had decided Judy's name. I did not know, until many years later, this was the name of his first girlfriend, Judy. Mama and Arlene agreed that she looked like a little rosebud, so her middle name became Rose. Therefore, she was dubbed, "Judy Rose." When she was finally placed in my arms, her head fit perfectly in the palm of my hand, and her feet just barely reached the crease of the bend of my arm. When she was tucked in the jump seat to go home, she was so tiny, you would have barely known there was a baby there. She was able to be discharged when she reached five pounds. Mama said, "She isn't any bigger than a five-pound bag of sugar!

"High Fever"

My sweet baby, Judy, was so sick! I paced the floor holding her close to me. Where was Freddie? He was never here when I needed him. I hollered to Eva and she came charging up over the stairs, "You better get her to the hospital," as she quickly assessed Judy's burning head, and watching her eyes roll back in her head. Eva went to Mrs. LoBozzo's, and called a cab, while I got Judy ready for her trip to the hospital. They kept her there, and I stayed till late in the night, and walked home to go to bed for a little bit, then walked to work the next day. I cried all the way home! It was about five miles from the hospital to home, and two miles one way to work.

At work, they allowed me to leave early so I could walk back to the hospital. Dear Mrs. Myles took care of Tammy. God had these beautiful people placed in my life to take care of me and my family. They were His human angels. They blessed me over and over again. My 10-month old baby girl was in the hospital, for eight days. I spent as much time as I could with her and continued to work. The nurses would get her fever down and back up it would go. The hospital staff were so good to her, and kept a constant vigil. I was so thankful when she was able to come home again, and from then on she seemed fine. Thank you, Jesus!

"Drinking Again"

Freddie's drinking abstinence had ended. During Judy's hospital stay he had been home once, just long enough to find out she was sick, then left again. He never went to see her. I remember one day he came home after a weekend drunk, and there was not a penny left in his pocket for food. I sat and cried! That next day, I walked to Drummond St. Market, (no longer in existence) as the meat there was known to be good and at a fair price. When I got to the checkout I didn't have enough money, so I began to tell the man to take some items back. He graciously told me to keep the items and pay him when I could. I went back about a month later to pay him, and he refused to take the money. God was always providing!

Freddie had a friend, Bob, who would come visit. It seemed he would show up when Freddie was gone drinking. He became a good friend, and I looked forward to his visits. He would make me laugh. Bud, Henrietta's uncle, would also drop by from time to time to check on me. His wife worked and he took care of their kids. They lived across the road from me. I was able to get Food Stamps for a while. when I applied to the State, I was surprised we got $105 that month. You would have thought I had won the sweepstakes! When it came time to reapply after 3 months, I never did as I actually didn't know you could reapply! I was thankful for those three months of plenty.

"Our Pet Canary and Washing Machines"

My friend from work, also named Joyce, gave me her yellow canary. She had named it Larry, and one day, Larry laid an egg, so the name was changed to Loretta! It was the only pet Freddie allowed me to have. I had also been given a washing machine. It had two tubs. one large one to wash the clothes in, and a smaller one that you transferred the clothes into to spin the water out.

That was so wonderful since I had a wringer washer before that. The wringer would snap off buttons and break zippers. I was so happy with this new washer. Before that, I scrubbed clothes in the shower on a scrub board. A year later I advanced to a pink automatic washer. It would spin so fast, since it was unevenly balanced, so it bounced all over the floor. I would sit on it when it spun, to try to keep it from rattling across the floor. It was in the kitchen, so as it got close to the stove, I would put my feet out, bracing myself with my feet on the stove, so it wouldn't go any further. Eva always knew when I was doing laundry. I had a nice back porch and a clothes line. I would stretch the cloth diapers after pinning them at the top, and straighten them to the very corners so they wouldn't be wrinkled. It was nice in the summer when there was a breeze, but in the winter they freeze dried.

"Trust and Obey"

Mrs. Myles babysat pretty much for nothing. I owed her money, and right now we were low on food again. I wasn't sure what we were going to have for supper. Not to mention the fact that the pot burner that kept us warm was almost out of oil, and I didn't know how I was going to keep heat in the apartment for the night. I couldn't depend on Freddie to help because it was Friday, and I knew he wouldn't be home as usual. It was snowing a light fluffy snow, as I walked home from work. I had my head hung down, but I was singing softly to myself, "Trust and obey for there is no other way, to be happy in Jesus, but to trust and obey. . . ." As I hummed and sang the words, that I could remember, over and over on that late afternoon after work, as I trudged my two-mile trek home, I looked up and saw something sticking up out of the freshly fallen snow ahead, "What is that?" I thought. "It looks like money." I said aloud to myself, "No, it must be play money." I continued to think. I got closer, and there in the snow as if someone placed it in the snow standing on end, was indeed money. I looked around! There was no one in sight, "Did someone lose it?" I asked myself, still in disbelief that it really was money. There were no foot prints in the snow. There were no tracks of any kind indicating that someone had recently lost it, and if they had, "Who? What? Where?" I was in a quandary. I gingerly picked it up! It was a $20 bill and two $10 dollar bills. There was no one around anywhere, and no place to take it to ask if someone might have lost it. I began to rationalize that possibly angels put it in my path. It had to have been for there was no other reason. I do not remember walking the rest of the way up the hill to Roak St. I think I flew!

I paid Mrs. Myles the $10 I owed her. I took the 5-gallon fuel can, and walked back down over the hill, and across the South bridge to Lewiston where the corner station had fuel oil. I carried it back over the hill, but before reaching home I stopped on Broad St., at the small grocery store, and ordered $20 worth of groceries, which they delivered for me. I praised God all the way with every step I took. I was still in shock at how God provided for me in a way that I could not even ever imagine. God is Jehovah-Jireh, the Provider and the answer to the prayers of my parents, and others that had been praying for me, God gave us food, heat, and a way to help those who were helping me with payment for babysitting. "Trust and Obey for there is no other way...."

"Spiritualism"

June, Freddie's sister's daughters, Renita and Jeanne, lived on two different streets nearby and I would go to visit them in the evenings, when Freddie did not show up. They would often come visit me, and tell stories of strange happenings that were eerie. At this time there was a popular soap opera called, "Dark Shadows," which promoted vampires. This particular actor called, Barnabas, depicted as a vampire, was actually a type of hero, even though he had a blood thirsty desire to have a beautiful maiden, as he would sink his teeth into her neck, causing her to become his vampire maiden or whatever the story plot was. I was hooked on the show. We had two TV's, one on top of the other. One had the voice and the other had the picture. I thought it was pretty ingenious. During Freddie's time of abstinence, he had taken a course in electronics, which I helped him with the reading and writing part. He only had an eighth grade education, and so was not good in reading, spelling, and writing. They were difficult for him, but with my help he did acquire his certificate in electronics, as he was very good with hands on projects.

Renita and Jeanne had said that if you left chairs out without pushing them under the table, it would call evil spirits to be there in the night. I always made sure before going to bed that the chairs were pushed in under the table. I didn't want to leave room for the possibility of an evil spirit to lurk. They were very superstitious, and it rubbed off on me. I had started reading books on spiritualism and paperback books promoting things of the unknown and questionings about things, such as the grave, and the dead coming back. I read books written by Stephen King, which promoted the supernatural as being the lurking of evil. Renita brought me, one of his books, "Salem's Lot," as she was convinced it was demon possessed and wanted me to burn it. I think she was fearful that if she did it a curse would be on her.

By now Tammy began doing strange things. She would talk on her little toy telephone, as if to her daddy, and each time she would say, "You not coming home tonight?" and sure enough he wouldn't come home. This used to freak me out! It kept getting stronger until I decided to go to a woman in Lewiston who told fortunes. I had been told she was the best, and I went with Jeanne. At one point, during the session of her predicting my future, she told me I was going to have five children. I knew that wasn't possible since I had my tubes tied. Yet, she was so convincing, I thought there was a baby swinging in the doorway behind me. Then she told me someone very close to me, dressed in white, was going to die. All these things left me pondering events and wondering. I felt uneasy about all of these things, and decided I should stop reading these books that were filling my head with fear. I threw them all away, and never have I read any books pertaining to matters of the supernatural beyond the grave. The Bible teaches that "the dead know nothing, and they have no more reward....." *(see Ecclesiastes 9:5-6 NKJV)*

"Waiting and Then...."

We had a 1962 Chevy Impala, black and sleek compared to the Barracuda, and the old Ford truck we had owned. We were on our way to visit Ma & Father, and were supposed to meet Ed & his family there. However, Freddie decided to stop to visit Shorty, living on Hampshire St., and he said he would only be a few minutes. Judy was about 8 months old, and Tammy, was a rambunctious, one-and-a-half-year-old! We sat in the laundry-mat parking lot, on a Sunday afternoon, waiting and waiting. It was close to forty-five minutes, and I was getting extremely perturbed, and decided he should watch the girls for a while. I marched Tammy by the hand, with Judy in my arms, across the street from where the car was parked, and entered the first floor apartment without knocking. Fred and Shorty were sitting there as I entered. Fred on the couch, and Shorty in a chair next to him drinking. I put Judy in Freddie's arms, and plunked Tammy on the couch next to him, and said defiantly, "There, now you watch them for a while." With that, I turned on my heel, and marched back out to the car, and took off for his parents' home.

When I reached Hamden St., where his parents lived, his brother Ed and his family had already arrived. When I walked in, Ed's first question to me was, "Where is brother Fred and the kids?" I said with emphasis, "At Shorty's having a few, so I left the girls with him!" I had barely finished my sentence when Ed bolted out the door, and jumped in his car, leaving his family at Ma's. I raced back out to the car, and took off after him, but never caught up until I reached Shorty's. Ed was already in the apartment, and by the time I got inside, he was pounding the daylights out of Freddie. The second he saw me he said, "Get the girls and go home." I located Tammy and Judy on Shorty's bed, still fully clothed, and just lying there. I scooped them up and took them home!

It wasn't too long when Ed dragged Freddie up the stairs and dropped him on the kitchen floor of our apartment, with anger in his voice and a firm demand to, "Never leave those girls alone with him again." After that he left Fred where he was, and went back out the door without further words. I was feeling great uncertainty! I helped Fred to the bed with bleeding lip and battered face. I said to him, "Are you sick?" His reply to me that day was, "You have no idea how sick I am." He then passed out, and I let him sleep it off. I never knew the hidden meaning of those words, and Ed never mentioned anything further to me again concerning it, and neither did Freddie.

"My Teeth"

I hated the dentist with a passion, and I would rather have done most anything other than to go to the dentist. I was scared of them! I had double eye teeth since my mouth was too small to house all my teeth. My second child had taken all the calcium from me, and my teeth suffered greatly, especially, since I had no vitamins during my pregnancy or pre-natal care. I had several cavities so I made an appointment to see a dentist. It was Dr. Violet, and she said I needed to have my eye teeth extracted, and I would have to get a partial plate. At that juncture of my life a partial plate would have cost far more than to have all my teeth out on the top, and have a full plate put in. I opted to have my top teeth pulled, and have a full plate put in at age 20. I went to an oral surgeon, Dr. Lebel, and he put me to sleep. He extracted all my top teeth for $50, and that was a lot of money then. It was going to cost another $50 for a denture plate. I waited six months, with no top teeth before I had enough money to get the teeth made. Dr. Miller, a wonderful dentist, made my top plate which lasted 30 years before I had a new plate made. During the time that I had this done, I barely went anywhere or spoke due to no teeth. Freddie used to do all he could to make me laugh just so it would show I had no teeth. This was a big joke with him at my expense.

"The Rolling Pin"

My dear friend, Alyce visited and brought along all sorts of things for the kids. Diapers, food, outfits and much more. I was so happy to have her visit. Then Fred, came in drunk once again, and things got rowdy. Alyce's husband, was not always nice, and was always a womanizer, and since he knew me from back home, he thought I was an easy target. He had always made passes at me, and being in the presence of his wife, didn't seem to make a difference with him. I was filled with anger, and I told him straight up, "If you touch me, I will take my cigarette, and burn your eyes out." He guffawed at that, as if it were a hilarious joke, but he never persisted with his passes again. I think he didn't quite dare to see if I would make good on my threat.

Freddie had one too many to drink, and was acting like a complete fool. I told him if he didn't stop I would take the wooden rolling pin, that happened to be resting on the top of the stove, and lambaste him with it. Just as I said that, he looked at me, drawling out of a thick drunken mouth, "You wouldn't dare." Without even a thought, I picked up the wooden rolling pin, and struck him beside the head. He crumpled to the floor, and I was sure I had killed him! Alyce's husband reassured me he was still breathing, and picked him up, and placed him on the bed in our bedroom. He calmly told me to just let him sleep it off, then he and Alyce left. It was not too long after they left, Freddie awoke and he was angry as a bear. He tore out the door, and went down over the stairs to the outside, and got in his car. I was right behind him, and was trying to talk to him, when he doubled his fist and hit me so hard that I landed on the other side of the street. I can actually say that I saw stars, as I landed propped against the tree when I came to. Freddie was gone and it was several days before I saw him again.

"My Children's Serenity"

I have no right to share my sorrow
With the innocence of a child.
I have prayed for their happiness
beyond all tomorrow;
And that all their sadness be mild.
But yet I found myself clutching at their tenderness,
And heard their whimpers for my tears.
Their little arms gave me gentle caress,
And they tried to soothe my fears.
I clung to them for assurance of love and hope.
I prayed in their arms for their faith and grace.
I felt I would scream for the blessings to love and cope,
With the ultimate forces beyond my pace.
I breathed for my children's life-
And then I marred their innocence and left a scar
With tears and sadness and struggle of strife,
Just for my comfort and pride by far.
What right did I have to tear into their souls?
What mercy can God give me for
the intrusion of their peace?
"O ye of little faith," yes little faith
to set your own goals,
And carry your own cross
To suffer the worthless dross
In the time left to lease for eternity's sake.
(Written by Joyce Robinson—June 12, 1970)
(pregnant for child number 3)

Chapter Nineteen

My Third Child

*"He rescued me from my powerful enemy,
from my foes who were too strong for me.
They confronted me in the day of my disaster,
but the Lord was my support."*

(Psalms 18:17 & 18 NIV)

I had learned, by now, without some form of contraceptive, you got pregnant! I used many forms, except I never took birth control pills as my mother had counseled me that these were not good for you. So I tried other forms to keep from getting pregnant such as the foam, douches and other methods! I never, particularly, enjoyed my sexual life, since I had to worry about getting pregnant. I often watched TV, while in the act, as I never knew the ecstasy of the sexual encounter. I remember the night I conceived my third child. I was interested in the movie, and that movie took precedence over going to have the douche, and because of the spontaneity, there was no foam used. I was too tired to bother and I was pregnant—just like that!

This pregnancy was different than my first two. I didn't gain hardly any weight and I carried very low. I had problems with my legs, and especially my right leg. I had what Dr. Cabelin called "Milk Leg" or Phlebitis. It swelled twice the size of my other leg and I often had to drag it.

I now had a phone, and I had called Mama, since I was feeling very blue and depressed. My due date was November 12, 1970, and it was now November 11, Veterans Day. While talking to Mama, she said, "Your father and I will be right there." I argued that she didn't need to come the distance; I would be fine as, they lived in Center Conway, New Hampshire, a good hour or more away. She wouldn't take "no" for an answer, and before I knew it, she and daddy were at the door. I was feeling squeamish by now, and I decided before going to the hospital, I needed to wash my feet, as I often walked around barefoot, change my underwear and brush my teeth. Mama checked my dirty underwear, and said immediately with concern in her voice, "We need to hurry." I thought she was being a little hasty. Daddy drove us to the General Hospital, and watched the girls in the car, while Mama and I went in. "My daughter is in active labor," she, confidently, explained to the admitting nurse, who looked at me and didn't see me in any distress, so she ignored Mama's urgency. However, when Mama was right, she was right, and "no one" could stop her from making her point. This nurse was no match for Mama, and she conceded, and I was examined. The examining nurse, ran from the room, and came charging back with a stretcher, "What are you doing?" I asked in alarm, "You are having your baby," the nurse shrieked! Wide eyed, and fully panicked, I shrieked back, "I'm not ready." Emphatically, the nurse briefly admonished, "Yes, you are!" while she continued to prepare me.

It was 12:10 p.m. when we were at the admissions desk, and number three child was born at 12:17 p.m. They placed a gas mask on me, which made me sick, but put me out quickly, as they were rushing the doctor in to finish the delivery! It was a boy!

Somehow Mama and Daddy located Freddie. They took the girls home with them for a few days. Tammy was three, Judy was two. Now a baby brother! It was a process to decide a name, but we tossed the name David around, and finally agreed on Robert. I was good with that since my dad's brother, was called Robert, and I knew him as Uncle Bob. My third child was Robert Thomas. He was 7 lbs. 13.5 oz. and 22 inches long. My biggest baby and the easiest to deliver! Freddie was delighted! He brought me home from the hospital to 90 Roak St., and my neighbor Eva and landlady, Mary LaBozzo were there to greet us.

It wasn't too long after that, Mama & Daddy visited to see little "Robbie," as he was dubbed. He was such a sweet boy. Freddie was drinking heavily. I went back to work at New England Counter factory, and walking to and from work. Robbie's first Christmas, would never have been a Christmas, if it had not been for my parents. They came and brought gifts, a ball for the girls, some clothes, a rattle and stuffed toys for Robbie, and food. They never stopped caring for me, not once. Neither did they ever say, "I told you so." Life continued to be an upheaval with Freddie. I never knew when he would be home, or when he would have money to pay the bills and provide for the kids.

"TEA TIME"

It was a chilly day, and the pot burner was in full swing, warming our little apartment. I was changing Robbie on the cot in the living room and playing with him, while Tammy and Judy were playing with Tammy's little plastic tea set. She had watched me make tea so often, and boiling water on the stove, that this was a normal thing for her to play with her little tea set. She came rushing in to me with her golden curls bouncing, and pointed toward the pot burner "fire" she told me as if I should understand that the pot burner has fire in it. You could see the blue flame through the glass door of the pot burner, so I glanced around the corner, and seeing it still jumping up and down as it burned the oil to keep the apartment heated, I answered her with, "Yes, it is fire!" She ran off and returned with the same announcement. "fire," while again pointing toward the pot-burner. After the third time, I decided to check, and YES! there was fire. She had placed her plastic tea pot on the gas burner and turned it on. Fire had erupted and had filled the kitchen with smoke, by now, with the flames beginning to dance over the stove. I opened the door to the hall exit, and screamed so the neighbors in the building knew there was a FIRE! The upstairs neighbors called the fire department, and they were there in no time.

The smoke damage was the worst! They had really made a terrible mess, and I was left to clean. I was thankful that it was not any worse but the mess- Oh my! I called Mama! I had no cleaning aids and what was I going to do? She told me that vinegar and water would be helpful. It was and so my cleaning started, and I was able to get things taken care of. I was thankful I still had my little apartment, and that my children, and my wonderful neighbors were safe.

"A Rainy Night"

Daddy knew Fred was drinking heavily again, and often he would show up unexpectedly. Even my cousin Jim would come knocking at the door, when I least expected his visit, and always Freddie was not home, but their visits always brought me comfort, and cheered me when it seemed things were at their worst. This night the rain was coming down heavily and Daddy came by. I told him Freddie was out somewhere, and I wasn't sure where. Mrs. Myles stayed with the children, while Daddy and I went in search.

We discovered his car, parked just a short way from the front of the Knotty Pine Café. Daddy pulled in front of his vehicle, and instructed me to go lift the hood, grab hold of all the timing wires, and pull for all I was worth. When I returned, Daddy said, "I guarantee when he returns home, he will be sober. Don't let on that you know anything about this night." I did as Daddy said, and after he left me off at the apartment, I went in and went to bed, and slept soundly. Freddie came in about 7 a.m. that next morning, quite sober and angry as all get out! He rambled on and on how somebody had pulled the timing wires out, and it took him all night to get it back in working order. I never made a comment and he never noticed that I didn't seem concerned.

"Charmer"

Freddie hung around with his buddy, Al, who was part of his ex-wife's family. I went to their house looking for him. When I came in the kitchen, in a frenzy, because I had not heard a word of where he was, and could not locate him in any of the bar rooms. I expressed my frustration to Charmer, Al's sister, that was sitting there in the rocker. She retorted back to me in a snooty sarcastic tone, "If Freddie wanted you to know where he was, Freddie would have told you." My immediate reaction was blind fury, and I leaped at her, and clasped my hands around her neck, and kept banging her head on the back of the rocker she was sitting in. Her sister-in-law, Nancy, came in to pull me off of her, and screeched to get through my rage, "Joyce, she isn't worth it." With that I stopped, and stormed out with Nancy on my heels, and letting me know that Freddie was with Al. They had gone to Boston, and for whatever the reason was, no one ever told me. Evidently, Charmer was in on the secret.

There was another incident, when I was in search of Freddie, and I walked to Al's house on Goff St. Al told me that Freddie was upstairs in his house sleeping. I went up the stairs, and opened the door to find Charmer there, coming up from under the sheets. I didn't notice Freddie right away, so I left in tears, and I didn't fight back. He returned home later and said all the things that made it alright again. I believed him.

"New England Counter"

While working at New England Counter factory, (a business no longer in existence) I was attracted to Dan. He was a handsome black man. His dreamy brown eyes made me melt. I would walk to his machine, during breaks, and we would laugh and talk. I became infatuated with him! Maybe I was in love with the thought of him. He had one tooth, that was gold, from having it fixed, and it would gleam when he smiled. He knew I wasn't treated well, and I confided things, that made him have a desire to protect me. I would get jealous if Dan paid attention to another female worker. I called Danny "milk chocolate," as his complexation was creamy along with his dreamy brown eyes. When things became so bad at home, and I would think of leaving Freddie, and I had Dan anticipating that I would leave Freddie, but I decided that I should stay and work things out. I came in to work and Danny sauntered over to my machine. This was when I told him I was going to try to make a go of things with Freddie. He walked away from my machine, and walked down the long corridor. As I watched him, he stopped and turned around, and looked back at me with a lengthy gaze, then turned back and walked away. I never saw him again from that day to this. He left work and never returned and shortly after that I quit there as well.

I did piece work, and I was good, at my job. I molded counters for shoes. I placed different shaped counters in a steel fingered plate, with slots, that hold them in place. Then lifting the plate, with my left hand, after inserting the counter, with my right, to press it in on a solid steel plug, I would press the foot pedal, with my right foot, with the right timing, before the steel pressure plate would come down, and flatten the counter, at the precise measurement. This crafted the mold in a curved cup that was placed in the construction of the heel, of a shoe. There was a rhythm to this procedure so speed was a factor to make any money. I was able to get the rhythm going, sometimes so fast I didn't want to stop. I never worked a 40-hour week, as I made my quota plus, always within a 30-hour week. Danny, however, molded by hand, with fire behind the plug making it very hot. He didn't have the fingered plate, but used his hands to curve the counter around the hot plug. There were workers that lost fingers from this work. I was beside a co-worker that had her finger chopped off. It was dangerous, so they started incorporating the automatic machines that seemed to have more break downs. I worked there for six years, (1967-1973), and made a good pay check of $105 a week, which at that time was excellent money.

"Before Robert Was Born"

It was about 7 a.m., when Dot, Freddie's sister, burst through the apartment door, questioning, "Freddie hasn't come home yet, has he?" She never waited for an answer because she knew he hadn't come yet, since she knew where he was. It seemed like she loved to rub things in my face. That was just the way Dot was. Dot had a farmers' walk that was set with a mission, determined to set things right because she knew. Her jaw was set and her shrill voice peaked when she wanted to get the point across. "I'll show you, just to prove to you that I know, but I won't drop you off, because I don't want to get involved. I thought to myself, "Well aren't you already involved?" Dot continued in her shrill voice, "I wouldn't put up with this for a minute. I went through it with my first one, but if Junior ever acted like this, he'd be out the door."

It had been a long night. Weekends were always long and lonely. No car, two small children, and pregnant with a husband that was a weekend drunk, as during the week he never even kept a beer in the refrigerator. He never drank at home and he never drank alone. It was the same week after week. You could count on Friday morning, that when he left for work, he would faithfully promise that he would be right home after work, and every time he promised, I would believe him. He was convincing, and I didn't want to believe that he would lie to me, so I would make every conceivable excuse as to why he was late, week after week.

"Wait till I get the girls bundled up," I answered Dot, "I will only be a few minutes." Dot stood at the door with her pocketbook draped over her arm, waiting rather impatiently, as if she were in some big hurry, and not bothering to help me dress the girls. The girls, obediently, without fuss, listened. Tammy followed, while I carried Judy to Dot's car down over the stairs of the second floor apartment, and out the front door. Dot drove us across town to unfamiliar territory. She turned off on to a back street slowing down, and as we neared some small homes that were in need of repairs, there was no mistaking Fred's car parked in the driveway of the house on the end of the street. It appeared no one was up yet on this Sunday morning. There were no signs of life. "There," Dot seemed quite proud of herself that she had proved her point, and done her good deed for the day. She rattled on, "I wouldn't take this crap from him, if I were you," she exclaimed. "I can't drop you off," she protested, "I am not babysitting, and I don't want to get involved." "Heaven's no!" I thought to myself again; "I wouldn't want her to be saddled with two little kids, her nieces, and drop me off where her brother is, because it would cause a scene, and she doesn't want to get involved!" These were my silent thoughts storming through my mind, as Dot sped past the little house back to the apartment. Before dropping me off, she voiced her opinion once again, "It's up to you, but I wouldn't put up with it if I were you."

People seem to think that their opinion of what they would do is an easy fix to a bad situation. Yet, no one knows what they would do if they lived in the circumstances, and under the duress that faces someone who lives in fear of their lives or what will happen to their children and maybe. . . just maybe things will change. That seems to be a hope that is clung to like a life line. At this point, I felt like a caged lion back at the apartment pacing the floor. I went deaf to the needs of my girls. I thought out loud, "I wonder if I can get Mrs. Myles to babysit?" In no time my plan was in action. Mrs. Myles came lumbering down the third floor stairs to my apartment to watch the girls. She watched them throughout the week, and loved them, so to have her babysit never seemed like a chore to her. I called a cab, and was on my way to where Dot had just taken me. It was within a short walking distance, when I asked the cab driver to drop me off before my destination. I paid the $2.00 charge, and slipped out of the cab, running to the house, and sneaking up the rundown steps that led to the front door. I never knocked, but barged in the unlocked door as if I owned the place. I was ready to move a mountain with my anger.

The kitchen was the first room I entered, with an adjoining bedroom, marked by an open archway. From where I stood I heard movement from the bed, and as I tiptoed closer, a woman was sliding from the end of the bed where she obviously had been lying. As she looked up and stared face-to-face into my eyes, she gasped. Her mouth was trying to form words, but there was no sound. If there were sounds, I never heard them in my blind rage. Without a word, I bolted to the side of the bed where Freddie was laying still deep in his drunken sleep. I doubled my fist, and came down on the side of his face with all my strength, catching his ear and splitting it. In an instant he was standing. He was still dressed in his work clothes, and reeking of booze. I came at him in a wild frenzy, grabbing him, and spewing out venom in curses that overtook my soul. While in our scuffle, I tore his watch from his wrist, and it went flying to the corner of the room. This infuriated him to a full-fledged rage. I was not able to withstand his strength, so I ran to the door, and raced for the car in fear of his powerful thrusts as he was on my heels. I made it to the car, but couldn't get the windows up in time to keep him from unlocking the door. The car seemed unable to start, and everything went into slow motion, when he grabbed me by the throat and began banging my head on the tape deck in the car. I could hear the woman screaming, "Freddie stop! Remember she is pregnant! STOP! STOP!" She was pulling at him to stop, and I could feel his grip lessen. She was actually intervening on my behalf, and still in his half-witted senses, he quieted down, and calmly got in the passenger's side of the car, while I drove back to our apartment.

Since we had this horrible struggle, and in his drunken stupor, I assumed when I drove in the driveway of the back entrance to our apartment that he would naturally follow me up into the apartment, and go to bed to sleep off his drunkenness, and then we would hash the situation out once he was in his right mind. I began to ascend the back stairs leading to our back porch, shaking and angry. When I reached the top of the stairway, and turned to look back at him, he was fumbling to take over the driver's seat in preparation to leave again. I had left the keys in the ignition, as it was our practice to do that.

My adrenalin was on screech. With an instant compulsive thought, I opened the back door of the apartment that entered into our bedroom. This was also where his CB and Ham radio equipment were located as well. There was a 100-pound amplifier that I used to shove around, and drag across the floor to move it when cleaning, but at this moment, I picked it up without effort, and carried it out to the porch railing, lifting it high over my head, and with the force of a strong-man, I screamed his name, in a piercing screech. He looked up, as he was backing out of the driveway, I let the amplifier fall to the ground, as he watched his beloved amplifier come hurtling down and smash on the tarred driveway, where the car had been parked just a minute before. I raced back for another piece of equipment and disposed of that in the same manner, as he watched from the car. Surprisingly how quick his reflexes were as he whipped back into the driveway, and raced up the stairs, two at a time. I slammed the wooden storm door closed before he made it to the doorway, and locked it, shutting the next door, and double locking that as well. I was panicking as to what my next move would be, as his threats were strong as he pounded on the door. I now had a phone and I was ready to call the police should he break through. It was Mrs. Myles who came to the rescue, she was a tall, heavy set woman, who always wore her bandanna showing wisps of gray hair from under her head-dress. This was accented by her bulging blue eyes, that held a fierce gaze, as she stood in a stance of authority, unflinching, in the doorway, she opened it up for Freddie. She blocked his way like a bulldozer that could not be moved, meeting him face-to face without fear. She demanded with a stern, foreboding voice, "Freddie, enough is enough." She pointed to the bed and said, "You come in here and lie right down and sleep off that drunk before you say another word or do another thing!" Obediently he laid down and went to sleep.

"The Week-End Ritual"

It would begin on Friday night, consistently, the need to be able to locate Freddie before he could cash his check and spend it all.

Sometimes I wouldn't go looking as I could not and would just pray that maybe this time he would come home. Faithfully every hour I would re-heat his supper, covering it carefully to keep it warm awhile longer, just in case so it would be ready when he walked in the door. With every sound of a car that resembled his, I raced to the window to see if it was him, and it never was. "Tammy, go look out the window, I think I heard Daddy." Tammy, three years old, would run across the linoleum, turning her head this way and that bouncing her long blonde curls, as she strained to see where Daddy was and when she couldn't see him, she hurried back saying, "No Mummy, Daddy isn't home." Then as if her little toy telephone had rang, she quickly would answer it, "Hello?" Listening to the non-existent voice, return her quizzical "hello," she would look at me, and in a matter-of-fact reply, she somberly explained, "Daddy won't be here tonight."

Every time this happened, chills ran down my spine, for I knew my little girl was right. Supper would be put away, and replaced with hot angry tears, as the bitter hours lay ahead. It was the same from Friday night, and then all day Saturday and into Saturday night. I took my anger out with scrubbing the hard wood floors on my hands and knees. As I scrubbed the floors on my hands and knees, the diamond on my left hand, ring finger, glistened and sparkled, and this acted as a buffer to my pain. I would console myself that the diamond was a binding act of love for me, and convince myself that his love for me was real, and I would continue to endure the heartache. The sparkling diamond was my glimmer of hope.

"Knotty Pine Café"

I was angry! That was a mild statement. Too many times, Freddie came home after his paycheck had been cashed, and he was nowhere to be found for the entire week end. He would come home broke, Zip, Nada—no money—nothing! I had called the phone at the Knotty Pine Café, his regular haunt, and for some unknown reason the phone clicked in as if someone answered. I could hear everything going on there. I heard Freddie laughing and I heard back ground noises. No one was on the other end, and after listening for a good twenty minutes or so, it hung up. I was beside myself with anger. I tried to call again and no one answered. I decided the kids and I were going to hike across town, to see for myself, for I knew where he was for sure

With Robbie in the stroller, and the girls trotting along beside me, we got to the place on Bates St. in Lewiston, where the Café was located. Facing the establishment, from the opposite side of the street was a telephone booth. I stationed the kids there, and told the girls to stay with their brother, and I would only be a few minutes. I entered the Café, Freddie was slumped over his beer while sitting at the bar. I was cursing up a storm at him, but there was no reaction! I was angry that he wouldn't even acknowledge me, or that his children were outside waiting. I grabbed his beer, and dumped it, then hurled the empty glass at the mirror behind the bar. I said to the bar maid, "Put that on his tab." She set another glass up, and I threw that as well. And then another, and another till I had broken all the glasses, and the mirror that covered the wall as well. Angrily I turned on my heel, and called over my shoulder, "Put it on his tab," as I stormed out the door and grabbed hold of the stroller, and commanded the kids, "Let's go home." He never returned home the entire week end. It was the following week that the Café burned. I did have an alibi! And it was not me!

"Mrs. Myles Death"

My dear Mrs. Myles' countenance kept getting really gray. I pleaded with her to go to the doctor, which she finally did. She came back telling me a tale of what he said, and that she would be fine but as time progressed, she seemed to be getting worse. I called Dr. Malazzo, her doctor, and told him about her countenance and how concerned I was. He told me that he had told her that if she did not go to the hospital that she would be dead in a year. I approached her with this, and she continued to be in denial. The day came that I called the ambulance, and they took her out on a stretcher to the hospital. She was so full of cancer that they sewed her back up, as there was nothing they could do for her. I visited her as often as I could. I loved her! She and I enjoyed many hours of tea together, and her words of wisdom were a cup of cool water to me.

When she had taken all she could, she closed her eyes, and fell into the sleep of death. (see I *Thessalonians 4:13 NKJV*) I do not know what her beliefs were, but God is her Judge. I hope I will see her again in the Kingdom. I was not living the kind of life I should, and I was not a good witness to her, but I believe that God placed her in my life to be a help to me, and my two little girls. Tammy would sit on her knee, as she would sing songs to her, and love her as her own grandchild. She never had children of her own, so I took the place of a daughter, and my little ones filled her void for grandchildren. Only in the kingdom will God reveal His great plan, and all He puts in our path. I called her sister in Canada, and told her of her passing. She had a pauper's funeral, with only three of us there. Mrs. LoBozzo, our landlady, Eva and myself. There was one bouquet of flowers that Mrs. LoBozzo had for her. That door of my life closed in tears.

Chapter Twenty

1971-1972

"Thank God every morning when you get up that you have something to do, that must be done, whether you like it or not. Being forced to work, and do your best, will breed in you, temperance, self-control, strength of will, content and a hundred virtues that the idol will never know."

~Charles Kingsley~

Robbie was such a good little boy. He sat and played with pots and pans for hours. At three months old he blew his pacifier out, and that was the end of that! At ten months, he refused the bottle, and from then on it was a cup for him. He never cried or was a chore in any way. One night, as I held my precious little boy in my arms, I dedicated him to God as I had my girls. I had learned from my parents that dedicating a child from birth was important. Jesus was dedicated by his parents at the Temple as a baby. His life was the example for us to follow. Even though I didn't attend church, I was convicted on this sacred belief. (see *Luke 2:25-27 NKJV*) Verse 27 *"And when the parents brought in the Child Jesus to do for Him according to the custom of the law. . ."*

I was dedicated to God just as Hannah dedicated Samuel to God—as this was the custom. Parents who love God want their children to be dedicated to the work of God. I Samuel chapter one tells of this story. I was dedicated at the Concord, New

Hampshire Seventh-day Adventist Church, and held in the arms of the well-known Pastor William Fagel. Beside him stood the author of the popular Bible Story Books "Uncle Arthur's Bedtime Stories," Arthur Maxwell. My sister tells me I was in a pink outfit with a sweet pink matching bonnet.

On this night I was alone, and pondering about my children, and how I wanted them to love God and be used for His glory. So in my arms, I held Robbie close to myself as I had Tammy and Judy and asked God to keep His hand on them and help me to bring them up to know Him, and love Him with all their hearts.

I was told Robbie had asthma, but that he would probably grow out of it. Dr. Horacio Lichter was the Pediatrician that cared for my children. He counseled me, while examining Robbie, not to have any more children, as they had such severe health issues and I was in danger of having a child with mental challenges. At that time, they called it "retarded." I left his office in tears because I knew I was pregnant already. I said nothing to him. Freddie was actually waiting for me in the car when I came out of the office, and I never told him what was said. I kept it all to myself! The days ahead I tried to abort the baby I was carrying. I painted the kitchen, climbed up on ladders, and did everything I knew I probably should not do. I think the only thing it did was make the baby I was carrying stronger.

My Journal:

(November 24, 1971)

Thanksgiving eve—Freddie never came home until 3 a.m. He spent $23 unnecessarily.

My Prayer: Dear God, help us as a family to help each other to overcome and conquer that which drags us down. In the name of our precious Jesus I ask for Thy divine guidance. Amen.

(December 24, 1971)

Christmas Eve- I spent long lonely hours watching the Christmas lights blink on and off. The kids are sleeping and each minute seems like an eternity since he left at 1:30 this afternoon.

<u>My Prayer</u>: Dear God, how many tears more will I shed? How much more heartbreak can I withstand? Help me!

Freddie arrived home at 5 a.m. Christmas morning. Drunk! We had a terrible argument.

(January 1972)

This has started out as always to be a financially poor year. Our biggest problem this year is Internal Revenue. Outside of not having enough money, financially, we have had each other to rely on, and the enjoyment of our children, and most of all, a great deal of love. For the good moments in life I give thanks!

A letter my mother wrote to my Aunt Alta, who was Daddy's sister:

(January 8, 1972)

> *Dearest Alta and family,*
>   *We found out last Friday night that Stan has diabetes, and was on the verge of a diabetic coma. We thank God we went to the doctor's when we did. Then Monday, Stan lost his wallet with important papers plus money. He thought, at least $40, but later discovered it was $55,*
>   *He had been covering a cesspool for this ski lodge with a SeaTac, and decided when he found his pocketbook missing, that it could be five feet under the frozen earth and snow. He came and got me and it was dark and we could find nothing, but stopped by the tractor and had prayer as I recently read a book by Elder Coon that Virginia gave me when we were in Florida last summer entitled, "Youth Prays. . .. God Answers." It gave the ABC's of prayer, ask, believe, and*

claim his promises, and you will receive an answer to your prayer.

As we prayed, I remembered and felt I had faith enough that God would answer. But we found nothing that night, and when I said prayers with Stanley, our little son, I said, "we will pray that Jesus will help find daddy's wallet." The next day I didn't bother to look, but Stan looked, and he was feeling very blue and very hungry on his diabetic diet, and I was trying to count the blessings we do have, and I said to Stan, '" we are better off at this time than a good many other times that I know of.'" So the next day, I went out with him and while he was moving the dump truck around, I went over to where we said prayer on top of the cesspool and thought in my heart the ABC's of prayer. Surely God would answer! I just felt He would and it would help Stan's faith. I glanced around and there at my very feet was the edge of his wallet frozen in the ground. I waved and waved not daring to leave the spot, and he shut off his motor, and said,' "What do I need, a shovel?" But he needed an axe to chop it loose and he said,

"God bless you—you were determined, but I gave up." He kissed me but I said to our God, "Thank you, dear Father, thank you, thank you, over and over again." We counted the money and it was $55. We paid an extra tithe and took it to the Church Treasurer that night. Stan said, "it was nothing short of a miracle," as he had looked and looked and dragged back and forth there. (with the machinery he had) "I would be a very poor Christian if I ever lost faith."

I added this testimony of my mother's faith as I believe it was her prayers that God heard so many times for me, as I walked in the "valley of the shadow of death" so many times. (Psalms 23:4 in part NKJV)

(February 3, 1972)

Freddie didn't come home until 1:15 a.m. He slept in the car the rest of the night after an exchange of sarcasms and bitter words.

We had a very bad storm this night. My eyes burned so from so many tears. I smoked all night and my nerves are on edge. It seems at times there are only dreams to live on.

My Prayer: Dear God, give me strength for reality.

(February 4, 1972)—Judy's fourth birthday.

Received in the mail from my sister a card for Judy and a pair of mittens. I am making her a cake tomorrow. Four years have passed since her birth. It seems only yesterday I bore her to this world. Time passes so slowly yet so very quickly.

My Prayer: Father, help her to grow in good health, love and strong in character. Keep her safe! Within Your hands I place her life, and whatever You decide for her future to accept. Amen.

(February 10, 1972)

Freddie went over to Bill Smith's to have income tax made out. It cost $20, but was well worth it.

(February 11, 1972)

Mailed out the big Income tax return today for $798.00. They will probably deduct $90 of that from what we owe. Freddie came in around 4 a.m. Drunk again! A patrol car followed him to make sure he made it. He had put a nail in his hand at work and finally on— (February 12, 1972). Freddie went to the hospital around 2 p.m. for a tetanus shot. His hand and arm was quite swollen, red and stiff. I am thankful that he will be alright.

(February 15, 1972)

Robbie became very sick and I rushed him to the hospital in the middle of the night. His fever kept sky-rocketing. Fred stayed home and watched the girls. Robbie had infections in both ears that were causing him to be deaf. The pain he must have suffered and I never realized it. I didn't sleep this night.

(February 17, 1972)

Freddie went to work as usual, and never came home all night. He finally came in at 10:30 a.m. and slept most of the day away.

(February 18, 1972).

About 3:30 in the afternoon, Strouty called (co-worker and drinking buddy) and wanted Fred to come after him as his truck broke down. Freddie didn't return until 1:30 a.m. He had been drinking again.

(February 19, 1972)

I went to get groceries in the worst storm we had all winter. Snow and more snow! Terrible winds!

"May 1972"

We went to Dot's in the morning. We were going to have a cook out. By afternoon, I was having contractions, and ready for my next baby to be born. There was a parade going on as it was the day before Memorial Day. Freddie flew up Main St., in Lewiston, with me in the car holding on to the car arm rest as he dodged traffic, and people to one of the local hospitals. Dr. John James was at the hospital waiting. After an examination, they gave me a pill to stop my contractions. It seems the baby was not in the right position. I was there the entire evening, and by morning my contractions had begun again, and still the baby had not turned. Dr. James came in late in the day, and realizing I was in severe active pain, examined me again and left the room. Within a fairly short amount of time, he returned with a pair of scissors with blunt rounded ends. He positioned me on the bed, and, emphatically, said, "We are going to have this baby now, because if we don't your mother will be on the next plane here from Tennessee, and I don't want to meet her;" were his exact words. With that being said, he reached up into the vaginal cavity, and cut the water bag, and with his hand turned the head of my baby so it was facing the right direction as it was in posterior birth position, which would be detrimental to its birth and my well-being. Kathy Ann was born. I don't remember much of the delivery. I had a tubal ligation two days later.

Kathy Ann entered this world, May 31, 1972. My Tubal ligation was scheduled for June 2, which at the same time it was discovered my appendix was about to burst. An appendectomy was performed as well as the tubal ligation. I was quite ill for some time. My sister took Robbie with her, Henrietta kept Tammy and Judy for me. We had become friends through all the adversities we went through early on. My enemy had become my friend.

I am adding the contents of Mama's letter to Aunt Alta, Daddy's sister at that time. She was very close to Daddy's family. Mama was a real prayer warrior. I never realized until later in life just how much she depended on the power of prayer to change things. This letter is the last letter she ever wrote to Aunt Alta. Dated: June 12, 1972 (just 10 days after my surgery. She was coming back home to visit, and see her new grand-daughter, Kathy Ann, and I was so excited and happy!)

> *Dearest Alta,*
>
> *I have not forgotten you, as I have been so busy studying as I have been accepted for the nursing course at the University (of Tennessee) and I am thrilled! I got all B's this last quarter, but I have to take Philosophy and Political Science, and I am afraid I may not do as well. I can only try and if I pass, I will be so happy.*
>
> *We will go home the last of July, and stay a couple of weeks, but will come by your place on our way, because on our way back, we will be so loaded that I expect we will make tracks back here without any side trips. We thought we would sell our home up in New Hampshire, but Stan has diabetes and said, "If*

*I find I cannot swing things down here, I at least know
I have a roof over my head and the place is practically
paid for."*

Her letter continues with bits and pieces about the pets they have and my brother, Stanley, but she also continues with mentioning that my *"last baby is born, Kathy Ann,"* and that I was having my tubes tied, and my sister was not having anymore chidlren, so that was the end of her grandchildren, but she was pleased she has seven, a lucky number! She ended with reference to Stanley, that before he would have any children, *"that Jesus will come before that comes about."* The end of her letter to Aunt Alta was, *"I want Jesus to come soon!"*

My Journal continues: (June 5, 1972) I came home. My sister in law, Louise and her niece, Faye, came after me. So good to be back home, I can barely move!

"Henrietta and Me"

In the midst of all the trials, Henrietta and I became like sisters – always in the search for Freddie to get the money we needed to survive from one day to the next and, from one week to the next. I went to pick her up at her place about fifteen miles out of Auburn. I didn't have a driver's license, but drove anyway. I was pulled over after making a U-Turn that caused a police officer to stop me. I had missed the turn to Henrietta's and he came up behind me just as I was making the U-turn! He at first flirted a little bit with me about blondes having more fun. He was quite flattering toward me, and generously allowed me to continue to my destination, but with admonishment that I was to park the car after I arrived and find someone to drive it. I assured him I would and continued to Henrietta's.

We talked for a while about the situation, when I arrived at her place and then decided we would chance it so off we went toward the city to find Freddie. I do not remember if we found him or not that particular day, but on our way back to her place, she counseled me to take the back roads as there was never a cop on them. So I did.

Just as we rounded the corner which was just a few miles short of a being back to her place, there on that the same corner, that I was turning on was the same officer that stopped me previously. He shook his fist at me and screeched out his rolled down window for me to pull over, which I did. He whipped his cruiser around and pulled up behind us. He packed a verbal punch with no flatteries attached this time. He told me to park the car off the road. I flippantly told him to "park it himself." That didn't set well with him as he pointed to Henrietta asking if she had a license. No, she didn't either! So we were made to get out while he moved the car. We walked to the phone booth in front of the IGA store not too far away and Henrietta called her mother to come get us. Her mother was disgusted that she was with me and gave her a hard time. We walked back to the car and I drove it to her place. We then decided we had to go back to town and began walking with little Harvey in the stroller. After a few miles of walking, Henrietta's boyfriend was on his way to see her, so found us walking and saved the day!

From that time forward we were connected. She became my best friend and I was hers. We were inseparable. "A friend loves at all times, and a brother is born for adversity." (Proverbs 17:17 NIV)

Chapter Twenty-One

Mama, My Precious Mama

"I will both lie down in peace and sleep;
For you alone O Lord, make me dwell in safety."
(Psalms 4:8 NKJV)

Knock, knock, knock! I awoke abruptly, and someone was knocking on our bedroom door. I was the furthest distance from the door as I jumped out of bed, and without a thought, raced to the door glancing back at Freddie still sleeping. I opened the door that led to the outside without further consideration. When I flung the door open there was empty darkness on the other side of the wooden screen door. With a flashing thought that perhaps whoever had knocked on the door was not able to arouse anyone, and could still be in the driveway. I raced to the kitchen window that overlooked the driveway to see only the rays of a full moon filtering through the alley way of the surrounding buildings, illuminating the darkness with a path of light that left no trace that anyone had ever been there. I felt troubled! Could it have just been a dream? I checked on the children. They were sleeping soundly, with not even a twitch of their muscles. Freddie was still in a mindless sleep unaware of the commotion that was going on. Not even Kathy Ann, my precious little one, had even moved. I returned to bed and fell into a restless sleep.

When morning had dawned, Freddie went off to work, and I had the preliminaries of the day accomplished, I called to my neighbor, downstairs. "Eva, did you hear anyone climbing the back stairs in the night?" I quizzed. "No! no! she answered thoughtfully, I slept pretty well and I didn't hear a thing, Joysie," she called out loudly so I could hear her from her downstairs apartment through the banisters. "Joysie" was her pet name for me. "Wait," she called as an afterthought, "I will ask Junior if he heard anything." Sidney, called Junior, was her oldest son. "No!" she came back in a minute with the answer, "Junior didn't hear anything either. Why, what's the matter?" she questioned further.

I explained my questioning, and how everything unfolded in the night as she listened intently. She thought, and said for me not to worry about it, it was probably just a dream. But in the course of the day, a bird slammed into the bedroom window. "Eva," I shouted, "Did you see that?" I stood at the top of the stairway as we often left our doors open, and communicated throughout the day. "Eva," I shouted again. "No, Joysie, what is it?" she questioned back. "A bird just flew into my bedroom window, and I think it hurt itself and may be in the yard below. Eva went to check out the back bedroom window since she was on the first floor. "No Joysie, I don't see anything. It must have just stunned itself and flew off. You know," she continued in wary tones, "they say when a bird hits a window, someone is going to die." A flashback came to me, remembering the warning of the fortune teller that someone was going to die, unexpectedly. "Yeah" I replied vaguely, while deep in thought. My mind was searching; the thought was a possible maybe....my father-in-law. He does have heart trouble. Then I remembered, "No! she said someone close to me. "Who?" I pondered.

I knew I shouldn't be dwelling on this stuff; the Bible speaks against it. "*Do not listen to your false prophets, fortune tellers, interpreters of dreams, mediums or sorcerers . . .*" (see *Jeremiah 27:11 NLT*) (see also *Malachi 3:5 NLT*). I was not practicing what the Bible taught, and I knew I should not go to the fortune teller, but still some of the things she said seemed intriguing, and it was difficult to get that haunting out of my head. I had listened, intently in the late night to ghost stories that Freddie's nieces often talked about. Some of them were older than me, and I felt more like a close friend rather than an aunt. The stories were vivid, and it made the hairs stand up on the back of my neck. The superstitions were, curiously, fascinating. I often got those crazy instincts of things that were about to happen, like a premonition, and it never proved wrong. It somehow became an omen of the unknown, something you couldn't explain, and no matter how you tried to dismiss it, it was there. Satan was cast out of heaven along with one-third of the angels that followed him. And they have been given dominion over this earth until Jesus returns and vindicates His rights. (see Isaiah 14:12; Luke 10:18; Revelation 12:7-9; Revelation 12:3 NKJV) This explains so many supernatural incidents, for these evil angels hold dominion over the earth to destroy the truth of God's amazing love.

It was the next night at the same hour, just before midnight, the same as the night before, that the phone rang. "Hel-hello," I faltered as I spoke and feeling uneasy. After all who calls at this hour? Freddie was home and sleeping. "Joyce!" It was Daddy's voice. "Daddy?" I answered back as a question, as his voice sounded strange. "Joyce," he continued slowly, "your mother is dead." "Dead?" I questioned. "Mama! Dead!" I repeated, as the words were finally penetrating... he quickly told the story in short sentences. "She was driving home from school, and ran out of gas. A drunk driver hit her and she died. Your brother and I were home. I will call you later with the details. Call your sister." He hung up. In shock! I hung up the phone, and picked up the receiver again to dial my sister's number in New Hampshire. She answered groggily, in sleepy tones, of being awoken from her sleep. "Sister, I have bad news." I didn't wait for her to answer—I just rambled the details that Daddy had provided to me. I repeated his words, "A drunken driver killed Mama. She was in her car, and ran out of gas. Daddy will call later about arrangements." It was absurd! A drunk driver killed Mother. Nonsense! This didn't happen. It's a dream! I will wake up any minute. Thinking back, on the night before, when I raced to the door and no one was there. Maybe, I will wake up and it will just be dark and stillness all around, and

I will go back to bed. But everything around me says I am awake, and it is true. I don't remember my sister's response. She was in the same state of shock I was, and nothing made sense.

The light was glaring in my eyes, and tears had begun to flow endlessly. The reality was settling in. Mama was dead! She was coming home from Nashville, TN, July 13th, and that was just a couple weeks away. She would get to see her grandchildren. I had not mailed any pictures or written as I was going to tell her everything personally, while she held Kathy Ann in her arms. There was so much to catch up on, and I could hardly wait. I wanted to tell her how Tammy had begun Kindergarten, this past year, and was promoted to the first grade. Then there is Judy, and no one believes her age because she is so tiny. Mama loved her grandchildren, and I knew she was anxious to hold them and love them with hugs and kisses. This drunk driver took away our joy of life. He took my mother, my dearest friend, and my children's grand-mother.

The next few days were a blur. We stopped at Jimmy's gas station, (no longer exists) connected to the diner in Auburn, before we headed for Concord, New Hampshire. The attendant that pumped our gas, knew Freddie, and jokingly, made a comment on the maroon sports jacket that Fred was wearing, "Hey, Fred, all dressed up? You must be headed for church, Haw! Haw! Haw!" Freddie waved him off, and we drove away. The long ride was minutes in my mind, rather than hours. I entered Boutwell Mortuary, and Daddy was standing next to the casket with no shoes on. "Daddy, where are your shoes?" He looked at me like I had just asked a stupid question. "Shoes? What shoes?" He was totally oblivious that he had come in only in his stocking feet. Someone noticed at the same time, and came and ushered him quietly from beside the casket, and took him to a shoe store to buy a pair of shoes. And there I stood looking at my best friend, lying there..... cold and stiff. Mama faced death without friends or loved ones to stand next to her during her final hours. The woman who witnessed her death, provided a blanket to cover her and listen to her final instructions, but were there comforting words spoken before the final breath was taken, only God holds the answer. It was a horrific death, and now I was alone because she had become my life. Everything I went through, all the years I rebelled against her, all the disobedience I dished out, she not only forgave me, she loved me and I loved her. I was the queen of rebellion. And now I was the queen of remorse! She kissed away the boo boos that hurt, and held me close. She stood like a giant for her grandchildren...and now our time together had been stolen.

I knew she was asleep and waiting now, so when she opens her eyes again, she will see Jesus and her body will be made new. Her work here on this earth was done. (I *Thessalonians 4:16 & 17 NKJV*) *"For the Lord, Himself shall descend from heaven, with a shout, and with a voice of an archangel and the trumpet of God. And the dead in Christ shall rise first. Then we who are alive and remain shall be caught up together with them in the clouds, to meet the Lord in the air."* There is further proof in (*Ecclesiastes 9:5 & 6*), that *"the dead know nothing."* The basic teaching that many believe that because Jesus told the thief on the cross that *"I tell you, today you will be with Me in paradise,"* (see *Luke 23:42 & 43 NKJV*) is a confirmation to some that you go straight to heaven when you die.

It seems that Bible students aren't thinking clearly when they read this since Jesus did not ascend the day he died on the Cross. He rested in the tomb, and rose on the third day, then he was still here on this earth for a while until He went to the Mount of Transfiguration. Due to human error, the comma was put in the wrong place! I was brought up to study all Scripture and make sure what was being read was in conjunction, and complied with all Scripture, and not take one out of context. Therefore, I knew Mama was sleeping and *if* I start walking the path that I should walk, I will see her again.

At this moment, the room was spinning, and everyone around me was a faceless body. I felt like all the air was being choked out of me, and I raced out to the front porch of the building to breathe. I leaned over the railing and I heard a voice, "Are you going to be alright?" It was my mother's sister, Vesta.

She was a nurse and I had not seen her in a very long time. "Yes!" I answered, not really sure of myself. I didn't know how to relate to Aunt Vesta. To be alright I had to comprehend all that was happening, and, somehow, I just couldn't. I can see the young man who spoke the final words at Mama's funeral, but I don't remember who he was. He was someone I knew and was so happy he was there, but I don't remember what he said.

The procession to the gravesite in the little countryside cemetery, in North Pembroke, New Hampshire, is where she was laid to rest next to her parents, Willis and Emma Hutchinson. The cars were endless. Mama knew a lot of people who loved her. Town officials thought it was a dignitary who had died, and they were ready to bring the flags down to half-mast, questioning who was this person that had just passed, that they had not been informed about? It was Mama, my Mama! And even though I know I will see her again, I wasn't ready for her to leave me now. It was too soon. Oh my precious Mama, I will miss you! Around the gravesite they were singing, "Shall we gather at the river, where bright angel's feet have trod......" ending with "that flows by the Throne of God." This was all being sung in sweet unison. I couldn't sing, because that wasn't the song she wanted. I could hear her sweet, pleasing voice vibrate in my mind, "Beyond the Sunset, O blissful morning.... when with our Savoir, heaven is begun. Earth's toil is ended, O grand reunion, beyond the sunset, forevermore."

The spread of food that our cousin Betty put together, out on her front yard, was tremendous. There were hugs and tears. It was a glorious reunion with one-member missing. She would not ever be able to toss her grand babies in the air, and laughingly blow on their bellies. She would never be able to wipe their tears and hug them close. She was taken from her six-year-old son, her husband, my sister and me. There was no more reunion with her ever again on this earth. Her life was stolen by the enemy. Why? Why is the question I have asked throughout the years? But God makes no mistakes and I trust Him no matter what. I must see her again! Did He allow her life to be taken to reach me?

To bring me back into good standing with Him. I don't know, I am grasping. *'The living know that they shall die, but the dead know nothing, and they have no more reward, for the memory of them is forgotten. Also their love, their envy, their hatred have now perished; nevermore will they share in anything under the sun."* (Eccl. 9:5 & 6 NKJV) Even so it still hurts!

"*And God will wipe the tears from their eyes; and there shall be no more death neither sorrow, nor crying, neither shall there be any more pain; for the former things are passed away."* (see Revelation 21:4 NKJV) A year or more later, I had the same dream, viewing Mama being hurled through the air across a six lane highway, after having been hit in the back end of her car. The windows all being still up, as in the south it is warm, in June, and no doubt her air conditioner had been going until she ran out of gas.

When the crash from the drunk driver, a young man without a license, hit her so strongly, she was literally propelled from the driver's seat, out the rear window of her car, shredding her clothing as she landed across that huge highway. The woman who viewed this from her car, and related this story to Daddy, and told how Mama was able to stand and walk back across the road, collapsing by her car, just as a truck came down from the exit, and ran over her. This dear woman, went to Mama's aid, doing what she could to make her comfortable. Mama was rushed to the hospital where Aunt Thelma Lou, Daddy's sister was working in the emergency room. They were going to do a tracheotomy on her so she could breathe, but it was too late. If she had lived, she would have had a life that would have been unbearable for the family to watch as her insides were crushed. God in His infinite mercy let her go to sleep.

In my nightmare, I heard her scream; it was chilling as it replayed every time I closed my eyes. The mental torture was bad enough, but there was no comfort from human arms or sweet sympathetic words to bring a form of relief. Grief dries the bones and brings with it an emptiness that is difficult to fill, so the soul drenches in sorrow. Mama—my precious Mama's life did not end with a long life, nor without pain, it was not a silent killer of some disease, and it was not without tragic results, nor was there any kindness to her death, but taken with brutal force, stolen by careless, selfish thought and left with scars that will remain until Jesus' return.

"George's Bestest Friend"

After the nursing home closed to patient care, Priscilla became bored with inactivity, as she was always busy with something that needed to be done. She went to the County Public Health seeking a job. They hired her to go into the county to find any citizens that may need health care. She traveled all over the county. One day, she saw a drive that didn't look very traveled, and she debated whether to go down or not, as she was up in the mountains. Spontaneous as she was, she did go down the drive and came to a small country cottage. She knocked on the door, at first there was no answer, so she knocked louder, and she heard a weak call, "Come in." She entered, but she saw no one, so she kept calling, and followed the voice in a small bedroom, where she found where the voice was coming from.

It was an old man living alone, in bed with the covers up over his ears. She asked him what he was doing in bed this time of day, and he said that he was sick, that he thought he had the flu. She asked him if he had eaten. He hadn't. She said she would fix him something, so she scurried around, and found enough things to make soup and coffee. She helped him to get adjusted, to sit up, and take the nourishment. She explained who she was, and she asked him what kind of help would he need. He said that he didn't know what help he needed. She sat by his bedside, as he ate the soup and drank the coffee. She filled out the required visit papers, and told him she would be back tomorrow to check on him. He thanked her for her help and she left.

When she got back to town, she went to the grocery store, and the next stop was the Church Community Center (Dorcas Society). She got some supplies that she thought he might use. The next day when she returned, to see the old man, (his name was George), she cooked food for him, fixed a bath, and helped him out of bed, changed his bed while he bathed, she straightened up the house. He was very grateful for her help. She told him she would be back the next day (this was not part of her job.) The next day George looked improved, and after a short visit Priscilla told him that she would be back, in a week, to take him into town to get a health care checkup, start him on food stamps, and see if he is eligible for other assistance.

The next week George was able to go with Priscilla and the tasks were done. She made weekly visits for another month. As she was leaving she told him he needed to sit outside for fresh air every day, and to breathe deep to clear his lungs and this would make him feel better. He said there wasn't a place to sit, and she pointed to an old settee, made out of horsehair and in dilapidated condition. But she told him to sit in it anyway, and enjoy the beauty of the outdoors for a few minutes every day. George could only see the settee as useless, but Priscilla could see what it might be. As she was leaving George asked her if he could pay her for her work and time. She tried to explain that this was her job, and of course she refused any payment, but George insisted on giving her something then he said, "If you like that old settee so much, just take it with you, a couple of bolts and it will come apart, I'll drag me a chair out here to sit in." Because of his assistance, she did accept the offer. George had a neighbor that came by occasionally, and took him to town and sometimes he would ask him to stop by the Wetmore house to say hello to his "lifesaver."

Stan and Priscilla moved to Ohio and then to Tennessee. Priscilla decided that she wanted to fulfil her lifelong dream to become a Registered Nurse. She enrolled in the school of nursing in Nashville, TN. When coming home from class one night she was tragically killed in an automobile accident. Sister Ruth and I, (Thelma Lou) accompanied Stan and Stanley to New Hampshire for Priscilla's funeral. Her body was shipped by plane to New Hampshire. We stayed in the house that was once the nursing home. The following morning after our arrival, we were in the "summer kitchen" eating breakfast when we heard a knock at the front door. Stan answered the door and we overheard him say, "George come on in and have a cup of coffee." He followed Stan in and Stan introduced him, then George said, I saw your car in the drive so I dropped by hoping to see Priscilla. Where is she?" Stan handed him a cup of coffee, and said, George, I have bad news, Priscilla was killed in an automobile accident in Tennessee, and we are here for her *funeral."* George sat staring at the cup. It was silent in the room then George pushed back his chair, stood up and with bowed head, he said, *"she was the bestest friend I ever had,"* and he left.

The memory of the old man's broken heart still brings tears to my eyes. When Stan was back in Tennessee, and going through things, he told me that he was going to haul the old settee to the junk yard. I insisted what it could be made into, but he insisted that he had hauled it all over the country, and now he was bound to junk it. I said, "please don't" and he said... "you can have it," and at that point, I knew he meant it, so I offered to buy it. He laughed, and said, "$5.00." And I said, "Sold." And I took it home. Well, my husband, Bill, was upset with me because he shared Stan's feelings about the "piece of junk" as they called it. I began work on it right away, so they couldn't take it away after I had started work on it. I tore off the horsehair covering and refinished the wooden arms. Then I took the seat and back to have them covered. The agency made a seat and cushioned the back covering with antique green velvet. When it was put back together and brought home, I invited Stan over. When he saw it, he said, "Hey isn't that my settee?" I kept it for 35 years, and since I am getting old, I decided that one of Priscilla's offspring should have something of hers, and I offered it to Joyce. Joyce decided that her daughter, Judy should have it. I hope you enjoy it as long as it lasts. I loved Priscilla and I love you. Priscilla was also one of my "bestest friends" Aunt Thelma Lou"

Written by Thelma Lou Wetmore Pitt (Daddy's younger sister from Greenbrier, TN)

"The Old Settee"

The old settee has found its resting place in the home of my daughter Judy in TN—A piece of her grandmother and her Great Aunt Thelma Lou graces her home. It is a beautiful piece of furniture. We are so fortunate that God can see the beauty in us as we stand before him in "filthy rags." He isn't ready to discard us because we are tattered and torn, but "clothes us with rich robes." (See Zechariah 3:3-4 in part NKJV)

(June 28, 1972)

Priscilla H. Wetmore, 52, of 621 Meness Lane, Nashville, Tennessee, died in an automobile accident when returning from the University of Tennessee, where she was enrolled in the Advanced Course in Nursing. She was born in Concord, NH, and lived in Center Conway, NH, before going to Tennessee. She was a member of the Concord, NH Seventh-day Adventist Church, she leaves her husband, William Stanley Wetmore of Madison; two daughters, and their husbands, of Intervale, NH and Auburn, Maine; one son, Stanley Wetmore of Madison; her step-mother, Anna Hutchinson of Concord, NH, two sisters, Vesta Tobin of Pittsfield, NH and Eva Shea of Boston, Massachusetts. She left seven grandchildren, Anna, Neal and Ricky as well as Tammy, Judy, Robert and Kathy.

"My Eulogy to Mama"

"Let us pray and God will lead the way,"
These words ring loud within me
The undying words, "come what may"
The undying strength of whatever should be.
Your love reached out beyond all tomorrows. .
Your faith was strength for all sorrows.
You will forever live within my heart.
No human hand can touch the grief I depart.
Sleep Mama. O tender, tender sleep,
For now, you are forever in God's keep.
O Lord give me strength to bear this pain.
May the memories of her love eternally remain.
The horrors and the beauty of death
stealing through the night air-
How can I accept? How can I prepare?
The breath of angels whispered gently in your ear,

Your work has been well done, have no fear.
Sleep sweetly, Mama, till the glory of
the Lord shines forevermore.
I pray I will be there to hold your hand once more.
(In loving Memory of my mother—Joyce
Ann Wetmore Robinson, July 1972)

"Another Obituary in a Church Paper"

Priscilla Neva Ann Hutchinson Wetmore born March 11, 1920 in Concord, N.H., died in Madison Hospital June 28, 1972. She was educated in Concord Public School system. She had attended 2 years at Atlantic Union College, South Lancaster, MA in the Pre-medical course when she married William Stanley Wetmore of Salamanca, NY, who was also attending college.

They moved to Pembroke, NH and built a house, on a hill, in the country. They had two daughters. Later the family moved to Center Conway, NH where they opened and operated a nursing home for 11 years. In 1965 a new arrival, this time a boy, Stanley Marlon, was added to the family.

The 16-foot snow drifts in the winter, the great distance to church school, and Priscilla's burning desire to become a registered nurse uprooted the family with the decision to move south.

In 1971, the family moved to Madison, TN where all of Priscilla's dream came true—a nearby church school, beautiful church edifices, a modern immaculate hospital, all the things she held dear—and then the acceptance into the 1972 Fall nursing program at the university of TN. As she put it on a tape recording the morning of June 28— ".... everything is so beautiful, the mimosa trees, the magnolia blossoms, the campus church, I just love it here so much. . .. "

Then tragedy struck suddenly to stop all dreams. Priscilla died within the walls of the hospital she loved. But we are glad we knew her and loved her just as she loved others. It was her wish to be buried in the small cemetery a stone's throw from the home built in Pembroke, NH; that wish was granted. As her six-year-old son said, "Mudder is waiting for those beautiful lights, and Jesus, then I will run and hug her."

"My Final Tribute to Mama"

Many before me have said eloquent things
That stirs the heart of a mother and brings
A tender warm thought and radiant glow,
To the tribute of Mother, we recognize and know.
My tribute is to a mother who long prayed for me,
She agonized before her Savior for
the unruly girl I came to be.
I left my Christian home and held a stubborn heart.
I wouldn't give in and selfishness wouldn't part.
As the story goes of the prodigal son,
So as a daughter I became one.
While away in the far country, just down the road;
The guilt I carried became such a heavy load.
I reasoned and sanctified the life I came to live,
I hardened my heart and an inch I wouldn't give.
Satan taunted me on every side . . .
He said, "You can't go back, you
have too many sins to hide."
On the porch of my old home where
mother never ceased her prayer,
Was a light that kept burning, just in
case I should wander there.
She brought to me her labors of
love in so many little ways,
She never condemned or judged
during my prodigal days.

A JOURNEY OF TRIALS STRENGTHENED THROUGH FAITH

Then tragedy struck and plucked her from my life.

O such pain, it cut my heart like a knife.

I stumbled back in the darkness, then
began to focus on the light-

It gave me strength to go on even
in the darkest of the night.

The light on the porch had long since been burned;

The Light of Jesus was the way I turned.

I'm home! I'm home! Your prayers brought me here.

But Mother sleeps waiting for Jesus to come near.

And now I reflect on her unselfish
life, labored for others,

Oh the sacrifice of love in the life of Christian mothers.

When she awakens and cries,
"Lord where is my Joyce?"

May the reply sound out in that Great Day,

"She is coming now, in on the sea
of Glass, home to stay."

For it was my mother's intercessory
prayers that set me free,

That I may live for Jesus, Who gave His life for me."

By Joyce A. Wetmore-Robinson—1973

Chapter Twenty-Two

Am I Going to Die?

*"Fear not, for I am with you; Be not
dismayed, for I am your God.
I will strengthen you. Yes, I will help you.
I will hold you My righteous right hand."*
(Isaiah 41:10 NKJV)

After we returned home from the funeral, and all that took place, I began to feel ill. I had time off from work so I was able to stay home. I kept feeling worse and so to speed up my recovery I went to the doctor. He thought from my description of everything that I had the flu. He gave me an antibiotic. I took the entire prescription in a ten-day period of time, but I was not getting any better. I was getting worse, and I didn't want to return to that same doctor so I contacted another one that took me in right away. After explaining symptoms, he felt I had a relapse of the flu so he gave me another anti-biotic. I took this in its entirety and was not getting any better.

I had taken the free flu shot at work, a couple years prior, for Hong Kong Flu, to awaken the next morning unable to pick my head off the pillow. I had been very ill at that time, and each time I wasn't feeling well, Freddie seemed to disappear. I was fortunate enough, by the Grace of God, to have neighbors that cared for me, especially Eva, that lived downstairs.

I had finally come to a point where I felt that if I didn't get the help I needed, I would surely die. I made an appointment with Dr. Cabatingan. I entered his examining room and sat on the table. I was in tears as he entered! I exclaimed in sobs, "I feel like I am going to die." He looked at me and without even examining me, he clearly stated, "You are if you don't get help immediately." I was startled that he recognized my need so quickly. He said you have Mononucleosis. All the symptoms that mimicked the flu, which were fever, chills, body aches and pains, sore throat which worsened with each passing day into swollen lymph nodes, fatigue, and weakness that developed into loss of appetite, which was due to an enlargement of the spleen or liver, which then quickly begins to jaundice, which is the yellowing of the whites of the eyes and or a pale yellowing of the skin. I had reached all levels. The only thing I lacked was swollen tonsils, but since they had been removed at age sixteen, this was not a factor.

It was under the observant eye of Dr. Oscar Cabatingan, that brought me great relief with medical treatment that continued through six months of recovery. He wanted to hospitalize me. I pleaded with him to allow me to stay home and I would follow his instructions. My sister took Robbie and Freddie's x-wife, Henrietta, took Tammy and Judy, while I kept Kathy. She was such a good baby! I couldn't lift her or carry her. I did what was necessary and no more, as I was so ill. It was not determined how I contacted Mono. I was twenty-four years old and it seems this illness can leave an adult with chronic life threatening diseases associated with lymphoma, and Hodgkin lymphoma. I recently spoke with my primary physician about it. He said that everyone carries the Epstein-Barr-Barr virus, but it is not active in everyone. This can leave some individuals susceptible to getting sick easily. Throughout my life, I have always had low blood pressure as well as tiring easily and having a low immune symptom, which fits the symptoms of what I experienced. I have learned since that time, that Vitamin D deficiency is also a result of that illness, which I take Vitamin D daily to counteract the need. This also helps with depression, which often overtakes me. Other symptoms have manifested themselves as a result as well. It is suggested that legumes and blueberries can help with this disorder. Fortunately, I enjoy both.

God in His divine mercy kept me from the other diseases that could have easily been a defect from the illness and taken my life. I lost tremendous weight during this time. I always have had a tendency of being on the heavy side, so I was really happy that I had lost weight, but did not want to go through such a weight loss program again. However, once a person has been jaundiced, the Red Cross does not promote that person being able to give blood, as it could be potentially harmful to the donor as well as the recipient. *"Bless the Lord, O my soul, and forget not all His benefits; Who forgives all your iniquities, Who heals all your diseases."* (Psalms 103:2, 3 NKJV)

The fact of losing my mother, in such a horrific manner, and having such difficulty delivering my baby girl, as well as the surgery that followed from an infected appendix being removed has been medically noted that such illnesses, and traumas can be the results that can manifest themselves up to six months later, before the onset of the illness of Mono. If it had not been for the Hand of God over me I would have died.

"Fear of Dying"

It seems so dark out tonight,
Very lonely as if time has stood still.
What were once dreams, became buried out of sight;
I felt stalked just waiting for the kill,
And the midnight air left it's chill.
I felt so alone, afraid and torn.
I could hear emptiness echoing within
The very chambers of my being.
Within walls of pain where eyes were unseeing,
The futile life that is left in a shell,
But then—I awoke from the living hell.
(Written by Joyce A. Robinson-1972)

Chapter Twenty-Three

12 High St – Bog Hoot

"It is God who engineers our circumstances and whatever they may be, we must see that we face them while continually abiding in Him….. for Jesus Christ's honor is at stake in our bodily lives."

~ Oswald Chambers~

My girls, Tammy and Judy were mad at me for whatever reason, I cannot remember, but after I had distinctly told them "no" they went off hand in hand. The next thing I heard was the back screen door slam. I went to see where they were headed and they were nowhere in sight. I sent out the alert to Eva, Mrs. LaBozzo and to the upstairs neighbors. We all began walking up and down the street to find them, calling their names frantically. I was now in tears, picturing my two little girls walking hand in hand to heaven knows where, imagining some stranger picking them up and carting them off to an unknown destination and I would never see them again. I raced for the phone after every avenue had been searched. Dialing the phone for the police I leaned against the doorway, and gazing into their bedroom, to my joyous surprise, they were fast asleep in their beds. Relief! I did not wake them up to hug them, but I did cry tears of relief and thankfulness that God had not allowed them to take off, out the door and run off where they may never be found again.

Tammy had begun Kindergarten at the school just down the street from us, but I felt it was getting to be time to move. We lived at 90 Roak St. five years and my family was growing. I wanted to be in the country. There was no place for them to play, and I wanted them to have a yard where I wouldn't worry about them. The scare of them running away was enough to make that decision.

Henrietta, Freddie's x-wife, and I had become good friends. She had an apartment in Bog Hoot on the second floor, but the downstairs apartment had become available. She told me who to contact, which was Mr. Norton Woodsum, who owned a small grocery store in town, and was known for his good meat there. There was a lot of work to be done at this apartment so I spoke with him about it. He said he would be willing to give us a couple months' rent to paint and fix it up. It had three huge rooms and a large bathroom. The kitchen was very big and had an alcove off from the kitchen area, but still part of it. As you entered the hallway, the bathroom was to the left. It was roomy, and I had the washing machine in there as well. As you continued in the hallway, there was a doorway to the right that went into a large bedroom. Just before you entered that room there was a doorway leading down to the basement, which was also for our needs. Fred enjoyed going down there to putter around with electronic equipment. Just before you came to the end of the hallway, there was a doorway that went up the stairwell to the second floor. This was the back entrance to Henrietta's apartment. Then at the end of the short hallway, there was a huge living room that was used as a bedroom for the kids. Off from the living room/bedroom was an entry way coming in from the front door, but it was not used as anything more than a place to store things. However, there was enough room to go in and out the front door, if necessary, as it was also the entrance to this storage area. The side entrance, that entered into the kitchen, was the entrance that was always used.

I continued my job at New England Counter and traveled in my, beloved 1968 Oldsmobile. Henrietta became the babysitter for me, and since Freddie was living in the same apartment building, it was not hard to locate him for her child support payments. Freddie was working on construction with his brother, Ed, and, was usually, gone all week long and was home on weekends. Henrietta and I had become so close, and spent much time together. She was like another sister to me.

Just before moving in, I spent much time painting. While I was painting the window frames in the kitchen, all of a sudden a young man ran out of the building next door. It was so close by it was barely a shout away. This young man had a butcher knife and was running after the another guy in his underwear.

I screamed to Henrietta upstairs to call the police that someone was about to kill someone. Then I thought, "What am I doing? They can see me and I may be next!" I ran upstairs to Henrietta's apartment and she explained that our neighbors had some issues. These two young men lived with their mother and they had some mental health issues inherited from their father. I later learned that their mother was the local Tupperware dealer, the town gossip, and was also good friends with Henrietta's mother. They were both gossipers! I laid aside my fears, and we successfully made our move to 12 High St., Bog Hoot. There were promises to keep in touch with Eva and Mrs. LaBozzo. I did for a time, but life just stops a lot of our good intentions.

"The Axe"

Freddie was out drinking as usual, and Henrietta and I had gone down to the local restaurant "Christies" (no longer in existence) for a drink and to party. We would flirt and laugh and get feeling good. I had gotten to the point of drinking more than I should and looked forward to weekends to let loose for I never knew when Freddie would be home. Henrietta and I had planned if he came home, and got violent, I would, somehow, contact her and she would call the police.

He came in, in a rage, which wasn't uncommon. He would fall over in the bathroom and Robbie would climb over him to use the bathroom toilet and prop his feet on him while there. This night, he was sure I had been out doing something with someone, and so, as always, there was an argument and then the hitting, and the punching. It was really fierce this night. He had me by the throat banging my head on the table. I kept thinking that Henrietta was coming to my rescue any time, but that didn't happen. I broke loose when he grabbed an axe outside the door and smashed the rear window of my dear Oldsmobile. It was winter so I had to drive to work on that Monday with plastic on the back window. My co-workers were shocked and feared my even being around him. The outbreaks and the violence was getting worse.

"A Pig"

I was in a bad marriage and I had 4 children to feed. A friend of mine & I decided to raise pigs because they were cheap to raise, and there was a lot of meat on them. I thought I would have enough meat for my children to eat throughout the winter, and I would at least have food on the table. Often my children did not have the most healthful diet, but I wanted to provide for them. As the pig grew and got fatter and fatter, and as time grew nearer and nearer for slaughter, I realized I couldn't eat that pig and neither could I feed it to my children. How was I going to get out of this mess? Finally, the day came...... and there is always a day that comes when we least expect it. The prodigal son came to his senses (*see Luke 15:11-31 NKJV*) in the pigpen and the prodigal daughter came to her senses, while she was fattening a pig to eat that led to her being delivered out of the pigsty of life! I blurted out to my friend who was housing the pigs, and caring for them – "I can't eat that pig." She looked at me in disbelief, "What?" I stuttered, "I, I can't, I can't eat that pig." I couldn't believe what I was saying. It just blurted out of me without any for-thought as to what I should say. It was from that moment on that many things began to happen, and by the power of the Holy Spirit, it ended up that I didn't eat that pig and neither did my children or my friend.

"Tammy's Broken Leg"

Our neighbors, across the road, oldest daughter, would babysit for me often. There were the Harrison's just up the street from them. It was a very close neighborhood. The man in the house next to us, on the right as you entered our driveway, kept to himself. The only time I saw him was when he washed his car, which was every day. There was never any interaction with him. George, however, that I had seen chasing his brother with a butcher knife, became a frequent visitor. He was always bumming a cigarette from me. He would swing the kids around on the neighbor's lawn until they were dizzy and fall down. The day he began swinging Tammy, my seven-year-old, by the arms, he lost control and down she went with him landing on top of her, and his weight broke her leg. She had what was called a green-stick fracture. I raced her to the hospital and they kept her there for over a week.

My Journal: (July 26, 1974) 4:30 p.m.

Tammy broke her leg in two places. George was swinging her by the hands and let her fall. I rushed her to the hospital. I stopped at the job site on Minot Ave. where Freddie was working and he drove us the rest of the way. They admitted her at 7:30 p.m.

"While Tammy Was in The Hospital"

(July 27, 1974) Friday

I finished packing everything and left. I could take no more. His drunks and coldness were more than I could bear. I just couldn't live like this wondering from day to day whether he'll be home or not, whether he'll scream at me for something, anything. It was unreal! It was a horror! I couldn't live like this anymore!

I needed to find a place to go. Henrietta had a friend that was willing to take me in with the kids. Freddie was getting ready to leave for work, and I kissed him at the door, but as soon as he had backed out of the drive way, I packed everything I could carry and moved the kids and I to her friend's place. We were there about two weeks. I visited Tammy in between times. Freddie never went near the hospital. However, not having me around, changed his demeanor. He sent word through Henrietta that he would quit drinking and make a go of our marriage. I consented to meet him alone at the apartment. He dumped a bottle of whiskey that was almost full down the drain in front of me. That was, definitely, a first! Through a tearful, heartfelt confession, he made promises, and I believed he meant what he said. We moved back home. Tammy came home from the hospital and arrangements were made to pick her up and take her to school and bring her home while I worked. George made sure she was always supplied with coloring books and crayons. He felt so badly for what happened.

"Quit Smoking"

I had been a chain smoker and smoked close to four packs a day. Cigarettes cost about seventy-five cents a pack. I was determined to quit! I had been getting up in the night to smoke, and always had one in my hand or smoldering in an ash tray. However, Freddie was not ready to give up smoking. He had quit drinking, and that was the best he could do for right now. Friends that smoked would stop by and smoke. They would butt out their cigarettes in the ashtray, once they learned I wasn't smoking. When they left, I found myself scavenging through the trash to find their cigarette butt so I could smoke it, till one day, I thought to myself, "what am I doing?" I then started writing out scriptures and stationing them all through my kitchen. Every time I wanted a cigarette, I would quote a verse and claim that promise. The hardest part was when Freddie came home, and he would blow smoke in my face and continued for about two months, when he decided to quit too. We both became smoke free in 1974.

"Bible Studies & Baptism"

We began Bible studies with Rachael and Kenneth Lee from the Auburn Seventh-day Adventist Church. They came faithfully every Friday evening and sat at our kitchen table studying with us revealing Bible truths. The same truths I was brought up to believe and know, and which Freddie had never heard. Freddie accepted the teachings of the Seventh-day Bible Sabbath and all the doctrines that he learned on the trinity, state of the dead and the judgement. Because I had not been living the life I knew I should, I renewed my baptismal vows as well with being re-baptized. When you live in the world, unless you stay connected to God in a personal relationship, you tend to forget what the Bible teaches, and you quickly justify your actions and become like the world. Freddie was baptized and I was re-baptized, August 2, 1975, by Pastor Richardson. My Daddy, all my children, my sister and my brother, were there to witness the event along with the members of the church.

"Stanley Comes To Live With Us"

Daddy was going through a difficult time adjusting to single life with a little boy. Stanley was in the third grade and soon to go into the fourth. Daddy asked if he could leave Stanley, eight years old, with me for a while and I took him in. We made a room for Stan and Robbie to share a room in Henrietta's apartment, at the top of the stairs just as you entered her apartment from the back stairway.

He began the fourth grade at the local elementary school with Mrs. Williamson. He loved her and she was good to him. He had a struggle with his bed-wetting for quite some time, but all his trauma was laid to his dysfunction. I took him to Dr. Gilbert Grimes, and he gave me advice, and told me not to worry about it as this seems to be something that boys go through more than girls. Stan was part of the family and more like a brother to my children than an uncle. There came a time when it just seemed like too much for me to raise my brother and my four children. I let daddy know that Stanley needed him, and I could not be both father and mother to my brother. Daddy came and took Stanley back to Tennessee with him.

"Why Did You Give Me a Way?"

Harvey, my step-son, was also a part of the family. Wherever my kids went, Harvey was with us. If Henrietta was going out for the evening, I babysat. We had Thanksgiving, Christmas and birthdays together. It was not just my four children and Stanley, but Harvey as well. Then the day came when Harvey was ten years old, and he asked me quite solemnly, "Why did you give me away?" I was devastated! I sat down with him and explained that Henrietta was his mother, and I was his step-mother, and I loved him, but I was not his Mama. I think he felt better to know that I had not given him away, and he would always be a welcomed part of my life.

"Two Years Later"

Daddy had a few ladies that my sister and I had met and one in particular we really loved. She was so in love with Daddy, but he didn't feel that they would connect spiritually. We learned that he was remarried to Jean Begley. She had been in the church at one time, but had left. He felt he could be a good enough influence on her, and that she would return to church. My sister and I had not been as taken with Jean, but we accepted Daddy's marriage and made efforts to get to know Jean. They lived in Nashville, Tennessee. Daddy sold the old house in Center Conway, New Hampshire to my sister, and her husband. There was an old logging truck out back that was to be Stanley's but he never acquired it. Our brother-in-law sold it, feeling it wasn't profitable to keep it. It was an eye-sore on the property and I do not believe he felt I would be able to move it. I was quite upset for Stanley's sake for some time over the incident.

"Our First Dog"

We acquired a dog, which was a 9" Beagle, which meant she was nine inches high, I named her Sniffles, which was actually the name of my CB handle. Freddie's CB name was Scout. We used the CB quite frequently as this had been a hobby of Freddie's for several years. Sniffles, got loose and hooked up with a mongrel dog in the yard. They were "stuck" together." My neighbor was angry that these two dogs were displaying themselves in front of his children, and I wasn't doing anything about it! We exchanged a few angry words and I managed to get them separated with a pail of water. Sniffles ended up with nine beautiful pups. She was very protective of the pups and the kids and didn't want anyone near them. I tried to give them away as she was a thoroughbred, but the father was not, so I didn't feel I could sell them, but under someone's suggestion, I put an ad in the paper, and sold every one of them, within a week, for $25 each.

Chapter Twenty –Four

201 Main St
1977-1978

"All things work together for good to those who love God and are called according to His purpose." (Romans 8:28 NKJV)

I went in search for houses that could be fixed up and wondered how I might be able to buy one. My children needed a place to live, where they could have freedom to roam and enjoy outdoors. Twelve High Street had served its purpose, but there was no land that went with the property, so playing outside was extended to the neighbor's property. Robbie learned how to ride his first two-wheel bicycle, by teetering on the two wheels, while focusing on balancing, when trying to stop, he crashed into our neighbor's garage doors. Before that he rode his Hot Wheel, three-wheeler, down over the hill that crossed the road and into the IGA parking lot. He then would play horse shoes, with the old man that lived at the bottom of the hill, then come home and tell me he had been playing with the cops! I learned later on, the friendly town officers used to play horseshoes as well. They definitely needed to have a better place to play.

I would often pass by a rundown place on Main St. in Bog Hoot. Everyone said that there were rats in the well, and it was haunted and so the rumors went. It definitely needed some

TLC, but it had a nice piece of land with a run-down garage. I went to the Town Office to see who it belonged to. It seems, a man by the name of Toivo Tomilla owned it, in West Townsend, Massachusetts. His uncle had died and left the property to him, but he never lived there. That was all the information they had. He paid the taxes every year and no one ever bothered with the place. I decided to write a letter to this man, and without any other address than the name of the town and state, I sent my letter. I inquired if he wanted to sell it and explained that I had four children, no money for cash down, but asked if he would he be willing to sell as rent to buy? Within a couple weeks I received a reply. He met with me, made out paperwork to buy as rent for $50 a month until the sum of $5,000 with no interest.

Every $50 payment came off the selling price. Fred was working away on construction sites during the week, so I attended to all the affairs in whatever form they came. I truly believed that the letter reached Mr. Tomilla on angel wings and the amount was absolutely designed by God. There was much work to be done, as there was an old hand pump in the house, so that came out and replaced with faucets much like the ones that had been at Freddie's parents. The well was not drinkable as it was filled with clay and iron so it was not tasty to drink and had an orange color, so we hauled our water in milk jugs from the spring about two miles beyond our place. We were however able to do laundry, as there was plenty of water. There was a nice fertile plot of land so I had a wonderful garden. All the furniture in the house that I could not use, I put in a lawn sale and discovered later that I sold antiques for practically nothing. It didn't matter. My children had a place to play.

There was an attached structure on the house that had not been completed and was quite run down. This home was in essence, the house that "jack built." There were additions here and there of different sizes and added haphazardly, without any leveling to make sure everything was balanced. The foundation was held up on sauna tubes and if you looked under the house, they were all slanting sideways. I am not sure what kept the house up. It had a dormer upstairs that was evenly built that didn't fit the rest of the house. There was barely any insulation, so we lost a lot of heat. The garage ended up housing chickens, and the old run down shed out back was a place for the ducks, as we had a bog out back, that was their own watering and swimming hole. We even had large birds of different sects come in to drink from it.

It had been two happy years with Freddie going to church and being a family man. I enjoyed my marriage and tried to find innovative ways to show him how much I loved him and how happy I was to be his wife, his one and only.

"My New Job"

I quit my job after six years at New England Counter (which no longer exists) and began driving for the Town of Bog Hoot, picking up pre-school children from their homes and dropping them off at their place of learning, then returning for them at the designated time to pick them up from the school and return them to their homes. I had become friendly and well known with the Town Manager. He asked me if I would like to be a school bus driver. I thought about it, and decided this would be good, as I would be home with my children on vacations and summers. It wasn't long before I was introduced to Mr. Bisby. He went with me on the school bus and I learned all there was about school bus driving. He rode with me for several weeks until I went to take my test as bus-driver and acquire my license. My first trip to pick up for school, on Maple Lane Road was when a little black dog ran out from its home right under the wheels of the bus. I was devastated, but with Mr. Bisby's encouragement after that ordeal, I continued to drive.

"Renovations"

Freddie put in a new bathroom. We only had a toilet and sink under the stairway. The stairway was moved to the other side of the house, but until that happened, the toilet tipped from side to side when you sat on it, since the piping underneath the house was not stable, we had a rocking toilet! I was so excited to have a new bathroom. It was a pretty blue the pionite sheathing around the walls in the shower with sliding doors encompassing the shower. Another dormer was built on the opposite side of the house upstairs, so that there was more room for the kids' bedrooms. There were 4 small rooms upstairs that were unfinished. Tammy had her own room, Judy and Kathy were together in another room, and Robbie and Stan had their room, Fred & I had our room, furthest from the top of the stairs. Downstairs was the living room-dining room combination. Fred built a television and installed it in the wall. The bathroom was on the other side of a make-shift pantry, where the rocking toilet once was and extended into a laundry room as well. That room also had a holding tank, for the water pump and the hot water tank was next to it. The kitchen had a painted wood floor and shelves that I put together myself and connected them to the wall to be used as cupboards. I made curtains that hid the stacks of dishes and so forth from view. When you entered from the enclosed porch that was attached to the house, you came into the dining room. This was where the kitchen table was located, as the kitchen was too small to fit a table, and the floor was so warped, that it would have caused the table to warble.

"Our Pets"

We had two dogs, Sniffles, our 9" Beagle, then we acquired Travis. He seemed to be a husky, lab, shepherd mix that went got along with our chickens and ducks. We had plenty of eggs from our Rhode Island Reds and they kept ticks and ants out of the way. We had a pet bantam rooster, that sat on top of the freezer on the porch, which looked in the window and crowed every morning. He was colorful and a quite comical. We loved our pets. Travis used to lay in the middle of the road and cars would go around him. I got a letter from the Chief of Police in town asking me to make sure my dog stayed out of the road so cars could go by. It was a very nice letter.

"Plenty of Goodies"

The Kuykendall's had been a part of Freddie's new conversion experience and they kept us in baked breads, cookies and fudge. They brought a fresh supply every month. I would store the extras in the freezer out on the porch and dole them out as needed. Sabbath's were the day of plenty from their bounty they brought us and the kids always looked forward to it.

"Our 10th Anniversary"

There had been displays of severe anger issues that were manifesting themselves with Freddie. He worked away all week and was home during weekends. I reprimanded myself for complaining about his ugliness after all God had worked a miracle and given me a home and a husband that believed the same as I did and here I was complaining because he often found fault with little things. I scolded myself for forgetting how bad things used to be. On our 10th anniversary, October 28, 1977, we went out to Bonanza for dinner and had a nice time together. He loved going out to eat, but the poor waitress that served us took the brunt of his criticism if the meal was not perfectly prepared, and would be sent back until it returned to his satisfaction or he would create a scene.

The next day October 29th, I woke up with a sore throat. Each day that followed it got worse. I had laryngitis, swollen glands, headache and fever. Since I wasn't feeling well, Fred took the kids to Henrietta's grandparents Halloween Party. The kids had a wonderful time but they told me that "Daddy and another lady present there" were whispering a lot with each other. My sister visited me and I complained to her about not feeling well on November 1, 1977. She urged me to go to the doctor and I did call Dr. Cabatingan and he took me right in. I had Scarlet Fever. Everyone was put on penicillin to avoid getting sick. I was terribly ill for two weeks.

Daddy became quite concerned with my health and came to Maine to visit. I was in the hospital at that time for a D & C.

The doctors at first thought I may have cancer but thankfully I did not. Because I was so ill Daddy and my sister came to visit me. Daddy traveled from Tennessee to New Hampshire as he had things to attend to at the house as my sister was going to buy it from him. I had great admiration for my Daddy and I was so blessed to have him visit me.

"For Being My Dad"

*As a little girl growing up, you were
to me a giant among men.
I saw you handsome, strong brilliant
and absolutely awesome.
The sun rose and set as little girls
dream of daddies and then-
As I grew older, I sometimes shuddered at
your strength and sometimes questioned
From whence your advice came from.
It seems only teen-age daughters have
the ability to know what is best,
But regardless of intermingled love with fear,
Of rejection with respect; to me you
stood out among the rest.
You were my father and somehow
to me you grew more dear.
As years have passed with good and bad,
I sit as a woman thinking of how thankful I am,
For the values you taught me and for being my Dad!
By Joyce Ann Wetmore, 11-12-1977*

My Journal 1978

January 14—No church due to a Nor'easter. I rushed to untangle Angel (our St Bernard dog) so she could get in her house and stuffed more hay in her house so she would be warm. I came back in the house and could hardly catch my breath. My left arm ached and was in pain. I never told Fred any of my ailments as he just thought I was a hypochondriac.

January 16—Tammy wasn't feeling well. I called Dr. Grimes that afternoon to get an appointment and it was after that she broke out with chicken pox. Judy said, "Oh gross, I am not staying here. I am not getting that." It was just a matter of an hour and she began scratching. She had chicken pox.

January 17—Kathy came down with chicken pox. Robbie was feeling left out because he had to go to school alone.

January 19- Heavy snow warnings on the radio. I was having vise grip pain in my back that radiated to my stomach.

January 28- Fred decided he didn't want to go to church today. I yearn for the fellowship.

My Prayer: I pray that Fred will yearn for the fellowship in the church as I do.

January 29- thanking God for His strength and for the friendships I have.

Prayer: Lord, help me to keep my eyes fixed on You. Grant me calmness of spirit.

Robbie came down with chicken pox. Another two weeks' house bound.

January 30—babysitting Tara.

February 2—Robbie cried most of the night. His itching was so bad.

February 4- Fred took the girls to church & I stayed home with Robbie. Praying for friends that are in the hospital. I made Judy's birthday cake and we got her a new outfit and a beginner's sewing kit.

"February 7, 1978—Angel"

February 7- Wednesday, I brought Angel, our St. Bernard, in the house while we were going to be away. We had my friend's daughter, Dorie babysit and she was a little leery of Angel. I had her reach her hand for Angel to sniff so she would get to know Dorie. When she advanced toward Angel, the dog lunged at her. I had my hand on Angel's collar but her weight was more than I could control. Angel put one tooth in the cheek on one side of Dorie's face and another tooth on the other side of her face. She instantly backed away from Dorie, and Dorie just stood in shock with tears welled up in her eyes. I called her mother one of my dear friends right away. We had to have Angel laid away on the worst snow storm ever. Fortunately, we had an International Scout that made it through the snow. They had to keep her 10 days and then would lay her away. My heart was so heavy over this. This huge gentle dog was protecting me. I loved her so much, but we had to have this done. Dorie's parents were as grief stricken as I was over Angel for if she had really wanted to hurt Dorie she could have taken her face off. Instead she left the marks of her warning. To this day, Dorie has two dimples from Angel and has told me that Angel gave her, her dimples. I thank God for such precious neighbors that could have become my enemies over this or sued me, yet they had great compassion. I thank God for such dear people. Yet, with all of this my insides ached that I had to lay away this big dog that I loved so much.

Later a friend of mine offered me a white husky. I talked it over with Fred and he screamed "Never again will there be another dog in this house."

"Reflections In My Journal About My Children—1978"

Tammy, 11 years old is becoming quite the young lady. She is such a pretty girl. Judy 10 years old is so different from Tammy. Judy seems more carefree and devilish. She is very modest and secretive. Her plainness becomes her and gives an awe of wonder about her. Robert eight years old and handsome as well as very sensitive although he tries to rough and tough, and displays tremendous feelings of compassion for others. Kathy, six years old also seems to be sensitive, but not to the extent of Robbie. She has a knack for capturing the hearts of those around her even though she is loud and sometimes quite coarse. None of them are alike and yet I pray that their principles will be the same and to care for each other deeply. My prayer for them today is that God will stay close to their hearts and watch over them.

Journaling continued to February 16, 1978–I was having terrible pain in my back and it felt like my hips were being pulled.

My Prayer: Lord, help me to accept the things I cannot control or change and work my life around the inevitable. Teach me compassion and long suffering. Thank you for hearing my prayers and answering my sorrowful cries.

"Bus Driving Test—1978"

I took my bus driver's test at the nearest Maine Dept. of Transportation yard. The man who tested me was a former Sargent in the military. He clenched a little fat cigar between his teeth, and spoke with gruffness. He made me a nervous wreck. The traffic test, swerving around cones was a cinch. Then backing in and making sure you didn't hit the cone you couldn't see was a bit more heart throbbing. Parallel parking a 34-foot school bus, when you are only allowed a six-inch gap between the bus and the curb was a bigger test of your ability. You were allowed to get out once and make a visual check before the final parking. My hands were so sweaty, and I wiped them on my pant legs and dried them the best I could after I made that one visual check, then returned to my seat, buckling in and continued to park. I did it! I was so relieved, I felt ready to pass out, I had been shaking so much. I was apprehensive, as the instructor was not lenient and never gave you any indication that you passed or not. He very nicely told me I did a good job and I would receive my license to drive school bus. I was so excited. I think I even surprised him that I did it all so well. I had prayed and I am sure that made the difference.

"Driving Bus"

I drove school bus for Bog Hoot for two years and then transferred my driving adventures to the next Town over for Harry Bush, the owner and school bus contractor for this Town. He had called me several times to see if I would drive for him. He was quite well-known as a former State Police Officer. There were many rumors of his actions that were told in various circles, which painted an unorthodox method of his character, and I would not be surprised that they were probably true. He was ridged and if he gave you any leeway of being nice, you felt that somehow you earned brownie points. I transferred to drive for him as it was more hours, as well as more money. Harry was a character, that you wanted to stay on the good side of. I drove for Harry for five years before taking on other driving challenges. Driving the hilly regions of the area was a good experience in skillful driving.

"Driving Experiences"

It was a very snowy day and school had not been called off so going over White Oak Hill was a challenge. It was early morning and I had the high school students. As we were going down over White Oak Hill, it had not been sanded, and I was creeping down the hill, with the bus, when I hit ice. The entire end of the hill had not been sanded. I stood on the brake, literally, and prayed within myself. By the grace of God, we stopped at the bottom of the hill just before it went out into the main roadway where traffic was often heavy. I was shaking so badly, I put the bus in park and turned to my high school kids and asked if they were okay. They all had been silent. One spoke up very concerned and said, "The question is, are you okay?" I told him I would be in a few minutes as soon as I stopped shaking. They were a wonderful group of high school students.

We had another horrific storm and this time I was going up over Flint's Hill notorious for its steep grade and curve. Again it had not been sanded as it should have been. I could not make the hill, nor could I stop the bus from sliding backwards. Again, I literally, stood on the brake and sent up a silent prayer. At the foot of the hill was a small bridge and everyone was certain the bus was going to careen over the banking, and land in the waterway. Once again, angels kept that from happening and we stopped at the edge of the bridge-way, unharmed. I called Harry on the two-way radio and said I was taking the long way around as sand was needed to be brought in before anyone could safely ascend that hill.

Another snowy event on Route 11 coming off from the back side from Johnson Hill Rd., as I turned left onto Route 11 and entered over the hill, there was a car that was unable to make it over the hill. I had my eighth grade boys get out and push the car until he could grab enough traction to get over the hill. They thought that was a great adventure. The driver was grateful.

Often I would do adventurous things that the kids thought was fun. On Halloween one year I decided to do the entire elementary run in reverse of the normal, which the last person usually off became the first off and the first off became the last off. I had not let the parents know, so the last off being the first off was Sally. Her mother was a teacher and she called Harry wondering where Sally was. I later talked with her and she told me if I ever did that again to let her know so she wouldn't worry as otherwise she thought that was a fun thing to do as well. However, Harry didn't see the humor in it. I had on a clown hat that day and googly glasses, when I pulled in the yard to re-fuel. Harry stepped up on the first step of the bus as I opened the doors and gave me the old one-two about what I had done. He went a bit overboard in my estimation, so when he stepped down, I said, "Are you done?" He said, quite gruffly, "No, I am not." I replied to him, "Well, I am," and I shut the bus doors in his face, parked my bus and went home. The incident was never spoken of again. I was a good driver regardless of our differences, I was a challenge to Harry and he liked a challenge.

Harry had his flaws, but when it came to a Christmas party for his workers or a summer outing, he knew how to make it a specialty. There was always enough food for an army and anyone could take home leftovers, as he never ate food left over from the previous meal. He would throw it away. There were always a nice gift and a gag gift, as well, and we would buy for each other. We always looked forward to Harry's parties.

On one occasion I was allowed to drive Harry's personal vehicle. He explicitly warned me that if I happened to do any damage to his truck, I better be wearing cement boots rather than return. I never dared to drive his truck again. He paid his workers well and if there were any issues that came up and I did run across a few, he would back his drivers one hundred percent.

"Turning 30- 1978"

Thirty is considered to be a milestone in a person's life and I never felt this way. The kids made me breakfast in bed and did the dishes all day without a squabble. Tammy made a cake from scratch and did such a good job. She gave me some stationary, since I wrote a lot of letters and a card was signed by everyone. I received several phone calls from friends and family far and near. I rec'd a spice rack, a food steamer, dish towels and antihistamines for my cold. I spent the day on the couch, but despite not feeling well, it was a wonderful birthday. It made my heart light to be given so much love and thoughtfulness from so many.

"Undeserved Grace"

I have always been known as having a lead foot. An owner of a local gas station, and repair shop used to tease me by asking, "If I get the stock car, will you drive it?" I thought that was a big deal so, of course, I would drive. It happened I was on the last trek before being done driving school bus for the day, and I was on the back side of Megguire Hill Rd. speeding around those back road corners. I had one student on the bus when the blue lights began to flash, and I immediately pulled over thinking they wanted to go by, but instead the cruiser pulled up behind me. The officer knew me and I knew him, but that didn't stop him from producing a ticket for my speeding.

I sheepishly went back to the bus garage after dropping off the last student and went home. I was in deep repentance to God. I put the speeding ticket on the counter and the worse part was to let Fred know as he would be very angry and I would pay dearly for that fine. I knelt in tears before the throne of mercy. When I went to find the ticket, it was gone. I asked Fred if he saw a ticket on the counter. He said an officer came and asked for it and he gave it to him. Word got around and the Chief of Police in my town came and took the ticket back as if it never happened. God intervened for me while I was praying. *"For You have cast all my sins behind Your back."* (Isaiah 38:17b NKJV)

"My Friend Sue"

Sue and I were close friends. We went horseback riding together in New Hampshire. It was a riding stable, where you were able to take horses out and ride them with a guide through various trails. They gave me the gentlest horse they had. We started off following the guide on a trail that went through a groomed trail. I had ridden my Dad's work horse, but I never did do well with riding even when I went one time to my friend, Cherry's to ride as a teen-ager. I had not been on a horse since then. Everything seemed to be going well, when all of a sudden my horse decided to gallop. I did all the maneuvers I knew to get him to slow down, but he was not having any part of my commands. He went on a dead run, past my friend, and then on past the guide. He tried to catch up and take hold of the horse, but this gentle horse was on a mission to get me off and had me hanging on my side with my feet wrapped around his neck. You see my legs are too short to stay in the stirrups stable enough to direct with my feet, so the horse was in control and I was not. By the time the guide caught up to us, I was hanging on for dear life and he managed to grab the reigns until we returned back to the barn. My legs were shaking so badly I could barely walk. That was my last attempt to ride a horse.

Sue had three boys and I often babysat them. I loved them so much. She had been married to Fred's nephew, David. David and I had been close before he married Sue, and then he became an alcoholic and he didn't always treat Sue very well. They divorced and she took off for some time to find herself. It was awhile before we reconnected after that crisis in her life.

It was April 1978, when Sue came to my house with a little ball of fluff. Our cat, Beretta had died. It had left an emptiness in our home, so this little white kitten with black patches we named "Patches" filled the empty spot. Sue often spent a lot of time with us and she missed Beretta too, so she thought our home would be a good home for this little kitten, and it was.

"Haunted House & Roller Coaster"

My friend, Alyce, decided the kids and I needed to get away and have some fun time. She picked us up to go to a camping area near Old Orchard Beach called Pine Point. We left the younger kids with the older kids and went off to the carnival area where there were attractions that were considered to be the best of thrillers. Our first thing was the haunted house. As a child, I was always scared of being scared. At night I would make sure my hand or foot never went over the edge of the bed just in case something was under the bed and grabbed my hand or foot. I don't know what made that such a scary thing to me, never-the-less, it did. I would check all the closets and behind all the doors on the third floor before going to bed to make sure nothing was there that shouldn't be. So here we were at the haunted house, and upon entering, the floor tilted this way and that making it eerie to walk. The psychedelic lighting and the illusions that came out from the walls along with the hideous laughter and skeletons popping up here and there added to the fear factor and then the spiders and snakes.....oh no. The worst part was when we went through an area where a masked person dressed as a monster was caged in a cement pit with bars and reached out grabbing at whoever walked by, and to me this was really scary, Alyce was behind me as I led the way through this house of horrors. She was wearing a loose fitting shirt over her blouse and because I was so scared, I reached behind me and grabbed the shirt-tails of her shirt pulling her up as close to me as she could get while screaming the whole time. She was laughing hysterically as we came to the end of the nightmare, when someone in a monster mask jumped out in front of me. I instinctively grabbed the mask off his face. Of course he didn't expect that and it was the fear of no fear on my part that made me do it. He cursed me as we made our departure from the haunted house. I was glad to leave. I have never gone through a haunted house since.

The next adventure was the roller coaster, which was considered to be the highest and most thrill seeking in the New England. As soon as I was seated in a single car to begin my trek up to the top of the roller coaster, my first thought was, "what am I doing?" With the creaking of the iron and steel railings as the car I was in ascended to the top, I knew this may be a ride I would never forget. As I crested the top, the first descent went straight down and my next thought was "Lord, I don't want to die on this roller coaster? The force of the dissention literally took my breath away and made me fearful of the next climb and ultimately how would this ride end? I kept my eyes closed as I finished this ride and prayerfully pleaded that I would live to see the end of it. I was glad to get off and still be breathing. It wasn't long after that encounter that the entire roller coaster was banned from being used and dismantled due to safety factors and the accidents that had occurred. The remainder of our week of camping was more of a quiet time of playing the card game, Rummy and going to the beach area with the kids.

1979 - *Tragedy Strikes*

Reflect upon your present blessings of which every man has many, not upon your past misfortunes, of which all men have some."
~ Charles Dickens~

"Trip to Nashville"

We decided to visit Daddy at the beginning of the year (1979), at his home in Nashville, TN. We thought we could visit the Grand Ole' Opera among other events there in Nashville and stay with Daddy and his wife, Jean, while we were there. We traveled in our 1978 brown Subaru sedan with the four children squished together in the back seat. Judy spent most of her ride in the back window. (seat belts were not a requirement then). I remember looking out the passenger side window listening to Freddie grumble and find fault about everything from the traffic to the kids, complaints about those he worked with along with everything I did wrong sitting next to him. I thought to myself, "this is going to be a very long trip." Our layover was in Virginia where we got a room. I was so car sick I couldn't stand to have anyone touch me or even jiggle the bed when I laid down and wished I could die.

When we arrived in Nashville, Tennessee, we learned that Daddy was just released from the hospital. He worked as a welder for Nashville Bridge. He had been on the highest part of the bridge welding, and when he came down, he had a seizure. Someone from the company took him to the hospital and he went through a series of tests. He was released to go home. He was resting on the couch and he thought he had a pinched nerve or something insignificant. While we were talking to him he went through another seizure that scared me. He came out of it and seemed to be alright.

We did go to the Grand Ole' Opry and the Country Music Hall of Fame, the Wax Museum and a few other the places, and ended up traveling to Memphis, TN to see the Elvis Presley mansion. We didn't go in as it wasn't open to the public during that time. I did engrave my name on the wall surrounding the mansion, and so did all the kids.

During our week and a half at Daddy's, we slept upstairs. Kathy had her first sleep-walking experience there. There was a snowstorm while we were there, which only left a dusting to an inch of snow, but school closed for 2 days and all the stores closed. Fred & I was going to go shopping but everything was closed down due to the little bit of snow that fell. We thought that was pretty funny. We met Jean's children by her former marriage. They were grown and Mary, the oldest was the only one with children of her own. Jean's other two children were boys, Tom & Joey. They did not have any children. Joey was a musician, married to Carol who was rarely around. Kathy was smitten with Tom and followed him like a puppy dog. They were all into karate and were experts in it.

Daddy's home on Meness Lane was the home he had also shared with Mama. All the familiar furniture was there. Daddy seemed fine when we left and I took a picture of him and Jean standing on the walkway in front of their home when I left. It was difficult to say good bye and going back home in the little car was going to be another long trip.

"Two Months Later"

I received word that Daddy was back in the hospital. They found a brain tumor and they were going to remove it. I booked a flight to TN and took my first airplane flight alone. I was seated by a woman with her little girl, and the woman was drinking bourbon. The smell made me sick to my stomach and her little girl was obnoxious. I had the sensation of falling as we ascended into the sky, so I hung on for dear life to the arms of my seat. Other than that the flight was okay. My friend Sue was caring for the kids while I was away. I didn't plan on being gone for more than two weeks. Since she often stayed at the house I knew she was capable of caring for the kids. I never thought about Fred giving her a difficult time and she could only take so much of his questionable advances, and so she left the house and the kids. After her divorce from Fred's nephew, David, she became involved in a lesbian lifestyle, and Fred was determined that she needed a "good man" to help her get on the right track with whatever he tried to do, until she could take no more. I could not blame her, but wished she had found someone to replace her. I was so involved with Daddy and didn't feel I could leave him, after surgery. He returned home after having spent a week in the hospital. I had taken a cassette tape of Tammy and Judy singing, "The Savior Is Waiting." that they often sang special music at church and sounded well together. As he began listening to it, in his hospital room, he began to cry as Jean entered the room, she snatched it out of the player and said, "We will have none of that here." I was angry and I didn't want to cause a scene in front of Daddy so fled to a quiet room in the hospital in tears. Jean found me and I was still angry. She tried to appease me, but I slapped her with words meant to sting. "I have had him for thirty-two years, and you have only had him in your life for four, so how would you know what he likes and what he doesn't?" She tried to reason with me, and I would have none of it. Eventually I returned to Daddy and it was never discussed again.

 There was a gas crisis when he returned home and in his state of mind, he wanted me to go and fill all the gas cans I could find. "This is the end times and we need to be ready," were his words. I went and waited in long fuel lines to put gas in the car. He had a big Oldsmobile that was a gas guzzler. I thought

Daddy was going to be okay, and I knew I needed to get back home. Before I left, Daddy and I had a heart to heart talk alone. 'Sweetheart!" he began. I thought, sweetheart? He had never used such a tone of endearment. He continued. "Promise me that you will care for your brother, and bring him up in the way he should go." Emotions overwhelmed me, as I clutched his hand, "Daddy I promise I will care for him as my very own." Then, there was a solemn silence between us.

"July 1979"

The brain tumor that was removed grew back from the size of a pea to the size of a golf ball within a month's time. Daddy's dear sister, Thelma Lou sat in vigil by his bedside while he thrashed with high fever from the cancerous tumor that took his life. She carefully and gently used her nursing skills to attempt to keep him as comfortable as possible with cool cloths over his body to bring down the fever and when she knew that he was at that point of no return, she awoke Jean from her sleep. Jean called her children to come and they arrived just as he took his final breath. Daddy had a painful death. I couldn't be there to hold his hand, since I had already had my moments with him and now it was time to lay him to rest. His brother, my dear Uncle Walter and Aunt Florence drove us to TN for the funeral. I asked my sister to go with us and she said she didn't have the money to go. I said, "I will pay your way, this was our Daddy." Uncle Walter was used to long trips and all of us together in his roomy Chevy wagon was comfortable. We took food along so we had sandwiches along the way and fruit. I left the kids with friends and I was pretty certain there wouldn't be problems as there was before.

During the funeral service, my sister, and Jean got into an argument over Daddy's glasses. My sister wanted them on him and Jean did not. Jean wanted to keep them. I was so upset with the both of them, I said, "When he is resurrected he won't need them so what does it matter?" They finally settled over the matter. My sister was grieving as much if not more than Jean and was not dealing well with it because she had him even longer than I did being close to seven years older than me. Mama had only been gone six years and now Daddy. We felt like orphans. Strange no matter how old you are, when you lose both parents, somehow or another, you feel like you don't know where you belong and suddenly you have to face life on your own, even though you thought you had been doing that, without your parents, you realize just how vulnerable you are in this world without them.

It was a hot July day when we watched Daddy's casket being lowered into the ground. Usually they do that when the loved ones leave the cemetery. I was last to leave and sat there sorrowfully watching. I felt so alone. I don't remember anyone who was there. I know Daddy's brothers and sisters that were still living were there and I do not even remember them, just Uncle Walter and our return trip back to the north. Daddy had received his first Social Security check the day of his funeral and Jean put it in the bank right away before even going to the funeral, as it was retroactive from the time he took sick. She didn't want me taking Stanley's clothes and Uncle Walter intervened and said I was taking him back with me and his clothes. She didn't argue with him and we left. The only thing I remember about our ride back home was the rain came down in torrents and the windshield wipers stopped working. Uncle parked under an overpass on the turnpike and Stanley, was able to get the wipers fixed with Uncle's instructions since his hands were small enough to get into a tight area. That is my only memory of the trip home.

JOYCE A. LEONARD

"Daddy"

I didn't think it would end this way,
I wanted you to stay -
I wanted to hear you sing the song you always sung,
On Thanksgiving day over the
pumpkin pie the melody hung.
"Oh, I'd laugh I'd cry
I'd fight, I'd die,
For one big piece of pumpkin pie.
I'd sleep out in the snow and rain
And bum my way on a cattle train,
For one big piece of pumpkin pie."
The words still ring clear in my mind,
In the halls of my memory where I find,
Glimpses of Daddy here and there
Remembering how he really did care.
Wake up Daddy, wake up, it's time to go
To pray, to work, to sing, you know.
I said good- bye
But I didn't mean for you to die.
I will miss you, oh how I will miss you
Till Jesus comes to make you new.
And we will be together forever
And ever, you know.
(By Joyce A. Leonard January 2019)

Chapter Twenty-Six

Don't Cry Out-Loud

You keep track of all my sorrows.
You have collected all my tears in your bottle.
You have recorded each one in your book"
(Psalms 56:8 NLT)

"Who left all that toilet paper in the toilet?" Fred was storming when he went into the bathroom and had to use the plunger to flush the toilet. "Joyce, get in here and clean this mess. This place is for pigs. You are all pigs, effin pigs." Without taking a breath, he continued his demands. "From now on, I don't want you or anyone else in this household to use more than one sheet of toilet paper when they go to the bathroom. It isn't necessary." With that command and being left to clean the mess, my face was flushed, but I dared not to go against his wishes. Fred was a big man and when his anger rose, it seemed his size did too. Little Kathy overheard the words and secretly, when the coast was clear she came to me and said in her stuttering little voice, "Ma-ma-ma, wha-what am I go-going to-to do?" I assured her quietly. "Don't worry, when you need to wipe, just call me. She seemed all right with the thought that I would protect her and we didn't say anymore for fear that he would find us whispering.

It was a typical weekend when Fred was home. He worked away all week so the only time we had to contend with any of his demands were the weekend. It became so unbearable, I used to pray, "Lord, please let him have an accident and die before he gets home."

There were seven of us around the supper table. Tammy, the oldest, Judy next to Tammy, then Robert sat across from Judy and Kathy, the youngest sat next to Judy. Stan sat on the end opposite Fred and I always sat next to Fred. My brother, Stan, two years older than Tammy, and almost eighteen years younger than myself, was thrown into a family he hardly knew. He had been with me a year in the fourth grade and now he was twelve.

With five kids, there is always a zillion things to talk about especially at the supper table. The chatter was like humming bees in a nest interrupted by the volcanic explosion of Fred's voice. "You are spraying all over the food when you talk. When you are at the supper table I don't want one sound coming from your mouths." Instantly, the buzzing went to the clinking of the forks hitting the plates and total silence of voices except the degradation that Fred inflicted before he finished his food. "Effin pigs. You're all ignorant pigs." When he finished his meal, he rose from the table and went out the door. As soon as the door closed behind him and he wasn't within ear shot, the buzzing swept over the table like a heat wave, but the instant the door knob turned and Fred reentered the room, it diminished in the same fashion that it started.

It was Sunday evening when the girls went up to their room to do their homework for the next day. When they finished, they came down to watch T.V. before bedtime, but forgot to shut out the bedroom light before coming down the stairs. Fred noticed the light and chose Tammy, to dictate his orders. "The next time you leave your room with the light left on, I will cut the wires and you won't have a light. Then you will appreciate what you once had." It ultimately happened later on that someone left the light on and true to his word, Fred cut the wires so there could be no more lights in that room till he felt the lesson had been learned. After he had given an order, whether obeyed or not to his specifications, he always came back at me to make sure

I obeyed the order to keep its effect or I would pay. His finger was often pushed into my face backed with a threat, "If you can't make these kids do as I say, while I am away, you'll effin pay one way or another."

The old holding tank that held the water pumped in from the well fit in the corner of the room where the washer and dryer were located, which was off from the kitchen area. It was painted a flat bright blue from some old left over paint to help spruce up the corner. No one really ever noticed it unless they were heading for the bathroom or to get something from one of the shelves that was near the holding tank. The shelves served as a makeshift pantry. As you passed the shelves and the corner, the next thing was the electric hot water tank that could only be plugged in if someone had to use water that needed to be hot and that was for a limited time.

I liked the bathroom because it made me feel pretty. It was the nicest room in the house, and it had sliding glass doors that encased the light blue tub. There was a side board with an oval blue sink in the middle of it and a large mirror that extended from one corner of the wall to the other. The walls were also a light blue paneling that resembled tile with gold swirls traveling through it. Even though the floor was bare wooden boards, a scatter rug finished dressing it up. However, the holding tank held special significance in my mind because it was there I could squeeze in the small space between the tank and the wall to hide. It didn't make me go out of sight if someone came by that way, but the corner was dark even with the bright blue paint on the tank, which was darkened by dust and age. It was a safety zone where I hid, and within my mind, it was where I was safe.

I knew I needed to keep my tears from being exposed. I was petrified that I would be caught crying, for then I would hear, as I had often heard too many times, "Now what the eff are you crying about?" There was a popular song that played over the radio, "Don't cry out loud, just keep it inside...," (*by Melissa Manchester*) and I literally kept it inside by hearing those words within my mind, as I hid beside the holding tank crying inside, but never out loud.

Monday mornings never came too soon. I was always up at the crack of dawn, preparing his lunch for the day and making sure his suitcase was packed with clean clothes pressed shirts on hangers and pants draped evenly over the hangers under the shirts. He worked construction out of state and he took enough clothing to last the week. Everything was expected to be just so. I kissed him good bye at the door, after I had taken everything out and arranged it in the car for him and started it up so all he had to do was put it in reverse and drive away.

I would silently sip a cup of coffee and in the wee hours of the morning, relieved to have some serenity for another week. I cried again, but not out loud, because I didn't want to wake my sleeping children. I pondered within in a silent prayer, "How much longer must I endure?" The only answer that seemed to give relief to my emotional pain was wishing, "If only he would die."

Chapter Twenty-seven

Hope Drained - Emotions Torn

"God is the Master designer and He allows adversities into your life to see if you can jump over them properly."

"Be my God and I will leap over a wall." (Psalms 18:29 NLT)

~Oswald Chambers~

1979 was a year of turmoil after Daddy's death. My health seemed to be getting worse due to female complications, but until I knew what those were I was in abdominal pain that continued with my menstrual cycle three weeks out of four. I made an appointment with Dr. Katz, which after the examination, he determined that I needed surgery for a hysterectomy. My uterus was falling away by bits and pieces causing terrible pain that made me feel like my hips were being pulled out of their sockets and making every physical movement very difficult and painful. I went to the General Hospital in Lewiston and had my uterus removed, and to keep from going into the "change of life" at the age of thirty-one they left one tube and a half of an ovary.

While in the hospital, Fred sent in his ex-brother-in-law to bring in the items I needed. Fred, however, never came into see me the week I was in the hospital and Henrietta, his ex-wife, watched the kids for me. Fred was building new kitchen cabinets for her while I was ill, so he was there a good share of the time while the kids were there too. Henrietta's step-brother was going through some troubling times and was staying with Henrietta during this time since he had no other place to stay. He was quite religious as a former member of the church he attended. He had left there after finding out several discrepancies within the church. It seems that Fred felt that Henrietta's step brother and I would get along quite well since we were both religious. Fred had stopped going to church with me, and I made excuses for him to my church family, as I felt ashamed that he was living the kind of life that wasn't conductive to the vows he had taken to keep at baptism.

When it was time to come home from the hospital, it was Henrietta's step-brother who came and picked me up. When I had to go for doctor's appointments, again he was the one who took me. When Fred didn't want to be bothered with me, he would send him to attend to whatever my needs were. He would play Scrabble with me since I was house bound for six weeks and I loved the game, and it was always hard to find someone to play the game with me, and do the things I enjoyed. It was while doing these games that I decided I should be a witness to him and used the opportunity to discuss beliefs we both had, and some we differed on.

It was during this time that there was an evangelistic series going on at the Middle School in the auditorium, not far from the church, I attended. They were not held at my church since there was not enough room to accommodate the guests that came. My friend, Dave, drove me and the kids, as well as neighborhood young people in my fifteen passenger van to the meetings, which were held nightly for two weeks. Fred had returned to work away from home during the week, and was only home on weekends, so he didn't take part in any of the meetings.

There was major concern with the pastor of the church at the time, because I was coming to the evangelistic meetings with another man. Both the pastor and the evangelist came to visit me at my home to speak with me about their concerns. They cautioned me with counsel such as, "Turn a man upside down and they all look alike," which really insulted me. I could not believe what I was hearing, or the insinuations, because even though there was great contention and need for separation from my husband there had been nothing improper about my relationship. Since the hysterectomy I was not allowed to drive, do heavy lifting or go back to work until the six weeks was up. My health was evidently not their concern! I was very angry and I asked them to leave my home, while informing them that they had no idea about the circumstances of the abuse I and my family endured at my husband's hand for so many years.

I felt hurt and betrayed by the false accusations of these, Christians, from the church I loved. I had learned that you should keep your eyes on Jesus and not people. I am thankful that this did not persuade me to leave the church. *"I will instruct you and teach you in the way you should go; and I will counsel you and watch over you."* (Psalms 32:8 NIV)

"Fred's Threats"

It came to the point that I was uncertain what Fred would do next. He would say I said things I never said, trying to make me think I was losing my mind. After he had put me in a state of confusion, he would then become enraged screaming obscenities at me, then abruptly turn around in the middle of the floor while doubling his fist and come rushing at me and within inches of my face he would stop and begin laughing hideously, and would then back away while he continued to berate me. He may as well have tied me to fence and shot me, which would have been a lot easier than enduring the grief of making me think I had lost my mind, and that he was the only sane person in the household. When he came to this crescendo I would threaten to leave, but he then would reverse his attitude and persuade me that we were going to work things out. I was never sure of his next move and didn't dare to cross him. My self-esteem had been taken away to the point I agreed with whatever he said and then I began to believe that I wasn't worth anything, and there was no good reason that I was living.

We had gotten in the van to go to Henrietta's, and once I was in the van and we had left the yard, he said he was taking me somewhere to rape me! My brother had jumped on the back of the van as we had taken off, fearful of what Fred may do to me. We had just come into the center of town and when we slowed down to take the corner, I opened my door and jumped out, rolling on the ground. My brother jumped off as well and we walked back to the house. Fred kept going.

His harassment came to a point that when he walked in the door and began to scream at me for whatever issue was on his mind at the moment, whether it was the kids, housework, the animals or a made up accusation, I would pass out cold. It was my mechanism to be able to cope, and by the time I came to he would be gone. His terrorizing became so unbearable and still I covered for him to my church family. I didn't want them to know the monster he had become so I would say he was sick. I would explain that since he was gone all week working, that he was so tired when he got home that he just couldn't make it to church. The only friends we had, was a former co-worker of his, John, and his wife, Jeanne. I would confide in her about how terribly hateful he was to me but she never knew the extent of the abuse.

"The Secret Revealed"

Henrietta took me out for an evening meal and said she needed to talk to me. Very gently, and hesitantly, she began to unfold the story that during my stay in the hospital having the hysterectomy, that Fred was seeing another young woman in my bedroom. Promises had been made to her that he was going to marry her. She had some mental challenges and was sure that he was divorcing me and would be marrying her very soon. She had written down the exact time of their encounters, evidently taking note of the digital clock beside my bed. She had given explicit details as to their encounter with each other. She became convicted that I should know because I was a Christian, and had begun to feel guilty for her part with him, so confessed to Henrietta since she knew her and trusted her. Henrietta felt I should be made aware and I could make my decision as to what I would do next. I sat in jaw-dropped shock at the revealing evidence of this unsolicited, and hand printed confession.

"Divorce"

I finally decided that I could bear no more, and went to see a lawyer for a divorce. My lawyer was very sympathetic and caring. I had to meet him at night in his office as Fred accused me of having an affair with him. We had separated, and I did not know where he stayed, although I had a pretty good idea. It was later he confessed he had been seeing another woman during our entire marriage. Until we got a divorce, Fred would come over to the bus garage and threaten me. I left with him one day, after my morning bus run, to discuss our situation, and when he brought me back for the kindergarten run, he began screaming at me so intensely, that my boss, Harry heard him and came to the truck and opened the passenger door, just as I passed out with Harry holding on to me. I came to in time to hear Harry tell Fred to leave and never to come on the property again.

I was awakened one night with Fred at my bedside ready to punch me in the head as I slept, I awoke in time to get out of his way. I told my lawyer and he went to the police station and stayed there until they did something about him coming to the house to terrorize me. I often had to hide in the bus garage after hours, until I could call my pastor to come and take me home. I had to lock myself in the garage when I needed a place of refuge, and Harry let me know where the key was should I need to get in there. Harry cautioned me not to open the door to anyone unless it was my pastor or someone I knew could be trusted. Fred had padlocked the door to the house so I could not get in. I needed my clothes as well as the kid's clothes, so the pastor's wife helped me break the door down so I could get in. We never told anyone what we had done because we were fearful of getting into trouble.

After several confrontations, a male friend moved in to the house with me and slept on the floor in the boy's room as an assurance for protection. He became an uncle to the kids and I was thankful he was there. Then one night Fred came in ready to fight this friend, because he was an irritant having his presence at the home of his wife. I still remember the pale yellow shirt Freddie was wearing and how he rolled up his sleeves ready to battle my friend. The children were fearful of the fight that was about to begin. So there would be no confrontation for the children's sake, this friend left. It was not long after he left that Fred continued to take on a demeanor of accusations, causing more tears, and utter fright, with apprehension as to what was going to happen next. Then he left as abruptly as he came.

A couple days later he returned in the middle of the day and his attitude had changed from an attitude of violence to a quiet behavior of meekness so when he looked at me in calmness, he quietly said, "Joyce, let's stop all of this and start over." I heard myself say, "No, I can't it is too late." He turned toward the door and walked away. I watched him from the window and his shoulders were slumped forward as if he had been beaten, and for a moment, I wanted to run and stop him and tell him I would try one more time. But the fear factor came flooding back and I knew it wouldn't last, and I just could not take any more, yet with all that I had endured, it hurt. The separation that divorce brings is a tearing of two souls that were brought together as one, and regardless of the infliction brought on by another, the pain is still there. It is later that the anger sets in and the bitterness that follows, and the utter hatred begins to surface.

The memories of your marriage don't go away. You don't expect the torments to rear their ugly heads again so you relive the pain. He used the kids as his pawn, taking them out of school, while threatening me that I would never see them again. He bought a camper, taunting me that he would be going camping since he knew this was something I would enjoy, then he would attack my sanity, and threaten my existence while he flaunted his skills with renovating Henrietta's apartment. It was three months of tortured emotions; tears for the death of the marriage I had hoped would be forever. We were divorced May 7, 1980

Chapter Twenty-Eight

The Whispered Promise

"Singing psalms and hymns and spiritual songs among yourselves, and making music to the Lord in your hearts."

(Ephesians 5:19 NLT)

"Way down upon the Suwanee River; far, far away..." crackled her ninety-one-year-old voice as her crippled fingers flowed over the keyboard of her parlor grand piano. I sat enraptured by the melodious tones that came from the movement of her fingers that bulged with deformity caused by Rheumatoid arthritis, yet they fleeted gracefully without faltering racing from one end of the ivories to the other. Florence Barnes had been a patient in the Wetmore Nursing Home, my mother's nursing home, when she had arrived as a paid guest there, and the parlor grand piano sat in a small room with no other furniture around, only one window behind her piano bench and the doorway that entered the room. It was just big enough to be used to keep her talent awakened and her mental attitude alive. This was the room where I fantasized that one day I would play just like Miss Barnes.

But this wasn't the first development of my interest in the piano. It had begun when I was four years old when I used to visit Grampa Hutchinson and Anna, my sweet, precious step-grandmother. "Anna can I play the piano?" I would quiz Anna almost immediately as we came in the house to visit. Anna never denied me anything. "Why sure you can." It was always the same positive reply. As I situated myself at the piano stool and opened the hymn book to "The Old Rugged Cross," I would race my tiny short fingers over the keys of the piano, striking them randomly to a tune I was sure was accurate to the melody that flowed through my mind. I would even sing along with it. My other favorite piece I played was "In The Garden." No one else recognized my accomplished efforts but Anna always seemed to be able to guess right so I was sure I had done a good job with my talent. A little older now, I sat wide-eyed and cross-legged on the linoleum next to Miss Barnes as her captive audience. Miss Barnes played as if she were before an auditorium filled with spectators. My imagination, as an eight-year-old little girl, could easily be wistfully drawn into the vision of playing the piano in grandeur when enveloped in the presence of such a professional as Miss Barnes. She had been playing since age four and had played in many concerts in her day, even Carnage Hall! "Oh Miss Barnes," I would coo, "if only I could play like you." Always Miss Barnes would encourage, "You will, someday dear, but you must practice long hours every day." And then she would turn to the keys again, tickling them with interludes from Beethoven and Bach. There were two favorites that I liked best, "The Swanee River" and "Brahms Lullaby."

The sun was streaming in the window from behind Miss Barnes and the air was crisp drifting in the opened back door, airing out the stuffy little room when Miss Barnes whispered gently in her coarse, raspy voice, "One day this piano will be yours." I sat there in awe, my eyes sparkling in excitement with the awesome thought that just about took my breath away. A thought that I couldn't quite comprehend.

I went back in my mind to Grammie Anna's house. I could feel the cushioned blue carpet under my feet as I entered the living room and sat at that piano in the huge room that held the aura of majestic presence, which was my experience as I sat there at the piano. It was a dream that would come true and I would play the piano for everyone to listen to and applaud.

Times change when little girls become teen agers, and dreams change too. Fantasies change to reality and hopes become hopeless. Miss Barnes died and I had moved away and I married. The homestead was quiet for years and the parlor grand was quiet too. Mama had the keys and the strings taken out professionally to be renovated and replaced later, then saved for me one day when I would be able to have it as my own. Tragedy molested the dreams of "the whispered promise," Then Daddy sold the old house to my sister and her husband.

It was sort of a family reunion to look through the belongings that had been left dormant for so long. Here I was in the old house again and my brother-in-law was barking out orders as to what goes and what stays. He looked at the keyless, string-less parlor grand piano, then directing his comment straight at me, he said, "And that piece of junk has to go or I will chop it up for firewood." Instant frenzy burned within my soul as I glared back into his face without hesitation and with words defying his authority, I threatened, "Don't you dare." With a deep breath and an ire ready to axe his thoughts I continued, "If you dare to lay one finger on that piano to destroy it, I'll take an axe to you."

With that declaration, my brother-in-law, turned on his heel, put his head down, wagging it with mumbled un-pleasantries as he slammed out the screen door to the porch, heading for the barn. I had no place to store a piano of such magnitude in a small house with four children and my husband wasn't any help in making a decision to keep this monstrosity. The whispers echoed down from the past, "This will one day be yours," was a promise that would never materialize. I knew my dream was losing and it hurt. Mama had sent the "guts" of the piano to a professional restorer and tuner, but he also had died. She had planned on having it restrung and new ivories replaced in the mahogany beauty with its scroll carved legs and its majestic aura.

After phone calls and questions, I learned that it would cost a pretty penny to put this piano back in order, to the tune of $500 I would be able to restore it to its original state, but it would then be worth ten times that amount. But $500 was an unrealistic amount for a family with four children and bad credit. I had no choice...my dream had to die, but the man I contacted in Maine offered to transport the piano from Center Conway, New Hampshire, back to his place of business in Maine and deliver to my home, a reconditioned cherry wood, upright, Emerson piano. And there it sat in my humble living room.... a piano that was the product of my dreams that almost disappeared from reality.

John W. Schaum's pre-A book for beginners in piano became my focus at every spare moment when I could sit down, fingering the keys and with the scale and singing "Doe a deer, a female deer; ray, a golden drop of sun; me a name, I call myself; far, a long, long ways to run; sew, a needle pulling thread; la, a note to follow sew; tea, a drink with jam and bread, that will bring us back to doe; do, ri, mi, fa, sol, la, ti, do!" Then "I love coffee, I love tea," was most fluently played and often the variations as I practiced became the special audition of any who would listen. Mama had taught me the basics with the penciled names of the notes beginning with Middle C sketched clearly on the ivories. I quickly mastered, "Chief Thundercloud" all the way to "The Streamline Express" and advanced to John Thompson's, first grade book, and by carefully watching the finger arrangements in the fully illustrated pictures, I was able to figure the notes and could fluently play all the way up to the "Evening Bells," which was more complicated piece. The day came, when I had to sell that beloved piano to buy groceries for my children.

Years had passed, but God had not forgotten about my love for piano and my desire to play. A friend from the church needed a place to live for a while. She became our border. We had moved from the tiny house we once lived in, into a trailer in another part of town, and there was one room that could accommodate our friend. The kids were gone except for one and we were still paying tuition fees for back church school bills, so the extra money would be a blessing to the household. Then before she moved in, she asked hesitantly, "Can I bring my piano?" Without a thought of where it would go, I quickly answered, "Yes, by all means." My friend, Melody, had a desire to play the piano too, and also wanted to fill the need of a piano player in the church. Melody took lessons and practiced diligently, while I fumbled with the bits and pieces of music as I studied notes and picked out tunes that went with the songs that I knew. Melody lived in my home for a year before moving on, but before she left, she asked if I would keep her piano for her, but if I wanted to get rid of it to ask her first if she wanted it back. I said I would. It was an agreement that brought tears to my eyes. I was blessed.

It was a quiet day when no one was around and with only the ticking of the clock and the sun's rays filling the room with dust particles that I sat before the piano and prayed with tears trickling down my cheeks, "Lord, please help me to be able to put both hands together and coordinate them so that I can play for You." I have a problem with dyslexia, particularly with the right and left hand and numbers. It was fairly easy to plunk out notes with the right hand, but it just seemed impossible to match the left hand to the put the notes in the right perspective to sound as they should. After many hours of practice on hymns that were familiar I was able to slowly make out some similarity to a favorite hymn. Another friend from the church helped me out with about six, half hour lessons before she moved away from the area. Then it was just me and God. Money was too tight to be able to afford piano lessons. Each time I sat at the piano, I envisioned Miss Barnes playing, with her deformed hands striking, chords of music that could stir the saints. All I wanted was to play for Jesus!

With a prayer each time I sat at the piano, and placed my fingers on the keys of that old borrowed piano, I would feel the presence of the Spirit deep within my soul. The words to the hymns rang out new meaning, which I thrived on in bad circumstances, and my first accomplished piece was "Near The Cross." The second verse moved me as I learned the words fluently to accommodate the tune, "Near the cross, a trembling soul, Love and Mercy found me......," that was me. I was the trembling the soul. Mine was a life of sadness, and at each corner when a crisis occurred, I trembled within, and it was the love and mercy of my God that held me. Then, "What a Friend We

Have in Jesus" was next, and I changed the "we" to "ours" and the "I," to me and mine. The song took on new meaning and the accomplished piece was a revival of my spirit within. My fingers were able to put other songs together such as "Under His Wings" and "My Jesus I Love Thee."

Then as God spoke to me early one morning and I claimed His love for me, He gave me the song, "I Am Thine, O Lord," that continued to draw my heart with words, "I have heard Thy Voice as You spoke Thy love to me, but I long to rise in the arms of faith and be closer drawn to Thee." Even with these accomplished pieces, I have yet to conquer the fear of playing while others listen and try to sing with my playing. It is a fear of rejection, that I am not good enough and never will be. I know I am unaccomplished, unpolished, like a diamond in the rough and too deep to be hewn out.

Heaven holds a grand piano like no one has ever seen, and God will let me play one day with the angel's choir, with every note perfected in a grandeur that only the imagination of a little girl can inspire, and perhaps Miss Barnes will be there, with the fulfillment of the "whispered promise" that "one day the piano will be yours and you will play."

Chapter Twenty-Nine

Memories of Laughter and Tears

*"Reflect upon your present blessings,
of which every man has many,*

*not upon your past misfortunes of
which all men have some."*

~Charles Dickens~

"Wetmore Reunion 1980"

We piled into my 1973, 15 passenger Chevy van, with Uncle Walter driving and Aunt Florence next to him. There were their grandchildren, Jonathan and Melissa and their daughter-in-law, Alicia along with myself and my children, Tammy, Judy, Robert, Kathy and of course Stan. We headed for New York State to the Wetmore Family Reunion being held at the home of Aunt Alta and Uncle Howard Sampson. It seemed like we hadn't been on the road long, as everyone was excited and talkative about who would be at the reunion, when someone piped up, "I'm starving. What are we going to eat?" without taking a breath, the next question came, "Can we have cherries yet?" They all loved the sweet luscious, juicy cherries, and Aunt Florence calmly replied, "Pretty soon," which was followed by a stern "no" from Uncle Walter.

We were getting close to our destination and Uncle Walter was thinking out loud, "Let's see, if I remember right, we are looking for Eagle Road, wait, what did that sign say? Did anyone see it?" Stan was first to comment, "I think you passed it." Kathy and Alicia were thinking of their stomachs, "Oh no it is raining, now we can't eat in the rain," they lamented. Aunt Florence was always so balanced and calm. "Don't get upset, she quietly answered, we will eat." Tammy was getting concerned, "Now can we have cherries?" Uncle Walter was still in a quandary, "Nope that wasn't the road, I guess it is up further." Kathy began to whine, "Do you think we will find it by dinnertime?" Robert chimed in, "I hope so, I am hungry now." Melissa put her two cents in and directed, "Go back to sleep."

At last we arrived at Aunt Alta's and it was pouring out. It was a cloud burst and just rained river lets down the windows. "We can't get out now, Jonathan exclaimed, "so why don't we just eat now? he finished his thought. Aunt Florence gave the list of food available passing to each one what they wanted from her basket of goodies. "Let's see we have cherries, fruit, graham crackers, bread and peanut butter, what will you have?"

The rain stopped as abruptly as it started on this Friday night that was the beginning of the Wetmore reunion. You might say we only skimmed the surface as we began to get to know the loved ones which we had prayed for regularly, as well as those of whom we had lived on the memories of their lives. On Sabbath morning, we all got ready to attend the tiny Seventh-day Adventist church in Salamanca, New York State. There was only a handful of members, but the Wetmore clan brought the church alive. Among our talented group were pianists, leaders, teachers, minutemen, singers, and we were even handy at delivering a sermon.

First, cousin, Jim, tall and gaunt, with an impressionable mission story that he related from Elder Tucker, who had the Quiet Hour ministries. I watched and remembered how Jimmy had always come to my rescue during my marriage to Fred, and it always seemed that always at my lowest point, he arrived with the thoughts of encouragement and to pray. Oh the prayers he must have prayed for me! These thoughts were whirling about my mind in remembrance as I listened to him wind up his story. Then my thoughts turned to my sister, if only she could be here too. Instantly a prayer formed in my mind for her, "Please Lord, be with her today."

Uncle Bill, Aunt Thelma Lou's husband, always gave a riveting Sabbath School lesson study. I loved listening to him as he presented how Christ allows Satan to bring affliction on us and use good with evil to suit whatever His purpose may be, but He (God) will not allow Satan to take our lives. We should question good things as to whether they are from God or not and seek divine guidance on every matter that comes before us.

After church we reunited at Uncle Don's home for dinner. Aunt Fern was the best cook around and no one ever turned down a meal she put together. As the meal was being served, my mind traveled over the memories of being here in this old farmhouse that held so many memories for me. There was a time when Aunt Fern would tuck cousin Joanie and I in bed side by side and pray with us. Joanie and I were close. Joanie and Janice and Jim's sister was in church today. She was getting her life back together since her divorce. I pledged in my mind to add her to my prayer list. And there was my precious Aunt Ruth, the eldest of my aunts and uncles, and seeing her again flooded back the memories of our times together with her gracious, unconditional love for me and for all her family.

Someone called out, "Pictures everyone, gather round." Today was the anniversary of Daddy's burial July 12, 1980, just one year from the time we lowered him into the ground. For an instant I waited for Daddy to fill his spot next to his brothers and sisters. Aunt Ruth and Aunt Thelma Lou were ready to pose and laughingly called out to their sister Alta to join them, and Aunt Thelma Lou chided the youngest of their siblings, Alice, "Stop stuffing your face." Now for the brothers, I heard someone call out, and once again, I waited for Daddy to make his funny faces and begin to be the clown of the party, and the shadows of his memory faded, as the tears welled up in my eyes.

It was in agreement to go visit the old homestead on Bucktooth Run where the family grew up, and so we put on some old clothes and headed down memory lane to Bucktooth Run, and as we stood in front of the old farmhouse, with about thirty of us gathered in the road staring at the old homestead, when the owners called out, "Can I help you folks?" Several shouted back, "We are the Wetmore's." (la de dah) My aunts were already up the hill and had been invited in to see the old home. As I entered, and to my amazement, the living room held a familiarity. I could picture in my mind how the living room once looked when Gramma and Grampa lived there. How strange it seemed! It was like a mirage and then it was gone. It was Jimmy Riddle that lived here, my sister's old playmate. "My mother lives in the trailer next door if you would like to go visit her," he informed us.

Before we all gallivanted off to Mildred's (Jimmy's mother's place) Aunt Thelma Lou was already tromping down through the pasture to the main attraction, "the old swimming' hole." Here we were a herd of strangers stumbling over rocks, ruts and left overs from grazing cattle to get a glimpse of the infamous place considered hallowed ground of when they were kids. First to shriek was Aunt Thelma Lou, "What happened? It was over my head?" Uncle Walter retorted, "And how tall were you?" Aunt Thelma Lou still in awe, replied, "It was and we used to dive off the spring board." Uncle Don, with his wry humor, quipped, "Sure you did. Are you pipe dreamin'?" Certain of her assessment, she continued, "Wasn't it over our heads, Bob? Bob where are you?" as she looked around for a valid consultant. Uncle Bob was somewhere else so Aunt Thelma Lou turned to find another one of her siblings to confer with her and finding her views were not important to anyone but her she continued with, "Well there must have been a drought or something to dry everything up."

The next event was Mildred's and the countryside view was beautiful on this warm July day. It was a perfect setting for the ending of the day. Approaching Mildred's home, several called out to her, "Mildred how are you? We are having a family reunion and thought we would visit." Mildred was delighted and hugs and kisses were passed about in a reunion of her neighbors that had long been gone that she had once been close to. An elderly gentleman appeared from a back bedroom, asking, "Who are these people?" Mildred answered him, "Dad, these are the Wetmore's, remember they used to live next door?" He looked a bit bewildered, "Oh yes, glad to see you, come again," as he turned toward the kitchen. Mildred invited us in to sit and visit while her dad continued to be in confusion, "See you folks later" he waved at us again. Mildred was conveying how happy they are living here and how good it has been for them, as her dad again called out, "Good-bye! See you folks later, come again." Mildred was getting a little upset with her dad, who evidently was suffering from dementia, she said, "Oh dad, take a walk up the road."

The Sabbath hours ended after such a full day of memories filled with laughter and some silent tears for the missing members. Uncle Walter and Aunt Alta sang a duet as Aunt Alta played hymns on the organ. I listened to their voices blend in perfect harmony with each other and thought how beautiful it was with Uncle Walter's tenor voice accompanied by Aunt Alta's alto singing voice, and I was blessed. I am forever blessed with the memories of such a wonderful family that God gave me and I appreciate them now more than ever.

The old homestead is a sweet memory and two of my aunts are still living, at this writing, out of the nine siblings that grew up in a Christian home that revered God and His commandments. It has been their example throughout my life that had influenced me in so many ways for the love of God. The day will come when their reward will be spoken, *"Well done, good and faithful servant, you were faithful over few things, I will make you ruler over many things. Enter into the joy of your Lord."* (Matthew 25:21 NKJV)

Chapter Thirty

Gift Wrapped Words

"God. . . .is able to do far more than we would ever dare to ask or even dream of—infinitely beyond our highest prayers, desires, thoughts or hopes."

(Ephesians 3:20 TLB)

"Oh, what a lovely gift, all wrapped in shimmering paper and topped with a lovely bow!" one might exclaim, but the gift I have written is held in a book that is identified only as the "Book of Records," accurately recorded by heavenly angels. The words we speak and the words we don't speak portray what is in our hearts. We can use the past that has been recorded for we are held accountable for what has been written as well as what has not been written, for the Bible says, *"That which has already been, and what is to be has already been; And God requires an account of what is past."* (Ecclesiastes 3:15 NKJV) I leave the ending of this book with a chapter wrapped in the words from my heart. I have written according as to how I have remembered and before each chapter I claimed the promise, *"For the Holy Spirit will teach what needs to be said even as you are standing there."* (Luke 12:12 NKJV) I believe this includes that I will be directed even as I sit and write for I was commissioned by God to write.

The details of my life are to serve as an antidote to those who have been filled self-pity because they don't have or they have gone without, been mistreated, or abused and as the saying goes—each of us has a story. My story isn't unique or so out of the ordinary that it is to be revered or sympathized with, but whatever our circumstances may be or have become, there is a God in heaven that hears and answers *"exceedingly and abundantly above anything we could ever imagine or think according to the power that works in us."* (Ephesians 3:20 NKJV) *Prayer* was the magnified power that transformed my life to become a real child of the King. My words are gift-wrapped in the indelible ink of life. My life continues to be a struggle to keep the flames of love for the most beloved of my life, Jesus Christ. He is my all in all. The song. "Live Out Thy Life Within Me" (written by Frances Ridley Havergal 1836-1879) sums up the yearnings of my heart. The words are gift-wrapped in love for Jesus, and it is my heart's desire to serve Him. Oh how I surely fail over and over again, but with His mighty power and the hand of such tremendous long-suffering love, He picks me up and we begin again.

I cannot tell you that in the continued years of my life, I was dealt a hand of joy and comfort, but I can tell you that through every trial and each crisis in my life, that God never left me or forsook me. He used every avenue of the journey as a stepping stone to refine my character to be purified and become *"a watchman on the wall that (I) will never hold (my) peace day or night. . ."* ("I" and "my" is my injection to make it personal) (Isaiah 62:6 NKJV), to mentor others and pray for the salvation of family and friends and even those who have been misused and abused. Many have been placed in my path for me to be a mother to the motherless, a grandmother to those who have lost their grandmothers, to be a friend to the friendless, a beacon of hope to those who have no hope. I leave you with these words gift-wrapped by the Holy Spirit that *"the words of my mouth and the meditation of my heart will be acceptable in the sight of the Lord, my strength and my Redeemer,"* (Psalms 19:14 NKJV)

8 South St., Concord, NH the home of my grandparents

15 Pleasant St., Auburn, ME - Tammy's first home.

201 Main St. in Bog Hoot which is Mechanic Falls, ME

Angel - my St Bernard dog.

Joyce and my sister Carolyn in Bartlett, NH in front of our daddy's logging truck.

Joyce being guarded by Buster the dog.

Carolyn holding son Ricky My Mama holding my daughter Tammy. Stanley in front of me (Joyce) holding daughter Judy and nephew Neal beside me

My home growing up in Center Conway, NH

Post Office in Center Conway, NH

On Jockey Cap in Fryeburg, ME with daddy and friend Linda chipping garnets out of the rock.

Cousin Jeannie with her dog, Susie.

Daddy when he married Jean Begley

Daddy's truck

Daddy's truck at the paper mill in Berlin, NH

The front view of 8 South St. in Concord, NH

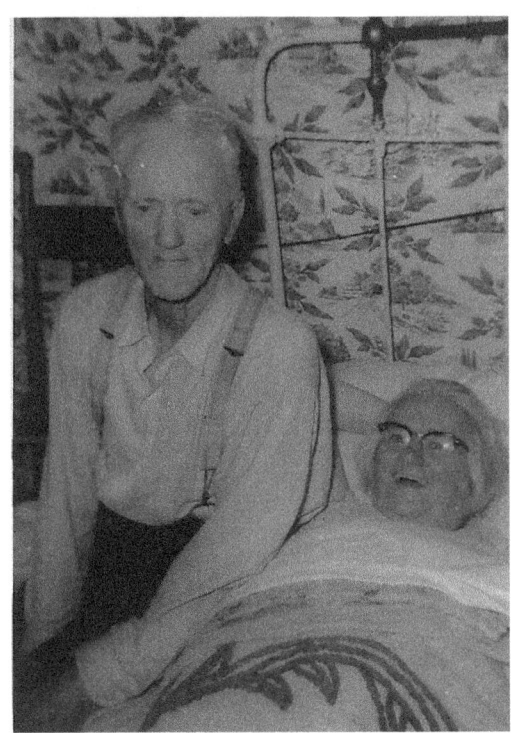

Gramma and Grandpa Wetmore

Grandpa and Grammie Hutchinson on the
steps of 8 So. St, Concord, NH

Grandpa and Grammie Hutchinson

Joyce with her doll Betty

Home in Center Conway, NH in the winter.

Bessie and Jennie

Joyce and Carolyn in front of the home daddy built on Blueberry Hill - N. Pembroke, NH

Joyce with her dog Lucky and pet raccoon, Pepper.

Funeral of Priscilla Wetmore

Joyce, Carolyn, Linda (who saved my life)
and my sister's friend, Marilyn

Back row: Stanley, Tammy and Judy.
Front row: Robbie and Kathy

Joyce the day she married Tom Robinson
(named Freddie in the book)

A JOURNEY OF TRIALS STRENGTHENED THROUGH FAITH

My first school bus I drove.

Baptized August 2, 1975 Carolyn, Ricky, Neal, Anna, Stanley, Robbie, Judy, Daddy, Tom, Kathy (littlest one) Tammy, Joyce in front of the Auburn, ME Seventh-day Adventist Church.

Tom Robinson - Pastor Richardson

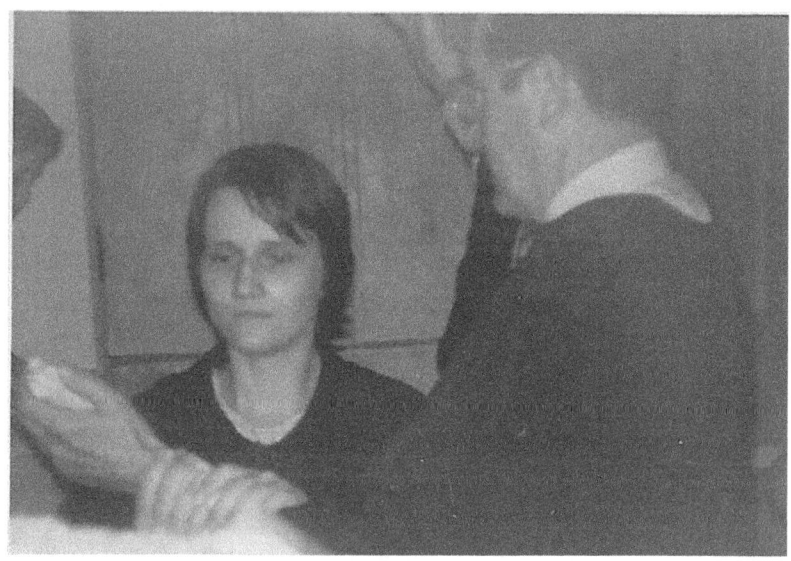

Joyce with Pastor Richardson

www.ingramcontent.com/pod-product-compliance
Ingram Content Group UK Ltd.
Pitfield, Milton Keynes, MK11 3LW, UK
UKHW022228230426
12048UKWH00016BA/1139